Critical Brass

Andrew Snyder

CRITICAL BRASS

Street Carnival and Musical Activism

in Olympic Rio de Janeiro

Wesleyan University Press   Middletown, Connecticut

Wesleyan University Press
Middletown CT 06459
www.wesleyan.edu/wespress
Text and photographs unless otherwise noted
© 2022 Andrew Graver Snyder
Manufactured in the United States of America
Designed by Mindy Basinger Hill
Typeset in Minion Pro

The publisher gratefully acknowledges the AMS 75 PAYS
Fund of the American Musicological Society, supported in part
by the National Endowment for the Humanities
and the Andrew W. Mellon Foundation

Library of Congress Cataloging-in-Publication Data
available at https://catalog.loc.gov/
cloth | ISBN 978-0-8195-0018-2
paper | ISBN 978-0-8195-0019-9
e-book | ISBN 978-0-8195-0020-5

5   4   3   2   1

FOR MY DAUGHTER, INA MABEL ELEANOR BISSLER

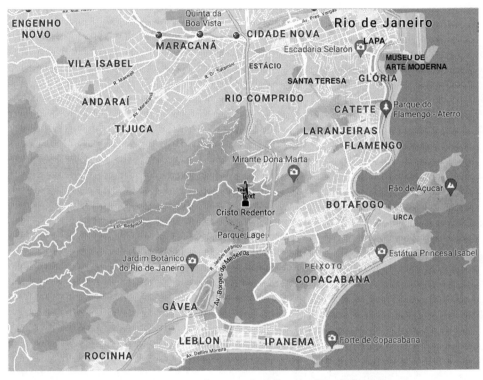

FIGURE 0.1 Map of center and south zone of Rio de Janeiro.

CONTENTS

ACKNOWLEDGMENTS

The prospect that a growing, internationally connected brass band movement that seeks to claim public space, spread inclusive musical education, and militate for a different world even existed in Rio de Janeiro was far from my mind when I entered graduate school in 2010. A first trip to the city in June 2013 at the height of the momentous protests that were to alter the course of Brazilian history introduced me to some of the brass musicians who at the time were musically helping to mobilize the protests. They took me in as one of their own when I began fieldwork between 2014 and 2016 as well as during subsequent trips.

I first want to thank, therefore, the musicians whose creative work made my research possible and who inspired me to believe that it is indeed possible to change the world with music. I owe an invaluable debt to the brass ensembles in Rio de Janeiro, especially the ones with which I had the most engagement, including Cordão do Boitatá, Céu na Terra, Orquestra Voadora, Bagunço, Fanfarrada, Damas de Ferro, Os Siderais, Favela Brass, and BlocAto do Nada. Special thanks to Juliano Pires and Clément Mombereau for providing various forms of access to the community. I wish to honor the memory of three young movement participants who left this world before this book was published, the second two of whom I interviewed: Pedro Dorigo, Chico Oliveira, and Bruno de Nicola. All the organizers of carnival brass blocos, brass bands, political actions, HONK! RiO, and all the HONK! and brass band festivals that are the subject of this book deserve thanks for doing what you do. The San Francisco Bay Area brass bands, who are linked in direct and indirect ways with the Brazilian scene, also gave me invaluable musical and political experiences. Thanks to all the musicians in the Brass Liberation Orchestra, Inspector Gadje, Extra Action Marching Band, East Bay Brass Band, Fanfare Zambaleta, and Mission Delirium.

Rio's brass musicians also helped me through the various challenges of living in in the city. After a production meeting for the HONK RiO! brass band festival, for example, three local musicians and I were robbed by a drive-by car with four men armed with guns, and my trumpet was stolen along with other friends' valuables. The brass band community took it upon itself to throw events called "HONK! Aid," a reference to Live Aid, and busked in the streets to fundraise and help us with the costs of replacing stolen property. In this spirit of mutual aid, I, like other gringo musicians in the movement, have brought from the United States musical products, which are much more expensive in Brazil due to import taxes, including a sousaphone. But no amount of tubas or acknowledgment can equal the warm reception and invitations these musicians gave me.

My mentors in graduate school at the University of California, Berkeley, who helped bring the writing of the dissertation on which this book is based to fruition, all bear influence in these pages. My dissertation advisor, Jocelyne Guilbault, provided caring, thoughtful, and demanding attention throughout the research and writing process. My dissertation committee—Christopher Dunn, T. Carlis Roberts, and Angela Marino—also provided years of intellectual engagement and support. Other scholars at many points in the research and writing process supported the development of this project, including Carla Brunet, Peter Glazer, Geoffrey Lee, Elena Schneider, Bonnie Wade, Martin Stokes, Candace Slater, Ben Brinner, Matt Sakakeeny, Sean Bellaviti, Emily Allen, Maria Sonevytsky, James McNally, and Dan Sharp. Brazilian scholars too provided immense support and resources; many thanks especially to Samuel Araújo who welcomed me into the intellectual community of ethnomusicologists in Brazil. I was fortunate to have been financially supported by Berkeley's Music Department to undertake graduate studies, and the financial support of the John L. Simpson Memorial Research Fellowship, Brazilian Studies Association (BRASA), Foreign Language and Area Studies (FLAS), and Berkeley Dissertation Completion Fellowship also helped make this project possible.

The transformation from dissertation to book owes thanks to many others beyond my time at Berkeley. Many thanks to Suzanna Tamminen, Jeremy Wallach, Alan Berolzheimer, Jim Schley, the editorial board at Wesleyan University Press, and the anonymous reviewers who worked assiduously to improve this book. Feedback on presentations given at the Society of Ethnomusicology, the Latin American Studies Association, the International Association of Popular Music Studies, the Society of American Music, and other conferences transformed my perspectives on the project. The responses of the editors and reviewers of the *Luso-Brazilian Review*, in which an earlier version of chapter two was published, and the *Latin American Musical Review*, in which an earlier version of chapter four was published, were vital in sharpening those book chapters. Related research not contained in this book was published in *Ethnomusicology*, the *Journal of Popular Music Studies*, and the *Journal of Festive Studies*, and those review processes also helped nuance the arguments in this book. My work with Reebee Garofalo and Erin Allen on our co-edited volume *HONK! A Street Band Renaissance of Music and Activism* helped produce vital perspectives on this project, as did my work with Brenda Romero, Susan Asai, David McDonald, and Katelyn Best on our co-edited volume *At the Crossroads of Music and Social Justice*. Looking further back, I am also extremely grateful to the faculty of Reed College—including David Schiff, Catherine Witt, Ginny Hancock, and Mark Burford—who gave me the tools to pursue ethnomusicology.

Salwa El-Shawan Castelo-Branco's position as visiting professor at UC–Berkeley in the last semester of my graduate studies gave me new perspectives to think about the neofanfarrismo movement in relation to heritage that are also present in this book. She invited me to present my research at the Instituto de Etnomusicologia, of which she is the founder, at the Universidade Nova de Lisboa in Lisbon, Portugal. This trip led to a successful application for the postdoctoral position of Investigador Júnior, as a recipient of the Concurso Estímulo ao Emprego Científico Individual funded by Portugal's Fundação para a Ciência e a Tecnologia, at Lisbon's Instituto de Etnomusicologia beginning in 2020. This research position here in Lisbon has provided the time and focus to finish this book and embark on related and new research projects.

My last thanks goes to my family who support my eccentric endeavors. A multitude of thanks to my parents, Liz Bryant and George Snyder, and my "stepparents," Peggy Hendrix and Bob Goodman, whose strong involvements in traditional music communities in the United States instilled in me a passion for ethnomusicology and engagement with a diversity of musical communities from an early age. Thanks, Dad, for visiting the brass parades of Rio de Janeiro before you got sick, and I'm sorry you couldn't live to see this book materialize. I am grateful to my wife, Claire Haas, trombonist and community organizer, without whom I might well have never picked back up the trumpet and joined a radical brass band in the Bay Area. Thank you for being an integral part of the fieldwork, my musical life, the revision of this book, and more conversations than you would have liked to have about this project. Thanks to our (currently) little daughter, Ina Bissler for helping me remember that there are other things in life besides academic endeavors. I hope you too feel the intoxicating exhilaration of musicians animating crowds in the streets.

Andrew Snyder
LISBON, PORTUGAL

COMPANION WEBSITE

Audio and visual examples discussed in this book are provided on the author's website (www.andrewsnydermusic.com), at the site's *Critical Brass* page under the Writing tab.

At the bottom of this page, there are links to resources for specific chapters, including all the musical examples referenced in text and endnotes. Examples are identified in the book and on the website by a shorthand for "Companion Website.Chapter.Example": for instance, CW.Int.Ex2 refers to the second example of the introduction, and CW.Ch1.Ex1 refers to the first example of chapter 1.

The links relevant to chapter 3's discussion of the performances of Fela Kuti's song may be of particular pedagogical value. Please note that some of documentaries featured are not in English.

Other writing and performances by the author are also featured on the website.

INTRODUCTION

An Alternative Movement
in an Olympic City

In the summer heat of the carnival Tuesday of 2019, Orquestra Voadora's three hundred brass and percussion musicians play to an estimated one hundred thousand people on the grassy park that lines the coast of Rio de Janeiro's Guanabara Bay. Voadora has entertained carnival crowds annually since 2009 with a diverse set of music. Balkan brass, New Orleans second line, countercultural songs from the rebellious Tropicália movement of the 1960s, and much more are mixed with Brazilian rhythms, from Rio's *samba* to Northeastern *frevo* and *maracatu*. Imaginatively created carnival costumes—superheroes, unicorns, and rainbows—disguise fraternizing musicians and revelers. They pass around beer, sugarcane liquor (*cachaça*), alcohol-laced popsicles (*sacolé*), and joints during the slowly rolling march through the park. Stilt walkers blow glitter into the air above the musicians, covering everyone in a sparkly rainbow dust.

Musicians have traveled from throughout the Americas and Europe to play in this participatory ensemble. Seasoned professional musicians play alongside those who enrolled the previous year with Orquestra Voadora's smaller professional band to learn their instruments. The latter have prepared in weekly classes with Voadora throughout the year, weekly rehearsals for five months before the event, and a seemingly constant series of informal brass jam sessions in the city streets. I am doing my best to play my parts loudly and make up for some of my fellow trumpet players who, despite having studied all year for this moment, are now struggling after having taken various drugs before the parade began. Despite some large variances in tuning audible from inside the ensemble, the

FIGURE I.1 Celebrations after Voadora's carnival performance.
Photo by author on February 9, 2016.

total sound created by the booming percussion and blaring horns heard from outside amid the audience is driving, rhythmic, and energizing to the multitude of people in attendance (figure 1.1).

Orquestra Voadora is one of hundreds of *blocos* of the city's "street carnival" (*carnaval de rua*), a movement of proliferation of free musical events in public spaces that has grown exponentially since the country's dictatorship fell in 1985. Blocos are mobile street music organizations associated with carnival that are often highly participatory with a wide range of instrumentation, and "street carnival" primarily refers to Rio's bloco scene rather than the city's more well-known samba school parades. Orquestra Voadora's bloco is one of the most popular of the brass and percussion ensembles that form a submovement of street carnival known as *neofanfarrismo*. Roughly translating to "neo-brass-bandism," the term emphasizes the community's innovative and alternative character by using "neo-" before the Portuguese term *fanfarra*. Here I translate fanfarra as "brass band," but in Rio fanfarra can refer to a variety of mobile ensembles of brass, woodwinds, and percussion of variable instrumentation and numbers.

Though neofanfarrismo emerged from carnival celebrations, its practitioners have increasingly come to regard the community as a social movement made up of committed musical activists, as the "-ismo" suffix suggests. Indeed, the opportunity of carnival not just for playful satire but for outright denunciation of Brazil's right wing and the status quo has become Voadora's yearly tradition. In the 2019 carnival, for example, the Orquestra Voadora bloco would receive notable coverage from media giant Globo for its politicized performance in homage to Marielle Franco, Rio de Janeiro's leftist, openly gay, Black city councilwoman who was assassinated the year before and whose image was memorialized around the city in the years after. This performance can be viewed on this book's companion website (CW) along with other audio-visual material referenced throughout in footnotes, which I encourage consulting to see these ensembles in action (CW. Int.Ex1).[1] In the parade of the 2016 carnival, the bloco had launched the event by calling out the city's government for the evictions and destruction in the Vila Autódromo *favela* where the Olympic Park was being built. Far from an obscure fringe of the city's cultural landscape, that year the bloco won Globo's coveted *Serpentina de Ouro* prize for best bloco of the city's street carnival.

Voadora's actions represent a trend of politicizing carnival as Brazil's crises—brought on by reckless mismanagement of mega-sporting events, precipitous economic decline, corruption scandals, and the rise of far-right populism—deepened during the 2010s. Over the same period, musicians who play with Voadora have carnivalized politics as well, incorporating carnivalesque repertoires into explosive protest settings. These brass musicians, for example, often break into Chiquinha Gonzaga's carnival march "Ó abre alas" (Open the Wings), a song traditionally used to launch street carnival marches, to push protesters forward amid the sounds of tear gas explosions and rubber bullets. This and other songs performed by brass and percussion musicians in the carnival season have made their way into spaces of political contestation, where strongly differing visions of Brazil's future have violently confronted each other. Musical activism in neofanfarrismo goes beyond explicit protest, with a wide variety of projects committed to inclusive musical education, while other bands within this largely middle-class movement have focused explicitly on fomenting the musical participation of marginalized populations, including women, Blacker communities, and those living in favelas.

The vision of an explicitly activist brass movement, as opposed to an ostensibly apolitical, carnivalesque manifestation, was consolidated with the founding of the annual HONK! RiO Festival of Activist Brass Bands in 2015. Originally inspired by a global network of alternative brass band "HONK! Festivals" that celebrate free and accessible musical culture in the public commons, Rio's festival has since spawned four other HONK! festivals in Brazil alone (see Snyder, Garofalo, and Allen 2020). HONK! RiO cast the city's carnivalesque brass community that emerged in the local carnival as a cosmopolitan, transnational, and activist movement. The festival has solidified its status as a definitive element of Rio's cultural landscape, and it was even cited as justification for the 2019 law that declared brass and military bands to be Intangible Cultural Heritage of the State of Rio de Janeiro.[2]

The politicization of carnival and the carnivalization of politics that typify much of the street carnival community and especially the neofanfarrismo movement represent not merely the overlapping of two distinct domains of social life between politics and music, but a continuum of cultural action and expression. Many neofanfarristas argue that the ritual of carnival—one that mythically valorizes inversion, equality, participation, and festivity—should be the rule, not a seasonal exception nor a mere performance. In this book, I tell the story of how this explosive carnival brass band community gave rise to an activist musical movement in Rio de Janeiro at a time of severe political crisis in Brazil. The chapters focus on *revival* of carnival practices, *experimentation* with carnival repertoires, *inclusion* of marginalized communities, *resistance* against hegemonic power, *diversification* of the movement, and finally *consolidation* of an avowedly activist movement. Through these lenses, I examine the processes of this transformation from carnivalesque to activist expressions by exploring the popularization of brass blocos during the post-dictatorship street carnival revival at the turn of the millennium to the explosion of HONK! festivals in the late 2010s. In doing so, I theorize carnival and the carnivalesque as constituting rationalizations and enactments of political critique and action, and I offer a case study in musical movement building. I ask what powers festive traditions in public space have to forge communities of opposition presenting vibrant alternatives that counter the unjust, violent, and unequal realities of urban life in a major neoliberal city confronting diverse forms of authoritarian oppression.

ETHICAL PRINCIPLES OF CARNIVAL

Orquestra Voadora's animated video, "Anthem of Orquestra Voadora" (2011), offers a creative, utopian answer to this question, suggesting that participatory music making in public space is indeed an effective mode of transforming capitalist urban society (CW.Int.Ex2).[3] The music is based on a fusion of a carnival march (*marchinha*) rhythm and the theme song of the Japanese superhero show *Spectreman*. It begins with a foreboding voice narrating over bleak urban images of trash, sanitary catastrophes, and urban chaos: "Like all metropolises, Rio de Janeiro meets the biggest enemy of humankind: pollution . . . Who will be able to intervene?" The beginning of a carnival march rhythm then accompanies a superhero image of Orquestra Voadora, which subsequently is embodied in a Transformer robot who fights a monster personifying urban chaos. The city's Christ the Redeemer statue launches to life and takes control of the Transformer in solidarity, and, as the monster punches the Transformer, musical instruments fly out of it into the hands of the terrorized people in the streets. As the people begin to play, the pollution monster is distracted and starts dancing, letting the Orquestra Voadora Transformer easily dispatch him. The Christ statue retakes its place on the iconic Corcovado mountain, and a new, beautiful day dawns on Rio de Janeiro. Such depictions of musicians as superheroes with the capacity to mobilize participatory music making that can transform social and political life are playful, but in neofanfarrismo these ideas are taken seriously, inspire action, and dramatize real practices. Indeed, Orquestra Voadora translates to "Flying Orchestra," and the image of flying is often spoken of in the community as a practice of freedom and going beyond what seems possible.

For many "alternative" Cariocas (residents of Rio de Janeiro), such ideas are inspirational, and the neofanfarrismo community has become an all-encompassing lifestyle. These mass musical events in the streets have provided a space for participation in carnival for middle-class residents many of whom were uninterested in, or even alienated by, the famous samba school parades—though, as we will see, the movement has been in a process of diversification on many fronts. Many middle-class musicians view the poorer and largely Afro-Brazilian samba schools as homogenous, commodified spectacles, and they do not consider them part of what many view as the "more authentic" street carnival due to the expensive entrance fee to the closed-off spectator space of the parade route (*sambódromo*). This view is espoused, for example, by one of neofanfarrismo's central actors, Juliano Pires, an enthusiastic musician who during my fieldwork showed up to almost every brass band event and stayed to the earliest hours of dawn. He playfully goes by "Juba," rhyming with "tuba," or "Ju Bones," for the trombone, which recalls the Brazilian tradition of musicians being known for the instruments they play. He explicitly describes street carnival as a liberatory, critical, and egalitarian practice in contrast to the samba schools:

I'm inspired by [Mikhail] Bakhtin who writes of carnival and street culture as forms of resistance. During carnival in the middle ages, laws were loosened and there wasn't so much hierarchy or domination. The nobles would go into the street and treated everyone as if they were equal. Carnival was a form of irony and subversion, of resistance to oppression . . . The sambódromo represents a false carnival according to the principles of carnival. The street carnival is the carnival in which you become equal with everyone together. The sambódromo is just a stage, with people observing, not participating. In carnival, you have to participate actively. Only in the street is there this possibility. (Interview 2014)[4]

In citing "principles of carnival" derived from the famous carnival theorist Mikhail Bakhtin, perhaps Pires is thinking of such passages from Bakhtin's *Rabelais and His World*: "Carnival is not a spectacle seen by the people: they live in it, and everyone participates because its very idea embraces all the people" (1984 [1941], 7), or "All were considered equal during carnival" (10). Bakhtin views carnival as constituting the people's "second life," all that is opposed to institutions, hierarchy, order, and spectatorship. This question of carnival's political potentials and efficacy has long been a debate of theorists, musicians, and politicians, toggling between Bakhtin's "resistance" theory and the "safety-valve" theory, which posits that carnival lets off steam to ultimately reassert the status quo (see, for example, Gluckman 1965). In recent decades, carnival scholars have generally moved past this either/or revolutionary vs. repressive debate and pointed instead to the "inherently equivocal nature of carnival" and its lack of universal meanings and functions (Godet 2020, 6). Likewise, I reject the notion that carnival has any inherent meaning or that these conventional theories can be neatly imposed on diverse practices as interpretive frameworks to understand them.

This debate fails, however, to engage with the central question posed by Pires, namely: how do the ideals of carnival inspire political and social engagement? As Brazilian sociologist Roberto DaMatta writes, "we are much closer to the participant when we look at Carnival in terms of what it suggests, presents, and offers by way of attraction" (1991 [1979], 24). In articulating a musical activism based in the practices of street carnival, or his "principles of carnival," Pires interprets Bakhtin's understanding of carnival as a revolutionary, participatory, and egalitarian tradition and reinterprets them as foundational ethics of activist praxis. Though Pires's words cannot be understood as entirely representative of the diffuse neofanfarrismo community, his conception of carnival as an activist practice is a prominent discourse in the street carnival and neofanfarrismo movements and is one he, in particular, helped to promote. For him and other neofanfarristas, it is not whether Bakhtin's insights into carnival are empirically true that is important. It is that they believe that they *should* be true.

It is worth noting, moreover, that Pires cites one of the foremost theorists of carnival, but one little known beyond humanities scholars. In this highly educated movement in Rio de Janeiro, one of the cultural capitals of the world, such scholarly references were not uncommon, and they point to the relatively privileged class position of the neofanfarrismo community. The movement emerged as a predominantly middle-class, Whiter,[5] and male community, but it has been in a long process of racial, class, and gender diversification, another transformation that this book explores, as the movement has increasingly framed itself as activist. Privileged leftist movements that view themselves as cultural and political vanguards and seek to unite with marginalized groups for common cause are, of course, not new. Alternative middle-class movements in Brazil and elsewhere, such as the 1960s' popular song movements, presented the middle-class artist as a populist figure who spoke, or sang, for the masses. As an instrumental movement, however, neofanfarrismo represents an example distinct from well-studied forms of musical activism whose critiques are based primarily in semiotics, representation, and mediation of lyrics. As Judith Butler writes about social movements, "it matters that bodies assemble, and . . . the political meanings enacted by demonstrations are not only those that are enacted by discourse" (2015, 7–8).

How might we evaluate the musical activism of a participatory musical movement that seeks to mobilize what Butler calls public assemblies by claiming public space through the affect of sound, a movement that does not only represent excluded Others through song but attempts to engage them as musicians, playing alongside and mobilizing them in city squares, streets, parks, favelas, and beaches? What obstacles and opportunities does a privileged musical community face in building a populist musical movement across the racial, class, and gendered lines that typify social life in Rio de Janeiro? I ultimately argue that such privileged festive activism can promote tangible alternatives to the neoliberal city even as it faces many challenges in an extremely unequal society. In this book, I look seriously at the possibilities, limitations, and contradictions of cultural social movements led by the more privileged sectors of society, sometimes called "vanguards," as they confront a world that is becoming more unequal, more violent, and more authoritarian.

FIGURE 1.2 Anti-World Cup street art shows a soccer ball removing a favela.
Photo by author on September 23, 2014.

AN OLYMPIC CITY IN CRISIS

In 2009, *The Economist* famously published an issue with a cover that showed a jet-fueled Christ Redeemer statue "taking off" from Rio de Janeiro to symbolize the country's optimism and global ascendance. Brazil was preparing to host the 2014 World Cup and 2016 Olympics in Rio, which were awarded in the 2000s in recognition of the country's economic and social advances through that decade. These events seemed destined to broadcast an international display of Brazil's promise to become the "country of the future" it has long hoped to become. Their realization was set also to be an achievement of the center-left Workers Party that had overseen this period of economic growth and decreasing levels of inequality. With enormous investments in urban infrastructure, the World Cup and the Olympics would create the city anew with massive new public works and infrastructure. Rio de Janeiro would be an "Olympic City," joining the "World Cities" of the Global North as the first South American city to hold the event. In the time that preceded these two mega-events, the revived street carnival and Rio's brass movement grew and flourished amid political, social, and economic advances.

But Brazil became increasingly politically unstable throughout the 2010s. At the beginning of what would be a deep economic recession, 2013 saw massive leftist protests that Idelber Avelar calls a "truly epochal, revolutionary, and unique event" (2017, 10). The protests drew millions of Brazilians to the streets, along with many neofanfarrista bands in musical support in Rio in opposition to the neoliberal logic of the World Cup's Fédération Internationale de Football Association (FIFA) and the International Olympic Committee (IOC) setting much of the country's policy priorities and regulating public space. Protesters argued that the mega-events had produced spikes in cost of living, deprioritization of public services, and violent police occupations of the favelas, as widely depicted in the city's street art, such as in figure I.2. They confronted what Theresa Williamson described as "a modern experiment in urban development and what has become the most debated case of mega-event impact in history" (2016, 143). In 2013, *The Economist* updated its cover with the Christ statue flying off kilter and on course to crash.

Examining the neofanfarrismo movement over this period presents a critical lens through which one can understand some of the effects of and citizens' responses to the massive transformations that occurred in Rio de Janeiro as the world's eye turned to Brazil in the middle of the 2010s. Or, as saxophonist and activist Tomás Ramos put it, "Rio de Janeiro between 2007 and 2016 has become a center of the global urban question. We have become a center of the transnational market, a laboratory of capitalism. If I were to sum up the movement, I would say that it is a critique of the model of development of the city that is in question. Another city is possible, and we want more democracy" (interview 2014).

My fieldwork on which this book is based occurred primarily between 2104 and 2016, during the period when Olympic Rio de Janeiro's central priority was to create the city that FIFA and the IOC envisaged to showcase to the world. Cultural practices like street carnival and neofanfarrismo were at once viewed as valuable economic resources but also as threatening and disruptive to the neoliberal project of revitalizing the city for the benefit of investors. Street culture was variably commodified and repressed, celebrated and derided by the authorities. My initial research was focused on neofanfarrismo and the street carnival revival in their engagements and confrontations with the "Olympic City," which is still an important line of inquiry here.

But 2016 was not merely the year of the Olympics in Rio de Janeiro. Instead of the Olympics being an event of celebration for the Workers Party, the head of state overseeing the events was President Michel Temer of the center-right Partido do Movimento Democrático Brasileiro, who came to office after a successful and extremely divisive right-wing impeachment earlier that year against Workers Party President Dilma Rousseff. Though she had been the handpicked successor of the massively popular President Lula da Silva, Rousseff's reputation had been badly damaged by corruption scandals, leftist dissatisfaction that came to a boil in June 2013, economic decline, and an uptick in violence through the 2010s. Under attack from the right, the party collapsed under its own "antagonisms, contradictions, and oxymorons" (Avelar 2017, 9), and the liberatory potential of the 2013 protests seemed in retrospect to have led to reactionary right-wing backlash and ascendancy instead. With no confirmed evidence of corruption against Rousseff, many of her supporters and international onlookers saw her impeachment as a legislative coup based on a technicality. The delegitimization of the populist Workers Party would open space for extreme right-wing politics in the form of Jair Bolsonaro's election in 2018. Of course, 2016 was also a watershed year in global politics with a lurch to right-wing authoritarian nationalism that upset the neoliberal global order. Brexit in the UK, Donald Trump's election in the US, and other global events that year portended a disruption of global politics and the end of Latin America's center-left "Pink Tide" of the early twenty-first century.

Writing this book with the benefit of hindsight, the larger national, and indeed global, significance of this period of mega-events has become clearer, as well as the privileged vantage point of Rio de Janeiro as a representative site of much broader conflicts. I view the "Olympic City" not as a singular event, therefore, but as a *process* that began much before 2016 and continues beyond. Olympic Rio de Janeiro is the urban context and trajectory in which neofanfarrismo emerged from the growing street carnival as the country has struggled with the challenges of democratization. Rather than cementing the Brazilian consensus of Lula, who left office in 2010 with 87 percent approval, and his Workers Party, the Olympic process emblematized the dissensus and polarization that emerged in Brazil through 2010s. This book is an ethnography of Rio de Janeiro at the end of a period that Cariocas have quickly come to view as a latter-day "época de ouro" (golden era). The years leading to the downfall of Rousseff comprised a period of cultural effervescence, relative political stability, and economic growth fol-lowing post-dictatorship decadence and preceding what looks by the early 2020s increasingly like a possible collapse of democracy in Brazil and the ascendance of right-wing strongmen worldwide.

CRITICAL BRASS AS CRITICAL THEORY AND PRACTICE

This book's title is a pun on the Critical Mass movement, known as "Massa crítica" in Rio de Janeiro. Critical Mass is a global movement founded in 1992 in San Francisco, where I wrote much of this book, of bicyclists who ritually take over public roads and spaces in direct actions to call for bicycle infrastructure and alternatives to car culture. *Critical Brass* was also the title of the third album (2005) of New York's Hungry March Band, a reference for alternative brass bands in Rio. Akin to Critical Mass, neofanfarrismo is globally connected to transna-tional networks that take a critical stance on hegemonic culture and politics by occupying the streets with alternative practices through instrumental force.

Beyond this pun, I suggest that neofanfarrismo is itself a critical theoretical practice that, like the intellectual tradition of post-Marxist criticism launched by the Frankfurt School in early twentieth-century Germany as fascism was on the rise, is concerned with the role of culture in fomenting revolutionary change. Just as the Frankfurt School sought not solely to explain the world but to change it in the Marxist tradition, neofanfarrismo is a radical critique of the neoliberal global city in which the movement is embedded and an active attempt to transform it. Like critical theory, neofanfarrismo is not an ideology with an absolute meaning to which participants sign on. The movement's meanings and values are determined by participants' diverse opinions; that is, neofanfarrismo is a debate with varying views, including the belief that the movement is not, in fact, activist at all.

My own narrative voice does not aim to give a definitive answer to these debates or portray any one actor as a central authority, but rather to put them in lively, comprehensible conversation with one another for the reader to understand how these debates have animated the movement's trajectory as participants have critically theorized their own movement. I draw on Eric Drott's view (2017) that music is not only an element of "contentious politics," but also part of a "politics of contention," in which participants debate the meanings, values, and questions that music brings with it. I base my analysis of this politics of contention primarily in the analytical frameworks of participants themselves, such as Pires's "principles of carnival." And I put these local theories in conversation with broader debates regarding musical activism, musical circulation, social movements, and authoritarian politics.

In the post-Communist world, leftist artists are left with no blueprint to respond to the crises of capitalism. Neofanfarrismo's politics are ambivalent and ambiguous, and its practices constitute a wildly experimental laboratory for determining contemporary meanings of leftist politics and aesthetics. By locating critical agency and political power in festive practices, I argue that public festivity can be a generative force of social and political critique and action. Unlike in protest song, the movement's critiques are enacted, rather than referenced, through the practice of alternative repertoires in the streets. Following these repertoires through their various performative scenarios throughout the book, I bring together three understandings of the word "repertoire."

First, in its most common musical usage, the repertoires of neofanfarrismo constitute the musical body of knowledge known by movement participants. These repertoires are widely variable but are based on particular classic and folkloric Brazilian genres that were codified during Rio de Janeiro's street carnival revival beginning in the mid-1990s and have expanded to include musical genres from throughout Brazil and the world.

Second, I draw on Diana Taylor's broader notion of repertoire as comprising enactments of "embodied memory: performances, gestures, orality, movement, dance, singing—in short, all those acts usually thought of as ephemeral, nonreproducible knowledge" (2003, 20). In neofanfarrismo, these repertoires include the communally held knowledge of how to act in the street in order to musically shepherd hundreds to thousands of people. Musicians and *foliões* (audience members, from the word *folia*, or revelry) know how to create human chains to protect musicians in dense carnival crowd settings. They know how to use the tactic of "mic check" (*microfone humano*) popularized in Occupy Wall Street to organize people in the streets. They know how to musically and organizationally respond to police encroachment.

As such, neofanfarristas employ these musical and extramusical repertoires as political strategies and tools of mobilization, and I therefore expand on Charles Tilly's "repertoire of contention," or the tools and knowledge available to social movements to challenge and contest hegemonic regimes (2010). What I call the movement's *musical repertoires of contention* constitute the body of expressive and sonic knowledge that neofanfarristas deploy in spaces of confrontation with hegemonic powers.

In neofanfarrismo, lines between political and cultural uses of these diverse repertoires are blurred and even nonexistent. Carnival songs were repurposed for the momentous 2013 protests. The Occupy Wall Street movement inspired the carnival bloco Ocupa Carnaval, critical of Brazilian politics. New Orleans jazz funeral songs are performatively used to memorialize the "death" of street carnival when a bloco is attacked by the police. Again following Diana Taylor, I interpret the diverse repertoires of neofanfarrismo as enacted in a variety of "scenarios." From carnival to protest, late-night jams in the streets to major stages in Rio and throughout the world, it is the shifting uses of these repertoires in changing scenarios that interest me—how neofanfarristas critically theorize and deploy their embodied knowledge to navigate changing realities.

MUSICAL SOCIAL MOVEMENTS

In locating political agency in cultural repertoires, the case of neofanfarrismo intervenes on a long debate about the role of culture in social movements.[6] Rather than understanding how social movements "mobilize" music, I show that here the relationship between festive and political practices is much more dynamic, interactive, and, in an important sense, inseparable. In the case of neofanfarrismo, the dominant theoretical paradigm of social movements using culture as a functionalist "resource" or propagandistic supplement is turned on its head. In Rio de Janeiro, politicized musical engagements in the brass band community largely arose from festive and carnivalesque practices and experiments in the streets. In this case, the question is not the standard "how do social movements use music?" but, rather, how do musical communities come to articulate themselves as social movements?

When communities of public festivity take on critical and alternative stances to the interests of governing regimes, I argue that they are themselves social movements, or *musical social movements* to underline their sonic and cultural components. Public festivity is not "prefigurative politics"—it is politics itself, or, as Angela Marino writes, "Fiesta is about governance: governance of land, people and place . . . [The fiesta can operate] as if it were the state to rehearse an alternative system of rules and conduct . . . Fiestas offer ways to move further towards how to govern ourselves" (2014, 70–71). Neofanfarrismo represents an alternative governance to that of the Olympic City.

In viewing neofanfarrismo as a musical social movement that has come to network with international musical and activist movements like HONK!, I contextualize the movement within recent Brazilian and global leftist, antineoliberal social movements in the post-Communist world, such as the global justice movement (or the antiglobalization movement), Britain's Reclaim the Streets, the Arab Spring, Spain's Indignados, Occupy Wall Street, Brazil's June 2013 protests, Black Lives Matter, and antifascist protests. According to social movements scholar Manuel Castells, these "networked social movements" are internationally networked but manifest physically in the local public space, which "is constructed as a hybrid space between the Internet social networks and the occupied urban space: connecting cyberspace and urban space in relentless interaction, constituting, technologically and culturally, instant communities of transformative practice" (2012, 11). Their organizing form, like the internet, is horizontal and "rhizomatic,"[7] and they are critical of the hierarchical forms of communist parties and earlier social movements. Departing from a concern with representational democracy, in their direct taking of public space and experimentation with new models of governance like public assemblies and consensus, these movements have sought new ways to embody democracy itself in conversation with translocal networks of resistance (Graeber 2013). Like these diverse movements, neofanfarristas have used the internet and social media to put musicians and crowds in public space, circumventing the city's cultural institutions and venues. They often proclaim "horizontal" organization, though the discourse of horizontalism is generally in tension with hidden and explicit power differentials. They are internationally connected and see themselves as part of a growing, mobile, and rhizomatic movement that seeks to reclaim public space with musical crowds. They perceive themselves as a political alternative and even a model of democracy in action.

While I recognize the transformational potential of all these critical engagements, I maintain a degree of caution about the possibility for enacting lasting political change through musical social movements. Such skepticism is best summed up by Gregório Duvivier, himself a participant in the neofanfarrismo movement, on his satirical HBO Brasil show *Greg News*, in which he portrays a potential carnivalesque protest against Rio's State Governor Wilson Witzel. Witzel had suggested that no one should go into the street armed for risk of being shot by police, but that carrying a Bible instead of a gun might keep people safe. Duvivier ironically portrays an enthusiastic musical activist: "Everyone, the governor is killing indiscriminately, but we are going to counterattack with a carnival march! We'll create the 'Don't Kill Me Because I'm Carrying a Bible' Bloco." Losing the character, Duvivier reflects on the strategy, "The Carioca is the king of humorous protest . . . It's great. I love it, but I don't know if it's working."[8]

CONTRADICTIONS OF AN ALTERNATIVE MOVEMENT

Part of this limited political potential, I suggest, is due to the positionality and contradictions inherent to a privileged, alternative movement. French trombonist Clément Mombereau, who has lived and played in Rio since 2011, mused: "The movement genuinely sees itself as alternative, but there is some basic incoherence that is part of it all and is inherent to any alternative artistic movement. You are at once against and inside the system. How much can you really be political with this kind of thing?" (interview 2014). This comment reveals an animating tension between the movement's embrace of the "alternative" as a relatively static and privileged identity marker on the one hand, and as a sign of dynamic transformation on the other.

The Alternative as an Identity Rooted in Race and Class

The broader demographic from which this ambitious musical social movement arose is often referred to as Rio de Janeiro's "alternative middle classes," whose lives and leisure activities are stitched into the spectacular urban geography of the city (see the map on page vi). Nestled between the Guanabara Bay and the hilly Tijuca rainforest, Rio's Center, where much of the brass band activity takes place, is a mix of dilapidated colonial architecture and high-rise office buildings. The area has become the entertainment destination since the revitalization of the Lapa neighborhood beginning in the 2000s. The most privileged Cariocas live in the South Zone neighborhoods, from roughly Santa Teresa to Leblon, with the more leftist and bohemian South Zone residents living closer to the Center. From the lower South Zone neighborhoods and west into Barra de Tijuca, where many of the Olympic games were held, residents are increasingly White, rich, and conservative. North of the Center, the city's poorer North Zone spreads out in a mix of working-class neighborhoods and Blacker favelas. Hillside favelas also rise above richer neighborhoods throughout the city creating a proximity of vastly unequal classes unique to Rio. Connecting the alternative neofanfarrismo community to the city's geography, trombonist Marco Serragrande explains that, "To be alternative here in Rio is to like vanguardish things—up and coming, still growing, new parties. Of course, in practice its majority is the middle class that lives in the South Zone, Lapa, and Santa Teresa, very much this cultural axis—Botafogo to the Center" (interview 2015).

Many neofanfarristas have had access to international travel and university education, and they have the privilege to play in outdoor spaces as well as the most important venues in the city, facing far less repression than poorer populations. Calling neofanfarrismo an expression of the "folkloric bourgeoisie," Mombereau suggests that the movement "is at the margins of the principal culture of the South Zone. It's 'alternative South Zone' because the mainstream South Zone is more the *playboyzinhos* and the *patricinhas*" (interview 2014). "Playboyzinhos" (from "playboy") and "patricinhas" are the respective male and female terms for the richer and "politically alienated" residents of the privileged South Zone, where the famed beaches of Ipanema and Copacabana are located. "Alternative South Zone" residents define themselves in opposition to such characters.

Neofanfarristas call attention to their class position more often than to the movement's racial demographics. Class remains the dominant analytical tool for understanding inequality in Brazil, and this is especially true in Rio de Janeiro where racial boundaries can appear more porous than class boundaries. From a North American perspective, neofanfarrismo would seem to be an extremely racially diverse movement, if mostly limited to the middle class. Class privilege in Brazil, however, still strongly correlates to race—as Stuart Hall famously wrote, "Race is the modality in which class is lived" (1996, 341). As a middle-class movement, neofanfarrismo is an expression of a demographic that I refer to as predominantly *Whiter* within Rio's and Brazil's racial spectrum.[9] Orquestra Voadora's saxophonist André Ramos positions the demographic of which neofanfarrismo is a part in distinction both to Blacker communities culturally fetishized in Brazil and to a conservative, Eurocentric White culture:

Brazil is huge, and the experience of people in the small [Afro-descendant] cities of Bahia is very different from our middle-class experience in Rio de Janeiro. Here the South Zone is very much the culture of the White man. Men don't dance here. Brazil has prejudices against homosexuality. We have all the problems of a Eurocentric society. We don't know how to dance like Afro-Brazilians . . . We have a dominant society that puts the United States and Europe above all others, but we don't belong to those places. We try to imitate [these foreign countries], but we will never be them. (Interview 2015)

Though neofanfarrismo is Whiter, there are many participants, and increasingly more as the movement diversifies, who are racialized as "Black" (*pretx/a/o* or *negrx/a/o*) or one of many terms in Brazil for mixed-race people, and the reader should under no circumstances presume that the movement is White or utterly lacking in People of Color. I refer to neofanfarrismo as "Whiter" rather than "White" in order not to reify stable racial identities which are in fact fluid and highly diverse. To note that the movement is "Whiter" is to note that it is Whiter not only than the Blacker (but also racially heterogenous) samba schools to which it portrays itself as an alternative, but also Whiter than many other popular scenes in Rio de Janeiro. Paying attention to racial demographics is important to understand how the movement relates to particular racialized repertoires, expressive practices, and communities in ways that a class-based analysis cannot fully capture on its own. More broadly, I suggest that the terms "Blacker" and "Whiter" can emphasize the relational element of racial formation in critical race studies, which often, especially in Brazil, cannot be divided cleanly into Black and White. Though I use the terms "Blacker" and "Whiter," I also use the less comparative terms "Blackness" and "Whiteness" to refer to racial formations as well as value and aesthetic systems in Brazil.[10]

Whiteness in Brazil is associated with a long legacy of privilege based in colonialism, slavery, eugenics, and postslavery immigration policies that explicitly sought to "Whiten" and "civilize" the country. Since President Getúlio Vargas's embrace of a mixed-raced country in the 1930s, "racial democracy"—a celebration of Brazil's supposed intimate racial harmony, mixing, equality—has dominated official discourses about race. The racial democracy has often been celebrated in Brazil in contrast to the United States' one-drop rule and official policies of racial segregation in order to proclaim that Brazil is more racially progressive and harmonious. The idea has been widely denounced as a "myth" that sustains racial and class disparities while depriving citizens of a vocabulary to denounce racism, and this critique has inspired diverse antiracist movements. Recognition of the myth has led to important studies of Blackness in Brazil, but studies on Whiteness are still relatively few even as critical race scholars have argued that examining Whiteness is crucial to understanding racism.

In what seems to be a new, toxic stage of Brazil's official racial discourses, Bolsonaro, with frequent disparaging remarks about indigenous and Blacker Brazilians, could be viewed as a *celebrant* of White supremacy in Brazil, with a bolder explicit identification with the privileges of Whiteness among the elite and denigration of all else. In this explicit embrace of *hegemonic Whiteness*, by which I mean a Whiter racial formation entrenched in the maintenance of its racial privileges, we are perhaps witnessing the dismantling of the racial democracy framework that has long disguised the hegemony of Whiteness.[11] In this book, I examine what I call neofanfarrismo's *alternative Whiteness*, by which I mean an intersection of a Whiter racial demographic with middle-class privilege and leftist politics. Drawing inspiration from the tendency in gender studies to view masculinities and femininities in the plural, I focus on multiple, conflicting Whitenesses in Brazil. I ask whether Whiteness can be anything other than a hegemonic category and what potential Whiter communities have to act in the realization of a society closer to genuine racial democracy. That is, in embracing the "alternative," can Whiteness decenter its own hegemonic position?[12]

Given that racial formations are relational, in identifying the movement's alternative Whiteness, I also examine how participants position themselves in relation to multiple forms of Blackness. Brazil shares with other postslavery countries of the Americas the paradoxical feature of being at once nations founded on White supremacy and postcolonial societies that culturally distinguished themselves through commodifying the repertoires of Blackness, such as jazz in the United States, *son* in Cuba, calypso in Trinidad, and, of course, samba in Brazil. In Rio de Janeiro, samba, and particularly the samba schools to which neofanfarrismo presents itself as a carnivalesque alternative, has been viewed as the authenticated and commodified heritage of the city. Though samba has always had many critical strains, the genre has been officially embraced since the 1930s as a celebration of what could be called a *hegemonic Blackness* that takes pride in Brazil's African heritage but has not generally contested the racial democracy paradigm and is rather emblematic of it, thereby supporting hegemonic Whiteness and the maintenance of structural racism. It is indeed partly the present and past connections to governmental and corporate power of the samba schools that is alienating to neofanfarristas. Though samba remains an important repertoire of neofanfarrismo, especially when it is celebrated for its critical legacies, many musicians are equally drawn to other Blacker repertoires—such as samba-reggae, funk Carioca, Afrobeat, and reggae—that manifest what I call *alternative Blackness*, which openly contests the racism of the Atlantic World and resists the conciliatory politics of hegemonic Blackness.

By virtue of its dominance, hegemonic Whiteness across the Atlantic World claimed access to and control of Blacker heritage even when it did not construct Whiter communities as heritage bearers, which Dylan Robinson critiques as dominant cultures' presumption of "inheritance" of the expressions of marginalized cultures (2020, 155). By contrast, I argue that the "alternativeness" of neofanfarrismo's prevailing middle-class Whiteness indicates what I call a strategy of *disinheritance*. Neofanfarristas seek to disinherit both the legacies of conservative, hegemonic Whiteness and the commodification of hegemonic Blackness, such as the samba schools that have been presented as the official heritage of the city, by playing a wide variety of musically eclectic repertoires. Neofanfarrismo is an expression of what I call the *alternative carnivalesque*, an ethic and aesthetic of critiquing and expanding the dominant repertoires of carnival. Because the ethos of carnival is celebrated as a counterdominant tradition, the alternative carnivalesque may appear redundant. But because carnival has been so often used and appropriated as a mode of hegemonic governmentality (Guilbault 2007), I consider the alternative carnivalesque as a mode of expression that aims to renew carnival's purported criticality and destabilize the ossification of tradition.

In identifying neofanfarrismo as belonging to a specific social demographic distinguishing itself from others through expressive practices, I suggest that in conflict with its populist intentions to grow and diversify are the social boundaries of "distinction" that it creates.[13] The movement's relational tastes, values, expressions, and vocabularies are based in the participants' particular class-racial-political intersections, which can be exclusionary to those outside of those boundaries. Neofanfarrismo manifests distinctive forms of sociality, and the movement's practices can be viewed as largely "rituals of intensification" of preexisting communities of sociality (Agier 1995). I do not discount the cases in which carnival has played a tangible role in subverting power relations or hybridizing distinct communities, and indeed I also document such cases here. But I recognize that the purpose of participating in carnival practices for many communities is primarily, but certainly not exclusively, to manifest their distinct cultural practices. In carnival cultures around the world, the opportunity to party in one's community through embracing the cultural expressions that bind its members is primarily what people look forward to all year, and neofanfarrismo is no different. In this sense, the word "alternative," like other alternative music scenes, designates a distinct demographic with particular tastes, as well as a market of financial opportunity surrounding it that includes sponsors, venues, producers, mobile beer sellers, and many other actors not strongly animated by activism.

The Alternative as Transformational

Yet only portraying neofanfarrismo's alternative stance as simply an expression of subcultural identity would fail to engage with its transformations, diversification, and aspirations. Though alternative movements do confront challenges in building beyond themselves due to the very situatedness of their identities, this book shows some of the pathways that alternative movements can take to gradually diversify beyond their original memberships and manifest critical practices. In contrast to its use as a marker of distinction, in its transformational and relational sense, I view the alternative as always "emergent" in Raymond Williams's sense (1977). Williams argues that certain "dominant" cultural formations permeate social and political structures. "Emergent" cultural formations can arise that may replace the dominant cultural formations, but the emergent can also be woven into the dominant cultural formation out of which new emergent cultural forms can arise. Importantly, though the emergent is merely "alternative" if it can be coopted and reincorporated into the dominant, some emergent formations can be actively "oppositional" to the dominant. Following this argument, I suggest that in its combative manifestations the alternative can turn "activist," a discourse that neofanfarrismo has increasingly embraced.

The emergent and dominant are, therefore, mutually constitutive, entwined, and dialogic discourses, dynamically creating new possibilities, but the question of how much the emergent has a truly transformative and oppositional capacity is what is at stake here. Clearly, these categories of emergent and dominant and the related categories of "alternative" and "hegemonic" have relationships to real material conditions of power, position, and inequality. Though I adapt Williams's model to understand the transformations of the movement, however, my analysis is not based on a classical materialist conception of cultural expression as dependent upon ruling and subjugated class confrontations, in which the hegemonic is conflated with the former and the alternative with the latter. By contrast, this book is instead an ethnography of a relatively privileged "alternative" community that often portrays marginalized traditions like the Blacker samba schools as "hegemonic." By examining the articulations of dominant and alternative value regimes within this musical community as theories and rationalizations of praxis, my inquiry is focused on musicians' animating *perceptions* of what is "dominant" or "hegemonic" and what is "Other" or "alternative," and the impact of these perceptions on the material world.

I suggest that cultural groups that view themselves as alternative are likely to embrace change and be continually emergent—that is, like Pires's "principles of carnival," the alternative is a performative and rationalizing discourse that creates an engine for cultural change. Once a formally emergent tradition has gained dominance, a cultural formation that views itself as alternative will likely continue the search for new alternatives. The history of Rio de Janeiro's brass movement in the past twenty years emblematizes such a dynamic process. "Alternative," culturally nationalist brass blocos emerged in the late 1990s as an alternative to the dominant samba schools. The diverse, international repertoires of the later neofanfarrismo movement were framed as an alternative to the cultural nationalism of the brass blocos. New alternatives, such as brass projects that highlight the role of women, the poor, and other historically excluded populations, have arisen within neofanfarrismo to challenge the privileged, Whiter, middle-class, and predominantly male profiles of the movement.

Because of the dependence of the emergent on the dominant, however, the transformational aspirations of alternative movements are inherently compromised and limited by the conditions that make their existence possible. All this is to say that neofanfarrismo is ensconced within the class, gender, racial, and geographic structures and conditions it seeks to challenge. It is emblematic of what DaMatta calls the "Brazilian dilemma," or the maintenance of social hierarchies despite the vibrant egalitarianism of the country's carnival traditions (1991 [1979]).[14] The diverse uses of the word alternative show that the goals of an alternative music scene are rarely reducible to one coherent cultural or political agenda. The emergence of neofanfarrismo as a self-proclaimed alternative movement has been a complex, contested, unfinished, and contradictory process. Alternative music scenes are in many cases animated by their *incoherence*—by their competing priorities and contested ideas.[15] The "alternative" is first and foremost a debate within a particular community, and my focus in this book is on the dynamic tensions between fragmentation and unity in the consolidation of the alternative musical social movement of neofanfarrismo.

CANNIBALIZING THE BRASS BAND

Any alternative movement will tell you just as much about what it isn't as about what it is, and neofanfarristas likewise self-consciously distance themselves from what the term "fanfarra" might evoke. Brass bands around the world are largely perceived as traditionalist, and in Brazil fanfarras can call to mind military and firemen bands, conservative civic ceremonies like Independence Day on September 7, and provincial bands from the "interior" away from the coastal cities. Neofanfarristas stress that their "new-brass" movement is alternative within the Brazilian context because of its musically eclectic repertoire, populist ethics, and "activist" engagements.[16] Juliano Pires, who attests to the principles of carnival discussed above, argues that neofanfarrismo represents a dual "cannibalization" (*antropofagia*) of the brass band, a transformation in a musical and ethical sense. In using the term "cannibalism," Pires draws on a Brazilian cultural discourse originally articulated by the modernist poet Oswald de Andrade's *Manifesto Antropófago* (1928), in which Andrade argues that Brazil's greatest artistic strength is the voracious consumption and transformation of all possible influences. The celebration of cannibalism parodies indigenous practices of eating and digesting foreign colonizers in order to take their power, and it has since played an important role in Brazilian arts as a prominent, historically Whiter, theory of Brazilian cosmopolitanism and modernism. Pires argues,

> In neofanfarrismo, we have two cannibalisms: the musical part is the cannibalism of changing the traditional format and music of the fanfarra. Generally, these ensembles play traditional music and we cannibalistically play contemporary music, whatever we like. And the other cannibalism is political and conceptual and comes from *fanfarrão*, because in Brazil a fanfarrão is someone who just parties and thinks everything is cool . . . We want to take responsibility. We want to assume that all art must have a political, social, and ecological [impact], especially when it is street art. The street is a privileged place because it has contact with all kinds of people. (Interview 2014)

According to Pires, the movement is, on the one hand, a rejection of the association of the ensemble with "traditional" music and, on the other, a critique of the politically "alienated" fanfarrão in favor of the *neofanfarrão*, the politically and socially engaged brass musician.[17]

Cannibalizing Carnival Music

Neofanfarrismo is a musical telling of stories about Carioca, Brazilian, and "world music." The movement not only frames itself as a departure from the traditional fanfarra, but also proclaims that carnival need not be associated with any particular genres, launching a radical critique of Rio de Janeiro's official carnival. Despite their values of spontaneity and freedom, pre-Lenten carnivals are in most places rites of traditionalism in which certain practices and genres gain auras of authenticity and heritage. Rio de Janeiro maintains significant investment in promoting particular carnival traditions as "authentic" manifestations of Brazilian culture, especially the Blacker samba schools. Most scholarly attention on the city's carnival has been paid to the samba schools and their roles in consolidating a singular, hegemonic national identity, or *brasilidade*, framed around African and mixed-race cultural roots.[18] Less attention has been paid to Rio's revived and explosive street carnival.[19] After a period of relative dormancy during the dictatorship (1964 to 1985), the city's blocos have been growing and constantly diversifying the repertoires of carnival. With over five hundred official blocos in 2020, and many more unofficial ones, the importance of the street carnival revival and its growing musical diversity rivals, and for many Cariocas eclipses, that of the samba schools. Both contribute to carnival now attracting approximately six million participants and holding the title of largest party on earth.

The initial musical critique of Rio's carnival by the brass bloco revival that began in the 1990s enlarged the admissible carnival repertoires beyond the characteristic samba and marchinha that had been framed as the authentic heritage repertoires of carnival. In celebrating the "alternative carnivalesque" and "disinheriting" the official Carioca carnival, these musicians launched an alternative heritage movement. They valorized a more "diversified cultural nationalism" as the aesthetic of a new "authentic" carnival through expanding repertoires to include other Brazilian genres, including *maxixe*, frevo, and *forró*, especially those perceived as "folkloric." In this initial stage, brass musicians articulated a discourse of *nationalist rescue* (*resgate*), one that had been deployed in earlier moments in Brazilian popular music history. "Rescue" is an expression of nostalgia that is devoted to the preservation and promotion of folkloric and national genres and is anxious about international influence.

Beginning in the mid-2000s, brass ensembles would further disinherit Rio's official carnival by embracing international and popular Brazilian genres beyond the folkloric pluralism of the earlier brass blocos. This diversification stands in stark contrast to mid twentieth-century efforts that used carnival to authenticate particular musical genres as heritage expressions of the singular national identity of brasilidade. In this alternative shift, musicians have employed the discourse of *internationalist cannibalism (antropofagia)*, putting their musical movement in historical dialogue with Brazilian artistic movements that sought to be in active engagement with the rest of the world, such as Tropicália. In their musically eclectic claim that one could "play anything" in carnival, Orquestra Voadora and the bands of neofanfarrismo sought to revolutionize and globalize the aesthetics of this gigantic festivity. Despite this voracious musical appetite, the movement reveals particular aesthetic affinities based in class and race positions, and I trace their aesthetic approximations to and distancing from particular cultural traditions and communities in the movement's articulation of itself as alternative.[20]

Cannibalism as Activism

While Brazilian cannibalism is often examined as a primarily aesthetic theory, it is important that Andrade's theory at its core was also ethical in its embrace of anticolonialism. Moving to the second of Pires's propositions about neofanfarrismo's cannibalism, that the movement represents a critique of the politically disengaged fanfarrão, this book engages the question of what constitutes musical activism in contemporary Rio de Janeiro. Saxophonist Mathias Mafort defines activism broadly: "Activism is a confrontation with reality. You can show another person that other things are possible beyond their closed reality. Everyone has their closed reality. And this reality can be opened up for something bigger" (interview 2015). Building on this expansive definition, I view neofanfarrismo's theorizing and practice of activism as a wide array of creative expressions of the alternative carnivalesque. Neofanfarrismo's activism is an extension of Pires's principles of carnival"—carnival as egalitarian, participatory, and even revolutionary—into an ethical guide for musical action.

Because the musical activism of the brass ensemble is not primarily based on the semantic content of lyrics, the focus of many studies of musical activism,[21] I use the term *instrumental activism* to examine the particular ways that instrumental ensembles manifest social and political power and how they might be instrumental to the realization of alternative possibilities. The power of music is in many cases, and certainly in instrumental music, defined more by the political, spatial, and musical relations it constructs in the act of performance than by its signifying content.[22] Beyond using musical repertoires to engage in *instrumental protest*, neofanfarrismo's musical activism aims, in the more utopian portraits of the movement such as the "Anthem of Orquestra Voadora" discussed above, at a musicalization of the entire city. In contrast to the spectated, neoliberal city, neofanfarristas demand a "right to the city" (Lefebvre 1968) by fostering what I call a *soundscape of public participation* that forges senses of belonging to the public body by playing music in the streets.[23] Through organizing open blocos and weekly classes (*oficinas*) as well as other inclusive strategies, musicians seek to democratize access to the production of music and integrate previously excluded populations, including women, Blacker communities, and favelados.

Pires's dual definition of the aesthetic and ethical cannibalisms of the movement reveals a classic split in alternative scenes between an "apolitical counterculture" and a "politicized left" to which I gestured above. Many studies tend to conflate the two categories or treat the countercultural as the cultural or aesthetic expression of leftist politics, while others dismiss the tangible impact of counterculture as political. In Brazil in the 1960s and '70s, counterculture was at times defended as a form of political action by the "festive left" (*esquerda festiva*). It was also viewed as explicitly disengaged from politics, an expression of an "'alternative Left,' which placed value on the subjective dimension of politics based on everyday experience" (Dunn 2016, 203). While I make no naïve distinction between the cultural and the political, neofanfarristas' own recognition of a divide between some devoted to parties and others to political struggle highlights tensions common to many alternative scenes and movements. The reality that much of the movement is composed of both activists and fanfarrões shows that the cultural element of musical social movements is at once the most animating force of movement expansion, as well as one of the biggest obstacles to forming a social movement that is more clearly oppositional.

RAIN, SWEAT, BEER, AND RESEARCH

Caetano Veloso's 1977 song "Chuva, suor, e cerveja," adapted and played by some of the brass blocos, captures well the corporal and hedonistic aspects of doing fieldwork on neofanfarrismo: in carnival, "We get drenched in rain, sweat, and beer." My ethnographic experiences often included being jammed in crowds of thousands while trying to execute passages on my trumpet, sprayed with beer, pushed up against other musicians, then alleviated on occasion by a light rain that cooled down Rio's persistent heat. I often thought of large blocos as carnivalesque bodies in Bakhtin's sense of being porous, grotesque, and full of laughter. Listening back to some of these recordings I made by leaving my recorder on while I played and roamed through the crowds of musicians for hours on end, my fieldwork itself sounds grotesque, capturing drinking and laughing, as well as the many mistakes musicians made trying to drunkenly execute musical passages. In musical ensembles that could range into the hundreds, my recordings from inside the bands and blocos could never capture the whole ensembles, but only the sounds of the various limbs of the grotesque musical body.

Researching a Participatory Movement

The neofanfarrismo scene is so internationally oriented that, though I was frequently reminded of my inexorable condition as a gringo in Brazil, I was a neofanfarrista as soon as I arrived with trumpet in hand. I joined the circuit of long-term creative international residents of the bohemian Santa Teresa neighborhood where brass band activity is particularly rich. My US nationality afforded me relative privilege and was often critiqued by my fellow neofanfarristas. But as a White, male, university-educated musician in a privileged internationalist movement, my relationships to my informants often felt closer to collaborations between social peers, rather than advocacy for an underprivileged community typical of much ethnomusicological scholarship.

My introduction to the neofanfarrismo community resulted from what felt like a haphazard series of encounters beginning with the Bay Area's Occupy movement in 2011, a series of events that makes more sense in retrospect as the encounters reflect transnational networks that I have come to understand better. Propelling many of the actions of Occupy Oakland was the Brass Liberation Orchestra (BLO), founded in 2002 during the mobilization against the Iraq War. I started playing trumpet with the BLO at protests all around the Bay Area, coming to know the networks and histories of activism for which the Bay cities are rightly known (Snyder forthcoming; 2015). In 2012, I toured with the BLO to the Boston HONK! Festival of Activist Street Bands where I found an emerging international network of alternative brass bands. Building on my experience with BLO, in 2013, I co-founded Mission Delirium, a professional brass band based in the Mission district of San Francisco that has shared bills with Rebirth, Soul Rebels, Kermit Ruffins, and Too Many Zoos (Snyder 2020a). Also in 2013, I noticed that the Carioca band Os Siderais was listed as a performing band in Boston's HONK!, and I discovered the band was part of the much larger musical community of neofanfarrismo in Rio de Janeiro around which I began to orient my research.

Neofanfarrismo is a movement of participation, and my experience as a trumpet player was the foundation upon which I was able to carry out this research. If I had not played a relevant instrument, I felt I would have had to start learning one to be taken seriously as a researcher, although valuable studies on street carnival have been undertaken from the perspective of foliões who raise other perspectives (see Andrade 2012). This book is based on my experience in most relevant musical situations being "inside the cord" (*dentro do cordão*), referring to the physical cord that is placed around the musicians in a bloco to protect them from the packed foliões, or to a human one composed by foliões holding hands to protect the musicians. Besides playing in the bands and blocos, I was asked to teach classes and run rehearsals for Orquestra Voadora and other bands, and I temporarily felt like a fixture of the neofanfarrismo scene. These relations facilitated creating research relationships as most neofanfarristas knew me as a fellow musician, one of many other gringos in the movement, before knowing of my research project.

Many of Rio's brass bands expand during carnival into open blocos and run open rehearsals in which sitting in and playing in carnival is encouraged. Carnival seasons were periods when I could access almost any relevant music project, and, in addition to street carnival, I paraded with the first samba school Estácio de Sá to gain a stronger sense of the institutions neofanfarristas so often critiqued. Outside of carnival season, I performed with several bands, gave lessons, sat in on rehearsals, went to shows, played at protests, and frequented the many brass jam sessions in the streets. I conducted over fifty formal interviews, which allowed me to construct an oral history of the movement as it developed before my fieldwork and to portray the complex debates that animate this book. Using social media was an integral part of the research process, both to contact potential interviewees and contacts as well as to follow the movement's self-documentation and propagation. Many Cariocas rely on Facebook, Whatsapp, and other social media networks to an extent I had not seen previously. These platforms are used to organize events in public spaces, sometimes quite spontaneously, without recourse to central venues or institutions (Bairros 2012), creating a hybrid dimension between physical space and social media in the movement (Sézérat and Andrade 2016).

Living in Santa Teresa with Juliano Pires, who had traveled to HONK! in Boston with Os Siderais in 2013 and returned determined create a Carioca version, I was part of the organizing committee of the HONK RiO! festival, which took place in August 2015 for the first time. The festival was largely organized at my house with different subcommittees coming in and out, and I produced a tour for my band Mission Delirium to the Brazilian HONK! festival. My wife, trombonist and community organizer Claire Haas, who came as a member of Mission Delirium to Rio de Janeiro and stayed throughout my fieldwork participating as a musician in the movement, has been an important companion in this project and is cited as one of many international participants. Building on my experiences with several HONK! festivals in the US and Brazil, I worked with Boston HONK! organizer Reebee Garofalo and Erin Allen to edit a volume of chapters about the increasingly transnational movements of alternative brass bands through the lens of the HONK! festival network, *HONK! A Street Band Renaissance of Music and Activism* (2020). In addition to visiting Rio since formal fieldwork and following these international networks, I have met up with Carioca bands in the United States as they have increased their touring to North American HONK! festivals, and I also toured for six weeks with the Brazilian neofanfarrista band Bagunço in France and Italy in the summer of 2016 and completed subsequent European tours with Mission Delirium.

Defining an Amorphous Movement

Who is a neofanfarrista, what bands count as part of the movement, and when did it start? Because "membership in a collective is rarely unified and stable but rather intermittent, provisional, and open-ended" (Sakakeeny 2010, 23), defining the boundaries of neofanfarrismo, a term with uncertain origin but likely attributable to Pires with his founding of Orquestra Voadora in 2008, is difficult. Neofanfarrismo refers to a dispersed network of professional to beginning musicians in Rio de Janeiro, and increasingly in other cities of Brazil, that integrates all musical levels in between. Some musicians have owned their instruments since childhood and trained in conservatory; others buy them the same year they begin to play in multiple blocos, inspired to learn them specifically to participate in carnival and neofanfarrismo. Some bands are crisp, professional, and arranged, even if they create spaces for amateur participation, while others are entirely anarchic.

Many groups manifest a range of activities along a spectrum of what Thomas Turino calls presentational to participatory performances, contributing to a high degree of porousness between groups during participatory manifestations (2008). During the year, bands develop their own repertoires in closed membership formations, performing presentationally in shows both in the street and on stage. These bands often create their own open, expandable, and participatory blocos in which they teach and disseminate their material. Orquestra Voadora, for example, is a closed stage band (*banda*) of twelve musicians performing throughout much of the year. But through its classes (oficinas) and bloco of four hundred musicians, the band has spread its material to hundreds of other musicians. During the "long carnival season," with carnival rehearsals beginning as early as five months before in the case of Voadora, musicians circulate between a series of mostly open blocos where they can learn a variety of songs.

Other musicians are only peripherally involved in neofanfarrismo. Some musicians involved in the more traditional brass blocos, especially percussionists, are also involved in the samba schools and other percussion blocos and are not at all present in the newer neofanfarrismo bands. Some neofanfarristas are completely uninterested in the traditional repertoires of the older brass blocos, which do not necessarily identify with the term neofanfarrismo. Other brass musicians only appear in the movement at carnival, otherwise playing in the symphony, military bands, jazz circuit, or not playing at all. The movement is a diffuse community, but the common identity around the term "neofanfarrismo" invites us to consider it as indeed a "movement," rather than merely a scene, and its processes of consolidation as such.

I have framed my investigation particularly around Orquestra Voadora, which has been the most popular and identifiable band associated with neofanfarrismo. Voadora is at once commercially successful, ambivalently views itself as activist, and sometimes engages in protest, and it therefore emblematizes the broader tensions between the diverse priorities of the movement. The band inaugurated the transformation from the carnival brass bloco revival toward an internationally oriented year-round brass band movement that came to be known as neofanfarrismo in the late 2000s. Using Voadora as a pivot has helped me trace the larger trajectory of the movement before and after the band's influence. However, in this book, this until recently all-male and Whiter band functions more as a window onto the larger movement of neofanfarrismo rather than as the book's central protagonist in order to consider the transformations and diversification of the movement. I also introduce the reader to selected case studies of other key bands and blocos, such as the blocos out of which Voadora was born as well as newer feminist groups and bands in favelas that later contested the movement's dominant identities. Because of the movement's openness and diversity of organizations, no one band should be understood as a discreet entity distinct from the larger community, but rather as a particular expression of an amorphous community with many distinct manifestations that feature many of the same actors.

The research and drafting for this book were finished right before the global calamity of the coronavirus pandemic hit Brazil soon after the 2020 carnival, which was viewed in retrospect as a site of contagion though the virus seemed a distant threat at the time. Beginning in March 2020, the mass events of social intimacy examined in this book largely ceased or went online, and the 2021 carnival was canceled in an unprecedented move, an effort that neofanfarristas and street carnival institutions supported in contrast to Bolsonaro's virus denialism (Snyder 2021b)—carnival in 2022 was postponed due to omicron but took place in April. The unprecedented development of the pandemic afforded a breaking point for my narrative, and the pandemic is largely not considered here but admittedly makes the book oddly dated, like watching a movie during the pandemic from the prepandemic world where no one is wearing a mask. This book, already a history, speaks to the dreams, struggles, and fears of the previrus world. Though I recognize that Covid-19 is a game changer—perhaps never again will beer and kisses be shared in carnival so liberally as before the virus—I doubt that the debates and lessons of the before times will be obsolete.

PARADE ROUTE

The organization of this book is based on Pires's above distinction between a musical and political transformation, or "double cannibalization," of Rio's brass ensembles. The first two chapters examine transformations in the emergence of the neofanfarrismo movement from the brass blocos of the street carnival revival and the bands' changing repertoires. The last four chapters explore the notion that neofanfarristas have transformed the brass ensemble from its apolitical, politically conservative, and merely festive functions into one preoccupied with social and political engagements from leftist perspectives, diversifying the participating demographics in the process.

In chapter 1, I discuss the reemergence of the street carnival at the turn of the millennium in relation to the broader cultural politics of Olympic Rio de Janeiro, a city permeated with discourses of *revival* as it set to cast itself on the world stage. I provide context regarding the longer history of Rio's carnival and the place of brass within it, and I examine how much of the revival of the street carnival positioned itself as alternative to the dominant carnival model of the samba schools. In chapter 2, I examine increasing *experimentation* with diverse repertoires, beginning with the "rescued" Brazilian repertoires of the brass bloco revival at the turn of the millennium, showing how they configured a diversified cultural nationalism as an alternative to the monocultural nationalism of the samba schools. Drawing on cannibalism, the subsequent neofanfarrismo movement later emerged into an all-year movement focused on international and mass-mediated popular styles of music.

Beginning a discussion of "instrumental activism," chapter 3 considers the movement's efforts toward *inclusion* in their forging of a "soundscape of public participation," critically examining the transformational possibilities involved in occupying public spaces with participatory music in the name of "the people." I show that while its strategies have integrated many new musicians, the populist activism of the Whiter middle-class demographic presents real challenges, limitations, and contradictions in integrating excluded populations. In chapter 4, I examine the expressions of *resistance* of neofanfarristas in protests, focusing on the ways they have used music strategically to support and mobilize protesters during a period of crisis in Brazilian politics. I show how moments of broader politicization have provided contexts for neofanfarristas to debate the political roles, functions, and priorities of brass ensembles.

Chapter 5 explores the movement's process of *diversification* by examining how its demographic limitations have provided the foundations upon which excluded groups—including women, Blacker communities, and favelados—have launched claims on the neofanfarrismo movement by founding their own musical projects. The diversification of the movement has led to critiques of cultural appropriation within it, leading to a continuing controversy that emerged in the 2017 carnival about politics of representation in the repertoires of neofanfarrismo and carnival. In chapter 6, I discuss the founding of the HONK! RiO Festival of Activist Brass Bands in 2015, and the challenges and consequences of the *consolidation* of a musical movement explicitly framed around activism. As HONK! festivals have since sprung up in four other Brazilian cities, neofanfarrismo, a movement mostly limited to Rio de Janeiro during my initial fieldwork, is becoming a genuinely national movement connected to the rapidly consolidating transna-

FIGURE I.3 A standard of Marielle Franco at rehearsal of Cordão do Boitatá. Photo by author on January 20, 2020.

tional HONK! movement. The conclusion evaluates the tangible impacts of the movement's instrumental activism, pointing to the contradictions, limits, and possibilities of musical social movements led by more privileged communities.

With neofanfarrismo's rapid rate of change and growth, it seems unpredictable to me what shape the movement may take in five, ten, or twenty years from now, how it will position itself politically, and around what frames it may consolidate itself in the future. As I have followed the movement since 2013, I have witnessed a gradual musical maturing, from beginning musicians initially learning all music by ear to the prominence of sheet music and more complex arrangements at bloco rehearsals. While some beginning musicians have come and gone through the oficinas, leaving music as a passing fancy, others have become world-touring professionals. Some neofanfarristas suggested to me that this stage of the past quarter century has only set the stage for the growth in the years to come of a truly original Brazilian artistic movement comparable to Tropicália.

The rapidly changing political contexts of Rio and Brazil will surely have consequences for the future of the movement. This research began in 2013, a period of reserved hope with the ascent of center-left governments and leftist social movements in Brazil, Latin America, and internationally. Post-Trump, post-Bolsonaro, postvirus, this book is born into a radically different world. Given Brazilian officials' casual threats of invoking something like AI-5, the 1968 Act of the dictatorship that launched the most oppressive period on the Brazilian left to date, neofanfarristas and their cultural practices existed in a highly precarious reality before the pandemic. While musical participation in protest was common during my initial fieldwork, during a trip in pre-Covid early 2020, protests had died down and musicians revealed that under Bolsonaro they feared protests could precipitate an excuse for a broader clampdown. As with Tropicália, a movement cut short by AI-5, Brazil's seemingly cyclical pattern of tolerance and repression may suffocate the potential futures of neofanfarrismo.

Whatever paths the movement, the country, or the world takes, the example of neofanfarrismo is a fundamentally hopeful one. Many assume that our postmodern and technophile existence will inevitably fracture senses of community and alienate us from the sociality of participatory, acoustic music making. Echoing a longer narrative of "festive decline" going back to Bakhtin's romanticization of the Middle Ages (Godet 2020), Barbara Ehrenreich, in her history of public festivity in the West, observes that "there appears to be no constituency today for collective joy itself. In fact, the very term *collective joy* is largely unfamiliar and exotic" (2006, 257). The example of a city in which music making in the commons has been growing at an exponential rate represents a testament to the resilience of human musicality and sociability, showing that Ehrenreich's pessimistic observation is, in an important sense, wrong.

In the streets of Rio de Janeiro, stickers from various bands and social movements adorn the instruments of neofanfarristas, including a line from a recent campaign of a popular party left of the Workers Party (Partido Socialismo e Liberdade, PSoL), "If the city were ours . . ." (*Se a cidade fosse nossa . . .*). The assassinated councilwoman Marielle Franco, memorialized on a standard at a carnival rehearsal in figure I.3, was a member of the party, and, upon her assassination, pictures swarmed social media of her wearing a T-shirt with the message. The line recalls Recife's famous carnival song "Vassourinhas" (The Street Sweepers), which imagines what street sweepers would do with the streets if they belonged to the workers themselves. It is often the final song played in the performances of the brass blocos of Rio's street carnival as foliões sing, "If this street were mine, I would pave it with brilliant stones for the street sweepers to pass." Neofanfarrismo is an imaginative debate and set of answers to the question: if the city were ours, what would we do with it?

ONE

Revival The Death and Life
of Street Carnival

In a short 2019 sketch by the satirical comedy show *Porta dos Fundos*, an exhausted man with a trombone, played by Gregório Duvivier, appears in a bloco surrounded by revelers (foliões) and asks a stranger what time the bloco will end. The other man played by Fábio Porchat, covered in glitter and wearing a tiara, responds, "Tomorrow! It's just started!"

"What do you mean?" asks Duvivier. "Isn't this Amigos da Onça?" referring to the popular, cult phenomenon of the neofanfarrismo movement.

"No!" responds Porchat. "This is 'What a Beautiful Thing.'"

Confused, Duvivier asks, "Where does this stop?"

"Vitória, Espírito Santo," referring to a city in the state north of the State of Rio de Janeiro. Seeing Duvivier's surprise, he asks, "Where did you think you were?"

"I thought I was in Rio, in the Lapa neighborhood!"

"There hasn't been carnival in Lapa since March. Are you crazy? Drunk? It's May!"

Duvivier rubs his eyes. "I didn't even know there were blocos in May."

"Of course! There's always blocos! There's precarnival, carnival, postcarnival, carnival hangover [*ressaca*], posthangover, and then there's the Mother's Day Bloco [in May]—lots of 'Mamãe eu quero.'" Porchat refers to the popular carnival march, "Mommy, I want," traditionally played by Rio's brass blocos.

Duvivier becomes extremely worried about returning to Rio and getting back to work. Porchat responds, "Work is a has been," pointing to a man dressed as a pirate who left a stable job at Brazil's oil company Petrobras to join the blocos, and then to a woman who lives off of selling alcoholic popsicles (sacolé) to other foliões: "There's no lack of work." Seeing that Duvivier really wants to leave, Porchat gives him carnivalesque directions to return: "Come with us for ten kilometers, and we will come across Boi Tolo," one of Rio's most unruly brass blocos. Porchat continues with a series of other blocos Duvivier must encounter, join, and follow to return to Rio, where Porchat tells him he'll see a huge crowd of people dressed in white.

"What bloco will that be?" Duvivier asks.

"That won't be a bloco. It's the March for Jesus. It's Rio de Janeiro. There are no more blocos there." Turning around, he yells, "Everyone, let's play 'Mamãe, eu quero!'"

Duvivier puts his trombone to his lips and remarks, "Screw it. I'll just stay here" (CW.Ch1.Ex1).[1]

———

As the calendar year turns, neofanfarristas increasingly proclaim that "carnival is arriving" (*o carnaval 'tá chegando!*), as if this enormous manifestation of human culture arrives as an uncontrollable force of nature. But for many, carnival also never dies. Blocos can last many hours, even an entire day, and where one bloco stops another starts to continue the revelry. Porchat's declaration in May that "there are always blocos" reflects a real movement, especially associated with neofanfarrismo, to expand carnivalesque street events beyond the carnival season to an all-year series of events, with carnival being the highlight and original inspiration.

The two characters are White, the carnival scene is filled with Whiter foliões, and the reference to a folião who left a good job at at the national gas company Petrobras shows that this bloco is far from a working-class manifestation. These disaffected foliões might find economic sustenance in the blocos' alternative economy of selling independent goods, such as artisan alcoholic popsicles. That the scene might be a familiar one to the Brazilian hipster demographic that watches *Porta dos Fundos* reflects the popularity of this neofanfarrista form of carnival among the Whiter alternative middle class, not only in Rio de Janeiro but beyond as other cities have followed the city's lead. The lead character, played by Gregório Duvivier, is a beloved legend of this demographic and a famous Brazilian comedian who also hosts HBO Brasil's *Greg News*, a leftist political comedy show inspired by John Oliver's *Last Week Tonight*. He studied trombone with Orquestra Voadora and has played with many of Rio's carnival blocos.

In 2016, Rio de Janeiro elected an evangelical bishop famous for his hatred of carnival, Marcelo Crivella, as mayor. In the 2019 Porta dos Fundos sketch, a carnival movement of alternative brass blocos that began in Rio lives on outside the city as a fantastical band of peripatetic wanders, as Rio de Janeiro has been taken over by fundamentalist Christians since carnival officially ended, as Porchat's reference to the March for Jesus implies. The foliões roam in a realm of continuous blocos from which Duvivier appears to be awaking as if from a dream. Upon recognizing current political realities, however, he chooses the dream instead, turning fantasy into reality.

REVIVING AND RESCUING RIO DE JANEIRO

When I began to attend such events in the real Rio de Janeiro, participants stressed that, despite the prominent declaration that street carnival is "traditional" and the popularity of old carnival songs such as "Mamãe, eu quero" referenced in the sketch, this world of cultural activity is quite new and constitutes a revival movement of something they believe to be akin to what might have existed in the past. In the face of what many viewed as a moribund street carnival culture during the military dictatorship (1964–85), musicians started to take back to the streets during the pre-Lenten celebrations beginning in the mid-1980s as the dictatorship collapsed. Many Cariocas refer to the revival of street carnival as a "rescue" of local and national traditions.[2]

Among the revival of other instrumental formations, the musicians of Cordão do Boitatá (1996) and Céu na Terra (2001) revived a somewhat forgotten tradition of brass blocos to create massive parades in the streets, and they played a diverse set of traditional Brazilian genres examined more fully in the next chapter. Because the term "neofanfarrismo" emerged later in the 2000s than the revivalist blocos considered in this chapter, I refer primarily to this earlier stage as the "brass bloco revival."[3] Brass instruments had been a major part of Rio's carnival in the earlier half of the twentieth century. As the ascent of the samba schools eclipsed other carnival activities by the 1970s in Rio de Janeiro, ensembles with brass declined in carnival along with the rise of a military dictatorship that was intolerant of unruly crowds in the streets. The revival of street carnival has been a major development in postdictatorship, Olympic Rio de Janeiro that has birthed many new cultural movements including neofanfarrismo. The reference to Christian conservatism having killed off the blocos in the sketch hints at the reality that street carnival again found itself in conflict with conservative sectors of Brazilian society by the end of the 2010s.

While neofanfarrismo now loosely defines a group of bands and blocos that play throughout the year, the *Porta dos Fundos* sketch shows that the movement cannot be understood independently of street carnival. Trombonist Gustavo Machado, constructing a family tree of the movement, explains that "[the brass bloco] Boitatá is the grandmother, Orquestra Voadora is the mother, and all its children are neofanfarrismo" (interview 2014), and trumpeter Leandro Joaquim pronounces that "all these events that have happened, they have just one root—the carnival" (interview 2015). In this chapter, I trace neofanfarrismo's lineage in the famous carnival of Rio de Janeiro, and I examine brass musicians' initial impulse to rescue "traditional" cultural resources as an expression of the "alternative carnivalesque." I provide historical context for the rise of the alternative brass movement through discussion of the histories of brass in Brazil and carnival's diverse manifestations in Rio de Janeiro. I situate the revival of street carnival within broader discourses of "reviving" and "rescuing" Rio de Janeiro since the 2000s, a city that had become known by the 1990s just as much for its violence and decadence as for its stunning beauty and vibrant culture. I argue that the brass blocos of the street carnival revival largely positioned themselves as an alternative form of revivalism to that promoted by city elites but that they are also inseparable from and contingent upon the larger cultural economy of the Olympic City, sometimes in conflict with and sometimes benefitting from the investments of Rio's revivalism.

Reviving the Marvelous City

As I walked all over the city and rode through it in buses and taxis, I witnessed a Rio de Janeiro between the 2014 World Cup and 2016 Olympics in constant reconstruction, only for the city to appear by the time of the Olympics newly polished with a vast array of new infrastructure. With the mega-events, the city government aimed to mark a stark contrast from the recent past. During my fieldwork, Cariocas portrayed postdictatorship Rio in the mid-1990s as a city mired in social, economic, and political chaos, having lost its status as the country's capital to Brasília and economic prowess to São Paulo decades before. For Carioca scholar Beatriz Jaguaribe, urban poverty, drug violence, and attacks on middle-class residents in the 1990s "seemed to endorse the portrait of a city on the brink of collapse" (2014, 113). Some of the most internationally visible symbols of Rio in the 2000s have been movies like *City of God* (2002) and *Elite Squad* (2007) that depict extreme urban violence in Rio's favelas.[4]

An expanding economy in the 2000s and the promise to host the World Cup and Olympics provided an opportunity to recast this image and revitalize the city. Rio de Janeiro became a site of immense investment with massive infrastructure projects, such as the reconstruction of the port (Porto Maravilha) that have reshaped the city. Jaguaribe argued at the time that "the Summer Olympics has served as the catalyst for a process of urban reinvention grounded in the production and (re)appropriation of urban space—a process that is simultaneously material and symbolic. It has focused on the strategically significant terrains, emblematic spaces that are critical to the city's rebirth in the global imaginary" (2016, 36), with the city "export[ing] the imaginaries and forms of consumption that circulate through varied media, tourism, and the market economy" (2014, 5). She suggests that since the turn of the millennium the city underwent a process of "branding" and renewal in its quest to become a "global city" as it harnessed the country's economic boom based on oil reserves. Through the Olympic process, Rio de Janeiro sought to regain its traditional role of mediating the marvels of Brazil in the international forum.

In this process of spectacular rebranding, colonial neighborhoods in the Center of the city—neighborhoods including Lapa, Centro, Santa Teresa, Saúde, and Gamboa—became musical destinations, supplanting the South Zone famously known for the birth of *bossa nova* and other genres in the latter half of the twentieth century. The central neighborhoods had been the cultural heart of the city before the development of the South Zone in the early twentieth century and a gradual shift of wealth southward. Like other cities throughout the world, investment and gentrification moved back into the central core of the city in the past decades. The Central neighborhood of Lapa became once again in the 2000s and 2010s the cultural heart of the city, with the opening of major cultural institutions like Fundição Progresso and Circo Voador alongside a wide array of samba clubs (Herschmann 2007). Following and provoking patterns of gentrification, the street carnival revival has been especially strong in the Center of the city, part of the larger revalorization of traditional, local culture in the area, and Lapa and its surrounding areas are also the heart of brass activities in the city.[5]

As a result of these various investments, and especially due to the Olympics, Rio has seen many new projects, especially focused in the Center of the city, that offer urban benefits to its citizens, such as an expanded metro system, a new light-rail system, and new museums, including the massive, futuristic, and popular Museu do Amanhã that educates visitors on the realities of climate change and the Anthropocene. The benefits of the Olympics, however, have not been equally shared. The expansion of the subway line, for example, links Ipanema with the rich suburb Barra de Tijuca, expanding access in the richer South Zone. No substantial transportation investments were afforded, however, for the poorer North Zone, and speculation caused the city to become much more expensive in the 2000s, leading to an affordability crisis that disproportionately affected the poor.

The story of the beloved Santa Teresa streetcar (*bonde*) emblematizes how many Cariocas viewed the investment in "public resources" as essentially investments in tourist infrastructure or services for the rich. The charming, hilly central neighborhood of working-class, bohemian Santa Teresa that overlooks Lapa has been served by a tram built in 1877 that links the neighborhood to the rest of the city from the Carioca metro station, over the Arches of Lapa, and into the curvy streets of Santa Teresa. After the trams in Brazil were largely replaced by the car economy in the mid-twentieth century, the Santa Teresa bonde stood as the only maintained tram system in Brazil, and it remains an icon of the city. It was much loved by the inhabitants of Santa Teresa and was far cheaper than the bus and metro system. Céu na Terra, a bloco that helped foment the revival of brass blocos, was known for leading the crowd of foliões by playing inside the tram itself.

In 2011, the tram was shut down after mismanagement that led it to derail and kill five people. Despite perpetual promises to reinstate service, it lay in disuse for four years, and a neighborhood social movement emerged to militate for its return. When I lived in Santa Teresa from 2014 to 2016, unfinished work sites adorned the streets, and residents came to believe that it would never return after a series of missed deadlines. Depictions of the face of the bonde with a tear falling from its headlight, anthropomorphized into an eye, were popular in vibrant street art appearing throughout the neighborhood. In August 2015, in time for the Olympics but late for the World Cup, the bonde did reopen but with a significantly shortened schedule and area of operation. In 2016, service was expanded, but users, including all Cariocas except Santa Teresa residents, were charged 20 reais (5 USD) for the privilege. As of 2020, full service still had not been reinstated, many believe the tram service will never serve the residents as it once did, and crying bonde art has not disappeared. The bonde has only been restored "for the English to see" (*pra inglês ver*), an old expression that captures how Brazilians and the Portuguese have long made efforts for colonizing interests to present their countries as "civilized" while continuing to mask real problems for locals. How long, Santa Teresa residents wondered, does it take to fix a neighborhood tram in a country capable of building stadiums?

Another challenge in Rio de Janeiro's branding as a safe place for international tourism was the images of extreme violence by the city's drug gangs that had come to control its many favelas. With the expectation of hosting the World Cup and Olympics, Rio set out on an effort to take control of the favelas in 2008, invading them with "pacifying police units" (UPPs). These occupations had the official aim of guaranteeing safety to favela residents, but they have been extremely violent and controversial, resulting in routine police killings of Blacker and poorer Cariocas. The UPPs have been stationed strategically in favelas primarily near the South Zones and Center in an effort to secure territories frequented by tourists and the rich. Some favelas experienced spikes in housing costs as they have begun to be gentrified, while favela tours for visitors treat them like "urban safaris." Journalist Dave Zirin described Olympic Rio as a city "where public space is dwindling, people are getting removed from their homes, and the poor are being marginalized in an effort to turn Rio into the megacity of the IMF's dreams" (2014, 3).[6]

Rio de Janeiro's largely neoliberal urban revival in the first decades of the twenty-first century occurred under the national reign of the center-left Workers Party from 2003 to 2016 and the broader "Pink Tide" ascendance of center-left governments in Latin America in the 2000s and 2010s. Before the party's reign, Brazil had come out of Latin America's "lost decade" of the 1980s with chronic inflation problems and privatization schemes touted by President Fernando Henrique Cardoso and others. But while the Workers Party had radical political and cultural roots in a wide array of social movements, Presidents Lula da Silva and Dilma Rousseff worked to build a state safety net largely within a neoliberal market framework and in alliance with conservative and center parties (the *centrão*). Rio de Janeiro's city government during the 2000s and 2010s was never led by the Workers Party or any leftist party, but by center and center-right parties. Despite the commitments to Brazilians' social and economic well-being of the Workers Party government, Zirin depicted Brazil in 2014 as a country "attempting to use the World Cup and Olympics to both present itself externally to the world as a grand new power of the twenty-first century and continue internally a process of state-directed neoliberalism that puts profiteering ahead of human needs" (18).[7] After the Olympics, as right-wing administrations took over in the city of Rio de Janeiro in 2016 and of the presidency in 2018, neoliberal neglect became explicit policy, and interest in urban renewal projects faded without the incentives of mega-events.

But the neoliberal rationale of urban renewal in this Olympic city was not unidirectional or totalizing, and the discourses and practices of revival have been contested and open for interpretation in diverse and contradictory ways. Street carnival, the brass bloco revival, and neofanfarrismo are manifestations of diverse, alternative reimaginings of a cultural revival in Rio de Janeiro occurring during the same period.

A Leftist Revival

As I sat in the back seat of cab on the way to the Boitatá parade, costumed as a communist devil with a Landless Workers (MST) red polo shirt, the cab driver broke the silence: "It's amazing. None of this existed until recently—I mean, it existed a long time ago, but it's come back with a vengeance," adding mildly dismissively, "especially with all these alternative types." Unsure of his politics, I nervously nodded my head in agreement.

Neofanfarristas likewise describe the "rescue" of the Carioca street carnival that emerged in the 1990s as embodying a critical opposition toward the city's dominant popular culture and cultural politics in postdictatorship Brazil. The desire to rescue traditional culture might seem a surprising stance coming from a leftist, cosmopolitan demographic that emerged from a period entrenched in the conservative nationalism of the dictatorship. But these musicians framed their interest in traditional culture as a critique of a commodified and homogenous carnival culture on the one hand and an overly Americanized dominant popular cultural sphere on the other. As cultural "rescuers," the early brass blocos of Cordão do Boitatá (1996) and Céu na Terra (2001) were animated by a folkloric desire to safeguard and preserve "authentic" Carioca and Brazilian traditions they feared of being lost.[8]

While "rescuing tradition" may be a discourse often employed by the right, there are plenty of examples of it being used by the left. In leftist movements for which traditional culture proved a positive resource, the nebulous category of the "people" (o povo) and their expressive cultures are constructed as vanguards of history. The left-wing folk revivals of the 1960s that occurred throughout the Americas—with figures such as Geraldo Vandré in Brazil, Bob Dylan in the United States, or Violeta Parra in Chile—positioned the expressive practices of the "folk" as resistant alternatives to conservative, authoritarian regimes.[9] In Brazilian terms, the brass blocos sought to "kill the nostalgia" (matar a saudade) for a carnival they viewed as having been disrupted and transformed by the right-wing dictatorship.[10] As Alexander Marković writes, "nostalgia articulates and makes sense of people's experiences of the present—often more than it faithfully describes what might have been in the past" (2017, 226). Neofanfarristas express nostalgic saudade for a range of Brazilian pasts, including classic carnivals of the 1930s, the 1960s Brazilian song festivals that critiqued the military regime, and the June 2013 protests.

These constructions of authentic lost carnival culture must also be viewed as articulations of social distinction of the particular demographic of Rio's alternative, Whiter middle class. Their expressions of approximation to and distancing from particular cultural traditions and communities are based in particular class and race positions. Neofanfarristas depicted "alienated" middle-class compatriots in the 1980s generally uninterested in Brazilian cultural traditions and infatuated instead with the rock movements of the United States and England.[11] In response to the perceived decadence and international orientation of the 1980s and '90s, many young, middle-class musicians at the end of the millennium looked back to an imagined golden age of Brazilian music and cultural nationalism. They drew on discourses of "radical nationalism" (Klubock 1998) that run deep in Latin America and position the postcolonial nation as a body of resistance against imperial capitalism. More broadly, the city's emergent cultural movements of this period that sought to revalorize local culture, including the street carnival revival, can be viewed as part of a broader cultural politics of the Pink Tide, which was also animated by concern for local culture and anxiety about foreign influence. Along with movements like the street carnival revival, the cultural manifestation of the Pink Tide in Brazil is perhaps best emblematized by Lula's choosing Gilberto Gil, icon of the countercultural Tropicália movement, as minister of culture.

This phase of repopularization of brass blocos and other street carnival traditions constituted a "music revival," what Tamara Livingston defines as "social movements which strive to 'restore' a musical system believed to be disappearing or completely relegated to the past for the benefit of contemporary society" (1999, 66). Caroline Bithell and Juniper Hill argue that music revivals, "motivated by dissatisfaction with the present" (2016, 4), often frame themselves as activist movements expressing opposition to the status quo. In addition to reviving specific repertoires and instrumental formations, many street carnival participants have sought to resurrect a more intangible "spirit" of carnival. This "alternative carnivalesque" critique of dominant carnivalesque forms is based on participants' normative conceptions of what Rio's "authentic" carnival should be. Neofanfarristas' ideas often resonated with prominent theorists of carnival, including Bakhtin, Turner, and DaMatta, who were themselves sometimes cited in my interviews.

Cultural theorists, of course, have deconstructed the notion of authenticity and have shown how the term conceals histories that establish some practices as more authentic and real than others in ways that are bound up in often problematic cultural politics (Bendix 1997).[12] Yet, as Maria Sonevytsky argues, "to many musicians, audiences, critics, and teachers the world over, 'authenticity' endures as a perpetual signifier of music that is competently performed or perceived to be aesthetically pure" (2019, 89–90). Indeed, authenticity has an affective truth that is worth taking seriously when claimed by musical communities for its capacity to inspire them. Accordingly, I focus on the folkloric project of these blocos and their particular practices that produced the brass bloco revival, and I show how they reconfigured the past as a critique of the present by framing their alternative practices as authentically carnivalesque.

While these concerns for heritage have often first been asserted by cultural activists, they can be subsumed by institutions, heritage regimes, and neoliberal profiteers. The brass bloco revival occurred within the context of what Rodney Harrison (2013) calls a global "heritage boom," in which UNESCO and other important institutions sought to safeguard "intangible cultural heritage," often in response to the homogenizing culture of a globalized world. In the contemporary neoliberal context, many local traditions around the world, far from being lost by globalized homogenization, have been reframed as "cultural expedients" (Yúdice 2003), or important economic resources for asserting local distinction on the global stage. In Rio de Janeiro, often in conflict with the radical nationalism of the brass blocos have been the neoliberal strategies to reframe the street carnival as a profitable cultural resource, part of the city's consumable heritage and a tourist commodity. These diverse rationales work in tense and often contradictory ways that complicate any appraisal of the brass blocos as inherently resistant to the forces that seek to control them. But before entering that discussion, if the brass of Rio's carnival is conceived of as a revived heritage, on what histories were these revivalists drawing?

DIVERSE ADAPTIONS OF A MILITARISTIC ENSEMBLE

In "A Banda" (1966), Chico Buarque sings of a brass band parading through town in a nostalgic portrait of Brazilian brass bands that brought happiness to all whom they passed by. As the band "sings things of love," "serious men" stop their business to appreciate it, a girl dreams that the band is playing just for her, and an old man forgets he is old and begins dancing. As soon as the band passes, to the singer's "disenchantment," the sweetness ends, everyone "takes their place," and "suffering" is again heard in the people's songs. The brass band, in Buarque's portrait, is an agent of temporary happiness, one that provides carnivalesque, momentary relief from the daily travails and pains of life.

Despite this carnivalesque and nostalgic portrait, brass bands worldwide, including in Brazil, are more often viewed as forces of cultural conservatism, militarism, and civic culture.[13] Portable and loud, horns and drums made effective companions for expeditions, their "calls" offering a useful symbology for attacks, hunting, calling attention, and revelry. Brazilian cornetist Luis Lopes, for example, has been memorialized for his decisive horn call during the campaign for Brazilian independence. Lopes defied Brazilian army orders to play the call to retreat for fear of losing the decisive 1822 Battle of Pirajá in Bahia, playing the call to advance that led the Brazilian army to victory instead, as seen in figure 1.1.

The modern form of the military band dates to the French Revolution, and it

FIGURE 1.1 Statue of Luis Lopes. Photo by author on January 23, 2020.

played a major role in articulating cultures of nationalism and their spectacles of domination. Civilian bands grew outside the military and helped forge emerging national cultures, as the brass band ensemble formats were standardized by the 1870s throughout Europe. European colonialism was at its peak in the latter half of the nineteenth century, and brass bands spread widely throughout colonized lands. Emerging nation states in Latin America that had already freed themselves from European rule, such as Brazil, also promoted the modern military bands, crafting their own cultural forms of state consolidation.

Brass bands were major vehicles of musical globalization, passing down a standard repertoire and set of performance practices throughout the world. Beyond their militaristic uses, they also provided a form of popular, mass, and globalized entertainment decades before recording technology existed (Reily and Brucher 2013, 10). They played European classical music in "lighter" forms, and they translated the music of operas, symphonies, and ballets to more recreational environments and dancing. While these events were meant to have a "civilizing," and Whitening, function—as citizens, enslaved people, and subjects witnessed the "primacy" of Western culture and entertainment—they also promoted pleasure, social relaxation, and class contact. Because of their loud and mobile nature, the bands led parades, processions, and other outdoor events that could draw in spectators and participants into open-air spaces, forging affective relationships of subjects to public places.

As these bands were integrated into many different kinds of institutions, their social and political purposes diversified. In many cases, working-class men enlisted into the bands and accessed musical training. Brass bands became important sites of musical fusion, as European musical repertoires and performance practices mixed with those of the colonized musicians, the subjects such ensembles were designed to discipline. All over the world, brass bands were ensembles in which colonized subjects learned and altered the musical languages of their masters, a widespread pattern of "indigenization" of the ensemble (Garofalo 2020), or, in neofanfarrista terms, cannibalization. Afro-diasporic, Romani, Indian, and many other musical concepts were blown through the restrictive chambers meant to produce the European chromatic scale, creating new distinctive repertoires. These musicians also used their instruments for pursuits anathema to colonial projects, as Robert Flaes quips: "It was one thing for the natives to learn and reproduce our music and our culture on our instruments. But that they should worship the local deities or chiefs with our instruments, dancing, smoking drugs, getting drunk and even having sex—that was never the intention" (2000, 10). In sum, despite their military origin, brass bands around the world have always had a ludic and populist side, and sometimes a subversive one, as masses of people were entrusted with loud portable instruments that had the capacity of taking space and calling attention.

Brass in Brazil

In the Lusophone world, Portugal served as a major disseminator for bands among its colonies, especially in Brazil with the arrival of the Portuguese court in Rio de Janeiro in 1808 (Pestana et al. 2020). Military bands (*bandas marciais*) gained prominence in Brazil beginning in the 1830s, with the founding of the National Guard and military police bands, which became especially popular during the Paraguayan War (1864–70). Civilian bands modeled themselves on military bands from the 1870s onward, predominantly playing *dobrados*, Brazil's traditional military march genre. Such bands are still a prominent element of military, police, and firefighter institutions where many Brazilians receive excellent musical training. They promoted a martial nationalism in public spaces throughout the country, playing for civic events like Independence Day celebrations. But, as in the United States with John Philip Sousa, by the close of the nineteenth century they were also increasingly public entertainers, playing extracts from operas and operettas and European popular dance forms, such as polka, waltzes, mazurkas, and schottisches.

In the era before electronic amplification, "hardly a public event took place [in Brazil] without a band" (Reily 2013, 109), and the dissemination of Brazilian brass bands could be considered the earliest manifestation of a national, popular music based on cultural mixing in the country.[14] Blacker and mixed-race musicians—in many cases enslaved and freed people and their descendants—were trained on wind instruments associated with European Whiteness, providing a vehicle for cultural validation. They played in public spaces in ways deemed more "acceptable" and "civilized" than the frequently repressed expressions of Afro-Brazilian culture, as "musical instruments were often associated with specific racialized bodies and carried with them the associations of the corresponding racial and social classes" (Brunet 2012, 27). Band leader and composer Anacleto de Medeiros, the son of a formerly enslaved person, was renowned in late nineteenth-century Rio de Janeiro. Saxophonist and teacher at Casa do Choro Pedro Paes explained to me, "The dobrados and *marchas* were appreciated by the public because every Sunday there was a band in the square playing these genres. Then it all started to mix with other cultures. The composers of the age mixed the European harmonic language with rhythms that had elements of African and indigenous influence" (interview 2015). By the 1920s, musicians of these bands formed "jazz bands," playing "waltzes, polkas, marches, foxtrots, and sambas" in dance halls and casinos before Brazilian popular music moved indelibly to more guitar-based genres (Reily 2013, 114).

Neofanfarristas often counterpose their alternative movement with what they view as the conservative band traditions that have survived particularly in the smaller cities of the "interior," away from the coastal population centers, such as the state of Minas Gerais. There, community-based *bandas de música* are still an important element of social life animating civic parades and religious processions, despite having declined in popularity since the mid-twentieth century. Many Brazilians still learn wind instruments in school fanfarras based in the military tradition, perhaps the most common association with the term fanfarra in Brazil. Some neofanfarristas who learned their instruments before involving themselves in the movement originally received training in such institutions. Many others had no previous contact with the larger world of Brazilian band traditions, and their primary inspirations to play wind instruments were the street carnival and neofanfarrismo movements.[15]

Brass in Brazilian Carnival

Despite the fact that brass bands are now certainly not the primary image of the world-famous Carioca carnival, wind ensembles played vital roles in the development of carnival music in Rio and around the country. One of the first major movies to dramatize Rio's carnival, the French-made *Black Orpheus* (1959), features in its first shots of the city's carnival preparations a brass band dressed in coordinated formal clothing and parading in the streets. Brass and wind instruments made their way into carnival from the beginning of the festivity's transformation from *entrudo*, the Portuguese tradition brought to Brazil in the seventeenth century that included throwing various liquids and powders on passersby, to the more musically based carnival traditions that emerged in the mid- to late nineteenth century (Queiroz 1992; Ferreira 2004). In the second half of the nineteenth century, the ascendant bourgeoisie's "great societies" (*grandes sociedades*) replaced the popular-class traditions of entrudo with elite carnival clubs that held masquerade balls and parades modeled on Venetian and Parisian traditions and accompanied by military bands, which were "an integral part of

Carnival in Recife, Salvador, and Rio de Janeiro" (Crook 2009, 50). Recently freed Blacker communities filled the streets of cities around the country with their own musical practices at the end of the nineteenth century (Queiroz 1992), and the early Republic waged diverse campaigns to civilize and Whiten the country and its capital city (Meade 1997). Associated with military discipline, the inclusion of marching bands and brass instruments in carnival was initially part of an effort to "civilize" the raucous festivities.

By the 1870s, popular-class carnival organizations emerged with the *cordões*, featuring percussion, string instruments, and singing in the streets, and they suffered persecution from the police because of their associations with formerly enslaved communities. In the 1890s, the *rancho*, a tradition from the Northeast of Brazil originally associated with religious processions, emerged in Rio, using wind, brass, string instruments, and percussion. The ranchos played complex arrangements of opera tunes and other popular music of the day, and they were viewed as a counterpoint to the unruly cordões. Samuel Araújo et al. (2005) argue that the ranchos served as "cultural mediators" by playing a wide diversity of music, including dobrados, maxixe, and marchas. With their flag bearers (*porta-bandeira*), original music (*enredos*), and linear parade formation, they served as a foundation for the organization of the samba schools in the 1920s. The term "bloco" emerged in the late nineteenth century loosely referring to a variety of ensembles but more closely linked with the unruly cordões than the "civilized" ranchos (Tinhorão 2013 [1974]), and the "blocos de sujo" (dirty blocos) were celebrated for their chaotic spontaneity and lack of formal structures (Fernandes 2019). Today "bloco" is the preeminent term of street carnival and generally refers to any mobile musical street carnival organization, as opposed to samba schools, club dances, public concerts, or other carnival manifestations.

With the emergence of radio, brass ensembles were contracted to play in the streets instrumental versions of songs that were broadcast on the new medium.[16] Brass and wind instruments were used in some of the first genres of what came to be known as Brazilian popular music, such as maxixe, *choro*, marchinha, and samba. Early recordings of the instrumental genre choro, an amalgam of European dance forms that had mixed with Afro-diasporic rhythms, feature a plethora of wind instruments. Early recordings of samba were often arranged with wind instrumentation, from early recordings, such as "Pelo telefone" (1917), to orchestrated *samba-canção* (samba song genre), such as the famous "Aquarela do Brasil" (1939). Like popular music around the Americas in the mid-twentieth century, brass fell out of use in Brazilian popular music with the rise of rock and the fall of big bands. Bossa nova promoted a more intimate aesthetic further developed by the musicians of *música popular brasileira* in contrast to the triumphant, orchestrated samba-canção that had preceded it.

With the rise of the military dictatorship (1964–85), expressions of street carnival, as well as many other kinds of public gatherings, became highly suspect and many songs were censored. The period is remembered by the South Zone middle classes as an emptying (*esvaziamento*) of carnival from the streets (Fernandes 2019). Ethnomusicologist and former musical director of the brass bloco Céu na Terra, Rafael Velloso, explained that during the dictatorship, "you couldn't go to the street with a group because you'd be accused of being a communist . . . If you went to the street, made noise, and blocked it, you were going to jail at that time, definitely. They built the sambódromo so they could get people out of the streets and perform in a safe area" (interview 2015).[17] By the early 2000s, journalist Ruy Castro, full of saudade, recounts that "The parade of open-top cars ended in the forties. The trams, on whose running boards the revelers would hang in bunches, stopped running in the sixties. The marchinhas too are going, going, gone—no one's composed them for decades . . . Carnival had lost its meaning. It seemed to be the end of a long beautiful tradition" (2004, 99).[18] When journalist Alma Guillermoprieto researched carnival at the end of the 1980s, she characterized South Zone middle-class acquaintances as highly dismissive of the festivities: "Carnival? Boring. Vulgar. Noisy, some people said, and recommended that I leave town for that horrible weekend . . . Was it true," she asks, "that carnival was something that happened principally in the slums?" (1990, 6). With the boom in street carnival and brass ensembles in the last couple of decades, however, Guillermoprieto's observations are out of date. Carioca scholar Micael Herschmann confirms that "street carnival, to a great extent, is a socio-cultural phenomenon of the middle class of the South Zone" (2013, 285).

SOUNDSCAPES OF CARIOCA CARNIVAL

Today Rio's carnival is gigantic. In 2018, six million people were expected to attend carnival festivities with 1.5 million tourists, generating 3.5 billion reais (1 billion USD) for the city (Mendonça, Figueiredo, and Neville 2018). In 2020, 731 official street carnival parades of more than 500 blocos were approved by Riotur, the city's tourism agency that also oversees the festivities. In a constant state of growth (until the pandemic), 294 new blocos were registered between 2000 and 2014 (Barroso and Gonçalves 2016). These large numbers do not include the many more unofficial blocos who reject the rules of authorization and are not counted by Riotur. "Street carnival" refers to this great diversity of free events, ranging from informal gatherings to the two million people who attend Bola Preta, including blocos based on the samba school model, outdoor stage shows, musicians on sound cars sometimes coordinating with ensembles below, suburban carnival traditions like *bate-bola*, and a great variety of mobile acoustic ensembles. In 2013, Mayor Eduardo Paes prohibited the use of demarcations to charge or exclude people from the festivities, further guaranteeing accessibility. The movement of brass blocos that emerged in the 1990s and would lead to neofanfarrismo should be taken as a notable but small piece of this gigantic festivity. And then, of course, there are the world-famous samba schools.

The Brass Blocos as Alternative to the Samba Schools

Given the enormity of present carnival activities, it was somewhat shocking to me that many neofanfarristas in their twenties, thirties, and forties claimed hyperbolically that in their childhood, there was, in fact, "no carnival," comments that resonate with Guillermoprieto's experience above. In the supposition that there was "no carnival," these musicians imply also that the world-famous samba school parades and other carnival events that did exist before the recent boom did not in fact qualify as valuable expressions of carnival for them. Tomás Ramos, a White saxophonist and activist who grew up between New York City and Rio de Janeiro and worked throughout his twenties with the PSoL (Partido Socialismo e Liberdade) explains, for example:

> When I was a child, people left Rio during carnival. Either you went to the sambódromo, or to Bahia, or to Minas Gerais. In Rio, there wasn't really street carnival. There was popular-class carnival in the Rio Branco Avenue and in the sambódromo, but the middle class would leave Rio. When this movement of neofanfarrismo began, a series of blocos started to parade again through the streets of Rio de Janeiro. People started to stay for Rio's carnival, and carnival was transformed into something marvelous. (Interview 2014)

Ramos's comment shows that middle-class youth largely did not perceive the sambódromo and other contemporary carnival manifestations as "their" carnival. The revived street carnival stands for many as an idealized alternative to the samba schools in particular.

Samba schools emerged in the late 1920s in Rio de Janeiro out of the blocos, cordões, and ranchos primarily in poorer mixed-race and Blacker neighborhoods, including favelas. While samba musicians had been persecuted and repressed earlier in the twentieth century, the populist government of Getúlio Vargas (1930–45) viewed them as vehicles for a postcolonial nation-building strategy that would prize mixed-race and African heritage as authentic expressions of Brazilian identity, or brasilidade. Building on the musical organizations from which they emerged, including the grandes sociedades, ranchos, cordões, and blocos, the samba schools grew highly formalized and structured with a myriad of rules governing instrumentation, nationalistic song themes, parading, and other elements. Emphasizing the Blackness of the genre in accord with the Vargas regime's cultural politics, even though samba also reflected the city's racial and cultural mixing, brass and wind sections were officially restricted from samba schools in 1934. The instrumentation of *bateria* (percussion ensemble), singer, and *cavaquinho* (high-pitched chordophone) was standardized (McCann 2004). Riotur, the department of tourism, took charge of the samba parades and restricted them to downtown where they would compete against one another, later moving them to the sambódromo built in 1984. As other elements of street carnival declined over the second half of the twentieth century, the schools became the preeminent expression of Rio's carnival by the 1970s and represented the city's dominant heritage regime, celebrating hegemonic Blackness and the racial democracy.[19]

For many in the street carnival movement today, the history of outsider involvement in the samba schools, from the Vargas government to the television company Globo, represents a history of commodification of artistic labor that has long compromised the carnivalesque "authenticity" of the samba schools. The transfer of the parade from the city's central avenue to the closed, expensive, spectator space of the sambódromo in 1984, occurring at the end of the dictatorship's reign, represents for many neofanfarristas a major repression against carnival. If, as Bakhtin writes, carnival is supposed to militate against official society and its practices and institutions, many street carnival participants question how the samba schools, with their highly orchestrated and commercialized events performed to a single style of samba, could be considered "truly" carnivalesque.[20]

By contrast, the street carnival represents to them a space of free and uncontrolled experimentation, egalitarianism, and radical self-expression. Brazilian anthropologist Roberto DaMatta (1991 [1979]) argues that Rio's street carnival creates experiences of *communitas* (Turner 1969) and equality for participants that stand in contrast to the structure and hierarchy of everyday life. Street carnival, for DaMatta, provides the possibility for open encounters with social Others that, outside of carnival, would be marked by social distinction and distance. It is created "by and for the society" (15), belonging to all, "without owners," and marked by decentralization:

> The fact that the blocos are organized in a far simpler way than the samba schools makes it possible for the former to distinguish themselves by saying, among other things, that the schools "no longer obey the Carnival tradition" ... that they are "for the tourists" rather than for the people, and that they put on a "show" instead of a spontaneous parade. The blocos claim to express purer Carnival values. (1991 [1979], 95–96)[21]

While street carnival participants celebrate freedom of expression and musical diversity, samba school participants have little to no control over the selection of the annual theme, the theme song (*samba-enredo*),[22] or their costumes (*fantasias*), which are decided by officials and designers high up in the schools' hierarchy. Many brass bloco participants find contemporary samba schools' songs homogenous, too fast, and lacking in rhythmic diversity. The sambódromo carnival is built around a competition, whereas street carnival blocos rarely aim at defeating their rivals (though Globo does award prizes to blocos). Though competitions and various forms of rivalry are part of many carnival and brass band traditions around the world, many brass bloco participants view competition to be anathema to the "principles of carnival," which they view as inclusive rather than factionalist. Street carnival stilt walker Raquel Potí proclaims, for example, that, in contrast to the sambódromo, street carnival is like "everyone at the Maracanã [soccer stadium] cheering for the same team" (interview 2016).

A song by Monobloco, "Arrastão da alegria" (Crowd of Happiness, 2013), captures well the attitude of many street carnival participants toward the samba schools. Monobloco, founded in 2000, was one of the first blocos that sought to stir up the musical diversity of the city's carnival by mixing a diversity of Brazilian and popular global rhythms. The group was also one of the first to hold oficinas (classes) to teach their eclectic musical styles in Lapa for students to participate in the yearly bloco, an educational format that has since proliferated in Rio and that neofanfarrista bands would later adopt. Monobloco now brings half a million to the streets for its carnival bloco:

I am, I am, I am
Monobloco.
My samba school is my bloco
My sambódromo is the street.
It is I who comes to invade the city
That burns and explodes under the sun and the moon.

Nailson Simões, professor of trumpet and Brazilian music at Uni-Rio and performer in many brass blocos, portrays the relationship between the resurgent street carnival and sambódromo as a revolt against commercialism:

> I got involved in the movement that was surging in the 1990s to create a street carnival with more quality and more diversity. People have been searching out street carnival because it's more spontaneous, like it was in the old days. There has been the growth of the samba schools, but that wasn't healthy for Rio because it's very commercial. It got to a point in Rio de Janeiro that was terrible. Carnival should be spontaneous . . . It's something completely out of the ordinary to go out into the street . . . It's the people's rejection of what is given to them. I believe this return to the street to be a social revolt. (Interview 2015)

These various "alternative carnivalesque" descriptions of street carnival, advanced by practitioners and scholars alike, as "spontaneous," "free," "open," "participatory," "anticommercial," "real," "authentic," and even "revolutionary" constitute an ethical belief system of what a pure and ideal carnival "should be." This belief system resonates with what trombonist Juliano Pires referred to in the introduction as "principles of carnival," from which samba schools supposedly departed long ago. In this view, the sambódromo is perceived as the dominant carnival of Rio de Janeiro against which the brass blocos with their participatory ethics articulate themselves as alternative. Percussionist Thaís Bezerra, who participates in samba schools, street carnival blocos, and neofanfarrista bands as a musician and musical director, describes the shift: "Today everybody wants to be part of the carnival. This is the goal. Twenty years ago everybody wanted to go to see the carnival, but now everybody wants to play" (interview 2016).

Like the supposition that there was "no carnival" before this expansion, however, global statements that dismiss the cultural imprint of the samba schools reveal particular class and racialized subject positions of the alternative Whiter middle classes who have sought spaces of belonging in a festivity marked by the commodification of Blackness, a strategy I have called disinheritance (Snyder

2021a). For the thousands of poorer people mobilized by the samba schools, each one with about three thousand participants, the notions that carnival "did not exist" and that samba schools are not participatory are absurd. Carla Brunet (2012) encourages us to view the samba schools as important institutions in the lives of Brazilian communities that are still "real" and important even as we recognize their commercialization and histories of appropriation. Claire Haas, who participated with me in the Estácio de Sá samba school, observed,

> There's some obliviousness about the fact that the samba schools are a lot more inclusive than neofanfarrismo. To participate in neofanfarrismo you first have to buy an instrument which will cost at least a thousand reais [300 USD]. Then you have to pay to go to the oficinas and learn how to play it. It's a very up-per middle-class group of people, and someone coming from a marginalized social group would feel this kind of social exclusion. Participating in a samba school doesn't have that barrier to entry. We paid fifty reais to participate in Estácio de Sá. You don't have to buy a drum to play in the bateria of a samba school . . . There are also lots of rehearsals in the streets . . . The critique of the samba schools, part of it is true: lots of money, putting culture on display for people who can pay for it . . . But it's thousands of people who do the parade per night. (Interview 2016)

Indeed, one could view the dismissals of the samba schools as based not only on a critique of commodification and spectacle, but as reflecting a more insidious middle-class dismissal of working-class culture and as an expression of social distinction.

Moreover, the dismissal of the schools as antiparticipatory is quite problematic. Both the samba schools and street carnival blocos stand as examples that are markedly distinct from ethnomusicologist Thomas Turino's model (2008), which distinguishes between presentational and participatory performance "fields."[23] In fact, both blocos and samba schools mix elements of both performance formats, and members of both the samba schools and the blocos could be understood either as participants or producers. Both ensembles animate foliões who could be understood as spectators, through consuming a performance, as well as participants, through singing along and dressing in costumes. While street carnival may be free for audiences, blocos can produce their own forms of exclusion by creating a space of middle-class sociality, ironically drawing the people most likely to afford a ticket to the samba schools. Though the price of attending the formal samba school parades may be inaccessible to many, samba schools hold many free and open opportunities to attend rehearsals inside school headquarters and in neighborhood streets. These are events that function as vital neighborhood social experiences in poorer, Blacker communities. My experience of parading with Estácio de Sá through the sambódromo as we performed the story of Rio's patron saint São Jorge during the formal carnival parade certainly felt like being part of a spectacle that I aimed not to ruin. But the building of relationships with a community distinct from that of neofanfarrismo over four months of rehearsals was forged through the social intimacy of musical participation.

Importantly, the incursions of money in the samba schools and the street carnival have not completely deprived either groups from the possibility for protest, showing that the fact of commodification does not clearly bend musical participants to the will of hegemonic power. The samba schools, though historically an arm of state propaganda, have recently enacted notable musical protests, such as a 2018 enredo that claimed that slavery in Brazil never ended and depicted then President Temer as a bloodsucking "neoliberal vampire," an homage to Marielle Franco in 2019, and in 2020 a veiled critique of Bolsonaro telling of the story of "Jesus of the people"—born in a favela with a Black face, Indigenous blood, and the body of a woman—who stands up to the "prophets of intolerance." Though the brass blocos' articulations of distinctiveness from the samba schools are important to take seriously in order to understand how they framed themselves as alternative, the samba schools are unique, complex, and dynamically creative institutions that cannot be dismissed out of hand.

The Brass Blocos as Alternative to the Rest of Street Carnival

Beyond their criticisms of the samba schools, the brass bloco revival promoted itself as an alternative within the landscape of the larger street carnival revival, as well as in contrast to middle-class indoor carnival club dances where brass ensembles most commonly played the traditional carnival marches that would be reinterpreted by the alternative brass blocos. When Boitatá and Céu na Terra were founded around the turn of the millennium, a few blocos had existed through the dictatorship, primarily in the North Zone, such as Cacique de Ramos.[24] There were also newer, critical blocos founded in the years after the dictatorship fell in 1985—including Simpatia é Quase Amor, Suvaco do Cristo, Bloco do Barbas, and Escravos do Mauá—whose birth marked the beginning of a street carnival revival movement in the South Zone and Center of the city. Most of these blocos are akin to miniature samba schools. They write and rehearse an original enredo for the year that they play in carnival over instrumentation based on the samba school model. Many of them formed the bloco league of Sebastiana in 2000 based in the Center and South Zone of the city, which was devoted to political satire, valorization of the past, free participation, Brazilian "authenticity," and promoting political causes (Fernandes 2019; Jaguaribe 2014).

There were also a few brass ensembles still in existence. Bola Preta, the oldest running brass bloco founded for the carnival of 1919 that was remembered for its cultural vibrance after the Spanish Flu pandemic had hit the previous year, has never stopped performing. The bloco now attracts two million people during carnival, giving it the title of the biggest bloco in the world over Recife's Gala da Madrugada. Banda de Ipanema was formed in 1965 with connections to antidictatorship movements.[25] Bola Preta and Banda de Ipanema today are, however, far outside of Rio's alternative brass community, with which I found almost no overlap, and numerous elements distinguish the brass bloco world that would birth neofanfarrismo from these more traditional ensembles. Instead of producers organizing and contracting musicians, the alternative brass blocos Cordão do Boitatá and Céu na Terra were organized by the musicians themselves. While Bola Preta played on sound cars (carros de som) above the audience, these newer ones played in the street acoustically, using cords around the group of musicians to protect them from foliões. While who can play in the older brass blocos is determined through contracting and closed membership, Boitatá and Céu na Terra created a participatory structure with a strong musical core by mixing contracted professionals with interested amateurs (CW.Ch1.Ex2 and CW.Ch1.Ex3).[26]

Unlike Bola Preta and Banda de Ipanema, the names of both Céu na Terra and Boitatá refer to multiple expressions along the continuum of participatory and presentational performance "fields" (Turino 2008). Both groups maintain closed presentational bands (bandas) who perform throughout the year as well as during carnival. Boitatá's eight-hour presentational stage show on the Sunday of carnival is attended by tens of thousands of foliões and features a who's who of contemporary Brazilian popular music. But these presentational, professional ensembles also host, rehearse, and lead relatively participatory blocos, open to those willing to attend rehearsal, or even jump over the cord during the carnival parade with an instrument (figure 1.2). They are formed by what Turino would call a musical "core" amplified by the "elaboration" of nonmember participants, who are generally less professional. This mixed-field approach would later be taken up by neofanfarrista bands who would create their own open blocos, and

FIGURE 1.2 The pre-carnival parade of Céu na Terra. Photo by author on January 30, 2016.

this format has been essential to the bands' ability to propogate knowledge of their repertoires, increase access to music education among the public, and simultaneously augment interest in their presentational performances.[27]

For Boitatá and Céu na Terra, creative and free use of fantasias (carnival costumes) were an important part of the alternative brass movement's critical departure from blocos like Bola Preta, Banda de Ipanema, and the other blocos of the street carnival. The prizing of individually chosen fantasias stands in stark contrast to the homogenous T-shirts (camisas) that many blocos outside the brass bloco community and all samba schools use to define who is and is not part of the organization. The example of Salvador's trio eléctricos,[28] in which T-shirts are used to keep track of who has paid to be inside or outside of the cord that defines the bloco, is a particularly negative example for the neofanfarrismo community. While many alternative brass blocos do have themes, participants are encouraged to imaginatively express their own interpretation of them through fantasias.

The colorful fantasias of the brass bloco revival are crucial to the playful carnival engagements denoted by the word "brincar," a term that has a child-like and innocent connotation. Carnival is conceived as a moment for adults to reengage with their capacities to play, in particular to play the characters they dress up as, resignifying possibilities for sociality. DaMatta explains that "the word brincar may also mean to 'enter into a relationship' by breaking down the barriers between social positions to create an atmosphere of unreality . . . we are dramatizing relations, possibilities, desires, and social positions" (1991 [1979], 109). When I asked professional fantasia maker and bass drummer in the neofanfarrismo movement, Helena Tyrrell, what the fantasia accomplishes in the play (brincadeira) of carnival, she replied,

> This is very serious business. The name of my brand is Panu Panu Dreams in Weaving. I don't sell clothes. I sell the dream of a person, the expression of a person. I think that with the carnival fantasia you have the space to play with this. Carnival is the great stage for you to express this freely. The carnival fantasia is your vehicle for you to put out what is inside you and what you want to explode. The carnival fantasia is a great form of expression of your id and of what facet of it you want to play with. (Interview 2016)[29]

Fantasias have perhaps reached their highest point of elaboration among the emerging stilt walkers who have become a formalized element of many blocos in the past decade, offering a mode of participation beyond music making. Raquel Potí, who is largely credited with popularizing the practice through elaborate performances and educational oficinas, has helped form sections of stilt walkers (alas de pernas de pau) in Boitatá and Orquestra Voadora, among many others (figure 1.3). These sections add a striking visual component to ensembles that make little use of stages or sound cars to elevate themselves above the audience, and they mark a strong contrast to the visual aesthetics of the samba schools, showing the increasingly independent and developed aesthetics of the street carnival. Potí describes fantasias as having their own agency to express the self: "I don't create fantasias. The fantasia creates me. I go to Saara[30] and things find me" (interview 2016). While the fantasias of the samba schools are certainly imaginative as well, they cannot be said to represent any kind of individual expression of the self, as they are part of a carefully designed mass performance designed by the school's designer (carnavalesco). When I participated in the Estácio de Sá samba school, I picked up my angel fantasia a week before the parade at the City of Samba factory (Cidade do Samba) without any choice in the matter.

For trombonist Gustavo Machado, this individually creative spirit represents a major difference between the brass blocos of the Center of the city and more mainstream blocos in the South Zone: "If you go to a bloco in Ipanema

FIGURE 1.3 Stilt walker Raquel Potí. Photo by Micael Hocherman
on January 30, 2017. Courtesy of Raquel Potí.

you will see very few people in fantasias. In the neofanfarrista movement, we
produce our own fantasias to create something beautiful, fantasias that interact
with other people. In Ipanema you don't see this. You see a shirtless man with
a little Antarctica [beer company] hat hitting on women" (interview 2014). In
contrast to neofanfarrismo, he associates lack of aesthetic imagination with crass
machismo and consumerism. The former musical director of Céu na Terra and
ethnomusicologist Rafael Velloso explains that all these aesthetic elements are
part of what constitutes the expression of alternative culture in the brass bloco
community, including for foliões:

> The way people related and came together in the streets was alternative. It's not
> just the music itself; it's the whole performance concept. The musicians aren't
> performing in a sound truck; [they're in the street] so people can sing along and
> dress in costumes. There are gardeners, pierrôs, clowns, people who get in the
> character [of the songs]. It's magical for the audience; they can be part of the
> thing. The "alternative" is related to the whole context. You go to the carnival
> and have fun and drink with your friends, and you bring the costumes and
> sing the songs. When you have five, six, or seven thousand people, they can't
> even hear [the music]. They're not there for the music, they're there for the

event. Young people don't want to go to a private party and listen to DJs play marchinhas and old stuff. This is not alternative. But going to the streets with bands playing the same songs with crazy people, drugs, alcohol and dressing in ways you invent yourself—that's alternative. (Interview 2015)

The brass blocos also design ornate standards (*estandartes*), a practice that neofanfarrista blocos and bands would adopt in the years following, rather than the flag (*bandeira*) more associated with the samba schools. Standards, which are also used in military and Catholic religious processions, are held by a standard bearer (*porta-estandarte*) who leads the parade. The standard bearer holds a position of power, privilege, and responsibility of leading potentially thousands of people (figure 1.4). Standards in the brass community are not industrially produced, and, like fantasias, a do-it-yourself ethos is celebrated in their construction. Helena Tyrrell, the fantasia designer who also makes standards for the brass blocos and bands, explains the mythos of the standard in defining a crowd as a bloco:

The standard is an instrument. The standard is a living symbol of the collective it represents. If you have a street carnival bloco and that standard is up, this means that that carnival bloco is there playing. If the standard goes down, there are just people there. It's not a carnival bloco. The collective of people has lost identity as a collective. This applies to carnival blocos just like an army in war. While the standard is up the war continues. It doesn't matter how many soldiers are standing. Same thing with a carnival bloco. If the standard is up, even if there are two musicians playing, it's a bloco. (Interview 2016)

In sum, free use of fantasias, playing acoustically, participatory musical structures, musicians taking roles as producers, and liberal occupation of city streets in the Center of the city were all elements that embodied alternative expressions of carnival in relation to the dominant forms of carnivalesque experiences that were available in the 1990s. The critiques participants levied against the samba schools and other expressions of carnival must, however, be understood within their particular class and racial context and how participants position themselves in relation to other communities. Though Whiter middle-class Cariocas had chosen to leave Rio during carnival during the dictatorship and its aftermath, they have since carved out a space within the festivities that they feel is authentically theirs by drawing on an imagined past.

FIGURE 1.4 Boi Tolo with standard. Photo by Andre Rola.

Managing Street Carnival

Street carnival has become a big business to manage. But the complaint of many participants is that blocos, "made by and for the people," mostly manage themselves, and the city profits from their labor. For example, on Tuesday nights throughout the year, Orquestra Voadora runs an oficina to teach brass and percussion and the band's repertoires to musicians interested in participating in the bloco. On Sundays beginning in September, the bloco holds weekly rehearsals with four hundred musicians and often thousands of audience members in the parks surrounding the Museu de Arte Moderna with no city authorization or services. The rehearsals are fueled by mobile beer and food vendors (*ambulantes*), usually working-class, Blacker people. Together with the Whiter, DIY vendors selling artisan cachaça and sacolé, they form an informal economic part of what is called the "productive chain" (*cadeia produtiva*) of street carnival. For the carnival parade itself, in 2020, Voadora budgeted 70,000 reais (20,000 USD) for the costs, with 30,000 coming from official carnival sponsors and the rest being generated by crowdfunding and a scramble for smaller sponsors. Despite the massive 3.5 billion reais generated for the city by carnival events in 2018, 90 percent of this sum was from hotel revenue, and free events make it difficult for blocos to make money from the event itself (Mendonça, Figueiredo, and Neville 2018). Especially as the economy worsened by the mid-2010s, brass blocos complained that they were barely able to make the events happen due to insufficient city investment.

Still, given the dependence of street carnival blocos on sponsor funds, street carnival cannot be simplistically celebrated as a purely resistant and autonomous manifestation separate from the profiteering logic governing the sambódromo. The growing popularity of street carnival led to the first decrees in 2009 by Mayor Eduardo Paes to regulate the festivities, creating a structure of city authorization and making the city government "street carnival's guardian" (Sézérat 2020). Henceforth, approved blocos had to follow guidelines of agreed parade times and routes, paying for official security, firemen, and porta-potties. As these costs are quite burdensome for individual blocos, the city, instead of viewing the blocos as a "public" investment administered through the Ministry of Culture, created public-private partnerships privileging particular sponsors. In exchange for covering some of the costs, private companies monopolized the commercialization of their products during official bloco events, creating an emerging privatization of free events in public space. As in the case of the 1991 Rouanet Law, which promotes private cultural investment with tax incentives, "the Brazilian government is essentially outsourcing its cultural policy" (Goldschmitt 2020, 195). Since 2011, Ambev, which also owns Budweiser and 25 percent of the beer market globally, has been given a monopoly of sponsorship of street carnival blocos to sell Antarctica beer, a Brazilian brand owned by the global company (Andrade 2012). In official street carnival blocos, the only beer allowed to be sold in public space is Antarctica. These various restrictions led to an "unofficial" movement of blocos in 2009 who viewed the new decrees as compromising the "principles of carnival," and they have refused to register themselves in the official system (chapter 3).[31]

While many musicians, especially amateurs, are willing to work for free and outside this profiteering system, professionals generally are not. The primary possibility for remuneration for professional musicians on which Cordão do Boitatá and Céu na Terra rely is through the funds offered by corporations like Antarctica. While much of the discourse of street carnival is revolutionary and proposes itself as a public alternative to the sambódromo, the existence of many blocos is predicated on the encroaching neoliberalization of street carnival, leaving their viability to private companies and individual initiative. This can lead to a wide gap between theory and practice. For example, Jean de Beyssac, producer of Céu na Terra, claims that street carnival is inherently a political act: "You don't need to be partisan [in a bloco]. You're in carnival. You are practicing a political act in its essence. You are occupying the street and exercising the power of intervening" (interview 2015).

During a Céu na Terra bloco rehearsal I attended in early 2016, however, videographers from Airbnb, a company that has faced extreme criticism for the spike in affordability of rental markets in cities worldwide and especially in Olympic Rio, were filming the rehearsal. They were making a commercial for the Olympics called "Stay with Me" and had paid Céu na Terra to include the bloco in the commercial. While many musicians in Céu na Terra had decried the gentrification and affordability crisis of the Olympic City in the 2013 protests, they were profiting from the financing of a company directly involved in such controversies. The producer of Céu na Terra spoke after the rehearsal, explaining that, while they did not view capitalist corporations as their friends, they were raising needed money for international exchanges. Samba schools, he explained, receive support from Riotur, but the blocos receive nothing but the sponsorship of Antarctica. Bruno Muller, a producer of the brass bloco Prata Preta near the Port area of the city, portrayed the challenging position in which the bloco found itself in trying to critique the capitalist system of the Olympic

City and also deriving their income from it: "We critique property speculation, but our biggest sponsor is the new Port. It's a dilemma because we as citizens have the right to benefit from cultural money. We have to take advantage. But at the same time, we are knocking on the door of the people who will screw us one day" (interview 2015).

Since 2016, in the "post-Olympic" city, Cariocas have confronted a worsening economic climate that has further limited the available funds for blocos, as well as an anticarnivalesque, conservative political climate that has revived worries of repression not present since the dictatorship. Rio de Janeiro's evangelical Mayor Crivella, who lost reelection in 2020, publicly decried carnival as a hedonistic event dangerous to Christian values, and he cut funding for the festivities in half in 2017 (Faiola and Kaiser 2017). In 2019, Crivella, justifying funding cuts in a statement that could not be less neoliberal, declared, "Carnaval is a big baby who needs to be weaned and walk with his own legs," and Bolsonaro likened carnival to a pornographic affair in a notorious Tweet the same year (Brown 2019).

Porta dos Fundos has followed these developments with their own satirical takes. In 2017, they depicted a samba school without funds from the city that has chosen the theme of "Carlos," in honor of a random man who had decided to sponsor the school in exchange for an enredo about him (CW.Ch1.Ex4).[32] In 2018, they depicted another school that chose "Devotion to Christ" as their enredo, by Crivella's suggestion, and imposed a ban on allegorical floats, which the Mayor viewed as pagan images (CW.Ch1.Ex5).[33] In 2019, they showed a samba school that had simply been taken over by a military general who promised to cut the eighty-minute parade to an efficient 3:12 minutes (CW.Ch1.Ex6).[34] In 2020, another school's theme, presciently entitled "Carnavírus" in reference to the encroaching coronavirus before it had impacted Brazil, would simply be a retrospective on the greatest moments of the country, since clearly the planet wouldn't last until carnival 2021 (CW.Ch1.Ex7).[35]

In these difficult political and economic times satirized by *Porta dos Fundos*, blocos have been forced to look for alternative methods of financing and keeping street carnival alive. Cordão do Boitatá in 2020 decided to organize their bloco completely autonomously, eschewing Antarctica and relying on crowdfunding campaigns publicly promoted by Gilberto Gil among others. Céu na Terra began to charge admission to attend their weekly rehearsals in the Fundição Progresso rather than rehearsing outdoors. Street carnival participants navigate the choices available to them, and the events reflect a diversity of often contradictory discourses, desires, and priorities.

A CONTESTED REVIVAL

Rio de Janeiro has undergone a major process of revitalization in the first decades of the twenty-first century, aggressively pursuing a status as a global city. The city has not only been innovating, but renovating: rescuing, revisiting, rebuilding, and recalling its past glories as it cast itself as an Olympic City. The act of newly reconstructing an old city parallels the newness of neofanfarrismo, an innovative musical movement based on an old instrumental format. This chapter has focused on the various performance practices and discourses of the street carnival revival at the turn of the millennium that, by "rescuing" models of the past, were proposed as alternatives to what participants viewed as dominant and even "inauthentic" carnival traditions. The brass bloco movement of the street carnival revival in many ways sought to contest the hegemonic discourses of the city's revivalism, offering alternative ideas and practices of what might constitute a revival of the city's "authentic" culture. They cast the brass ensemble, an earlier expression of Rio's carnival, as an alternative, liberatory, and authentic form of street carnival.

This rescue has been a contested and contradictory process and shows how utopian discourses are compromised by the subject positions and social structures that participants inhabit. Despite the movement's inclusive discourse and embrace of purported "principles of carnival" that resonate with prominent carnival theorists, the brass bloco revival remains limited mostly to the Whiter middle class and relies in many ways on neoliberal management. Its alternative Whiteness can be understood as a disinheritance of the commodified hegemonic Blackness of the city's official heritage regimes of the samba schools, as well as of the conservative hegemonic Whiteness of middle-class Cariocas who abhor carnival, prefer American cultural imports, or elect to patronize carnival's more commercialized manifestations. Brass bloco musicians navigate a neoliberal and authoritarian city in which their survival depends on acquiescence and financial support while they attempt to transform these systems. The next chapter discusses the musical choices of these blocos and of the emergent movement of neofanfarrismo, which eventually critiqued what these newer musicians viewed as the musical homogeneity of Rio's carnival, including the earlier brass blocos, by embracing an ever-expanding musical eclecticism.

The brass bloco Me Enterra na Quarta (Bury me on [Ash] Wednesday) provides a last hurrah of carnival for Rio's alternative brass movement, as musicians and revelers snake through the bohemian neighborhood of Santa Teresa. The "burial" references the death of carnival on Ash Wednesday—in many carnival cultures, a personified king of carnival ritually dies only to return for the following carnival in an annual triumph of virtue over vice that reverses the death and rebirth process of Easter. In Rio, however, the bloco Me Ressuscita no Sábado (Revive me on Saturday), with many of the same musicians and repertoire and also in Santa Teresa, "revives" carnival the following Saturday. These blocos are part of an extended season of postcarnival "hangover" events (ressaca) that can last up to a month after carnival, referenced in the sketch that began this chapter.

The implied joke of these related blocos is that carnival only dies between Ash Wednesday and the following Saturday and is alive throughout the rest of the year. As neofanfarrismo emerged as an independent movement from carnival in the late 2000s, the brass ensembles began creating massive parties in the streets outside of the pre-Lenten season, and the alternative carnivalesque became a mode of expression beyond carnival. The festivity would come to be viewed by many brass musicians and foliões as an all-year lifestyle, aesthetic, and series of events—a marked transition from the seasonal blocos of Céu na Terra and Boitatá. Though brass musicians would expand the repertoires and uses of brass ensembles beyond the carnival season in the next stage of neofanfarrismo, the association of brass ensembles with carnival and its aesthetics and ethics would not be shaken, as neofanfarristas would seek to "carnivalize" the entire year. Indeed, it is not uncommon to hear the performative quip, "It's already carnival!" (já é carnaval!) at brass band events in April, soon after the last carnival has passed.

TWO

Experimentation

To Play Anything

"Ferro velho! Ferro velho!" Syncopated shouts celebrating "old iron" in Portuguese emanate from the park spaces at the Orquestra Voadora carnival bloco rehearsal. Hundreds of musicians covered in glitter momentarily take their mouths off their instruments to scream this short refrain. In the recorded version of Voadora's original song "Ferro velho," the band overlays on top of the brass band a sampled recording of the mechanical and robot-like voice of the operator of a recycling truck. The truck routinely roams through Rio de Janeiro's bohemian hillside neighborhood of Santa Teresa, crying out "ferro velho" in search of old appliances, metals, and discarded materials. The band's website explains the song's origin story:

> The song . . . was created from the light sleep of Tim Malik (Tuba) interrupted by the auto-speakers that announce the arrival of the buyer of discarded materials that gave inspiration to the principal theme, the refrain of four words and the conviction that it is possible to transform the "industrial discard" of which the song speaks into dancing material. (Orquestra Voadora 2014, CW.Ch2.Ex1)[1]

Later in the performance, musicians yell out in chorus another of the truck driver's lines reused in the original song, *"qualquer metal"* (any metal). For Malik, the line resonated with the democratization of access to music making that the street carnival revival and neofanfarrismo made possible in millennial Rio de Janeiro. Furthermore, Malik explained to me that "metal" was meant to invoke both the materiality of brass instruments as well as aesthetics and ethics more reminiscent of punk music.

The Santa Teresa truck referenced in the song quite literally rescues local discarded material to recycle for new uses, and the song puts the discourse of cultural rescue (resgate) as a central foundation of the band's project. But there is also much in the song that is internationalist and in engagement with the model of Brazilian cannibalism of consuming Others and transforming them into new products. Tim Malik, the song's author, is one of the early core members of the band. He is an American tuba player who lived in Rio for eight years, and one can hear American popular musical conventions in the song's strong bass line and repetitive grooves not present in traditional Brazilian carnival or brass music. In overlaying the "ferro velho" sample in the recording, the band's aesthetic practices seem closer to the cannibalist movement of Tropicália with its imaginative sonic juxtapositions. The song title is the eponymous name of the band's first album, the cover art of which is reminiscent of the Beatles' *Yellow Submarine* (figure 2.1). It shows a flying object powered by brass instruments and carrying the various materials it has picked up—a brass tradition in motion. The song suggests that the innovative movement of neofanfarrismo has Rio's "old iron" at its core but is taking it to new places. By 2020, in a sign of the changing of the guard as a new generation of neofanfarrista bands had emerged out of the world Voadora created, the term "ferro velho" had come to affectionately refer to Voadora and other bands founded at the end of the 2000s as an "old guard" of reference and reverence.[2]

Focusing on the changing repertoires of the city's alternative brass movement in the past two decades, I argue in this chapter that the emergence of the musically eclectic movement of neofanfarrismo in the mid-2000s, emblematized by Orquestra Voadora, from the revivalist carnival blocos of Boitatá and Céu na Terra at the turn of the millennium involved a conceptual shift from nationalist rescue to internationalist cannibalism. "Ferro velho," however, shows the interdependence of these concepts: the desire to gain inspiration from the local past is in dialogue with influences that come from abroad and the contemporary world, marking a new stage in the history of the Rio's carnival, characterized by a dynamic embrace of musical experimentation.

When I began fieldwork in Rio de Janeiro in 2014, I initially referred to Orquestra Voadora's eclectic repertoire choices as a result of "globalization." Musicians bristled at the word, associating it with cultural homogenization, North American imperialism, and alienation from local traditions and agency. Voadora's trumpet player, Daniel Paiva, remarked, "We have always felt very colonized by

FIGURE 2.1 Cover art for Orquestra Voadora's 2013 album. Illustration by Danilo Lucas, design by Marina Taddei. Courtesy of André Ramos.

the United States in the last century. When this word globalization came into fashion, it was meant to seem 'cool,' but in fact it was a disguise of American domination" (interview 2014). Drawn to the band's rejection of the frame of globalization in their engagements with international genres, I became increasingly aware of the prominence of the discourses of "cannibalism" to describe their voracious hunger for diverse, often global repertoires on the one hand, and "rescue" to denote their fierce protectionism of local musical practices on the other. My analysis of neofanfarrismo's repertoires is based on participants' own key frameworks of rescue and cannibalism, and in this chapter I provide a genealogy of taste of the neofanfarrismo movement and argue for local and historicized theorizing of musical circulation.[3]

As animating theories of cultural production, rescue and cannibalism are in a tense and dynamic relationship. As "Ferro velho" illustrates, in Rio's brass movement, musical circulation is not only a matter of engaging with present, international resources, but with past, local references as well. Though I trace a shift from nationalist rescue in the first phase of the brass bloco revival to internationalist cannibalism in neofanfarrismo, I suggest that this gradual diversification of repertoires is not simply indicative of a movement of historical stages from national to postnational identity.[4] Rather, Rio's brass musicians have adapted these established Brazilian frameworks of rescue and cannibalism, which have long been employed strategically in relation to shifting cultural and political realities, to conceptualize their engagements with musical genres from Brazil and around the world in diverse ways.

I situate these debates within the broader racial formation of neofanfarrismo's alternative Whiteness which, as I argued in the introduction, "disinherits" both the cultural conservatism of hegemonic Whiteness as well as the commodification of Blackness in Brazil. Atlantic world carnivals have long functioned as nationalist "heritage industries" by appropriating repertoires associated with Blackness and representing them as authentic national heritage, a story emblematized in Rio de Janeiro by the city's samba schools. As I showed in chapter 1, Rio's Whiter middle classes did not feel represented by the heritage regimes as redemocratization began by the late 1980s.[5] By the 1990s, the heritage power of samba to represent the national body had also been weakened by the decentralization of media production and the proliferation of regional genres as well as popular ones including rock and funk. Hermano Vianna, in *The Mystery of Samba*, had asked about this development, "Does this also spell the end . . . of the version of Brazilian identity created with so much care and effort by many groups with a converging interest in 'things Brazilian'? What can now assure the unity—even if only the musical unity—of Brazil?" (1995, 106).

The implicit response of the revival movement of brass blocos to such a question was not to defensively hold on to the samba paradigm as the singular authentic expression of brasilidade, nor to uncritically celebrate globalization as a response. Rather, brass musicians initially disinherited the samba school model popular with other blocos and forged an alternative heritage movement that would reimagine the nation around the rescue of a multiplicity of Brazilian "popular," especially folkloric, traditions. Embracing a form of diversified cultural nationalism that represented the nation in its plurality beyond the singularity of the "samba paradigm," they mixed classic genres of the city's street carnival with Northeastern regional genres, claiming to "rescue" carnival itself from commercialism and a restricted representation of brasilidade.

Opening the second stage of the brass movement in the mid-2000s that musicians would call neofanfarrismo, brass players who had cut their chops in the street carnival began experimenting with sounds available through new mediations, including an influx of immigration, the internet, growing festival networks, and an increase in resources for traveling and touring. Drawing on cannibalist discourse and disinheriting the traditional notion that carnival is primarily a heritage event, even in the diversified form of the earlier brass blocos, musicians further expanded the boundaries of the earlier brass movement. They affirmed the belief that one could "play anything" (*tocar qualquer coisa*) in Rio's carnival. While continuing to draw on the earlier street carnival's Brazilian repertoires, they would also make street carnival a space for *cumbia*, Afrobeat, punk rock, and even video game music interpreted by brass, among many other genres.[6]

Given the predominance of cultural nationalism and heritage traditionalism in Rio de Janeiro's carnival and carnivals elsewhere, this second step was not necessarily an obvious stance to take and constitutes a radical shift in the aesthetics of the biggest musical festivity in the world. Despite neofanfarristas' claim to a wide-open musical eclecticism, however, I focus on the approximations to and distancing from other repertoires and communities based on racial and class identities in their aim to forge a socially and aesthetically distinct musical movement that has its own, often unspoken, boundaries. How might this contemporary musical diversity of carnival revise our understanding of the traditional role of Carioca carnival as enacting a singular national identity? What kinds of national and international affinities have been forged through these new fusions?

WHAT TO PLAY? A POSTCOLONIAL PREOCCUPATION

Like counterparts in many other countries in the Americas constructing national identity, Brazilian intellectuals in the 1920s rejected the elite's historically Eurocentric orientation, debating how Brazilian artists might create national art forms that would not be merely imitative of European models. The two positions of nationalist rescue and internationalist cannibalism emerged out of cosmopolitan Whiter intellectual scenes as ways of thinking about Brazilian artistic production in relation to the rest of the world that have resounded ever since. These two poles are well represented by the São Paulo intellectuals Mário de Andrade and Oswald de Andrade respectively (no relation) and their collective but distinct projects to forge innovative models of national cultural production. Part of the modernist movement that emerged with São Paulo's Brazilian Modern Art Week in 1922, they were influenced by the European avant-garde and particularly its fascination for primitivism.

Mário de Andrade fostered a discourse of nationalist rescue based in a search of diverse forms of Brazilian popular culture outside of metropolitan spaces. With trips to the interior of São Paulo, the Northeast, and Amazônia, he documented a variety of regional Brazilian cultural practices. He is viewed as Brazil's first ethnomusicologist, having accumulated substantial information about Brazilian folklore, and his book *Ensaio sobre a música brasileira* (*Essay on Brazil Music*) (1928) sets out a space for consideration of Brazilian music as a national product. Also in contrast to the pre-Vargas Whitening paradigm, the White intellectual

Gilberto Freyre of the Northeastern state of Pernambuco mounted a different and more conservative defense of racial mixing based on the supposedly "intimate" relationships between masters and the enslaved. It was with this latter intellectual scaffolding that cultural nationalism based in mixed-race identity became the official policy of the Getúlio Vargas dictatorship and its embrace of what would be called the "racial democracy." Vargas presided over Brazil's "golden age" of popular music in the 1930s and '40s, during which samba and choro became national genres and the samba schools went from being persecuted to nationally visible, government-sponsored organizations (McCann 2004).

In the *Manifesto Pau-Brasil (Brazilwood Manifesto)* (1924), Oswald de Andrade also celebrates national culture but from a different perspective, proclaiming Brazilian superiority over European culture with an exaltation of Carioca carnival: "Carnival in Rio is the religious event of our race[7] . . . Wagner is submerged before the carnival lines of Botafogo. Barbarous and ours" (Andrade and Rego 1986 [1924], 184). In his later *Manifesto antropófago* (1928), he is more concerned with absorbing and transforming cosmopolitan influences as resources for nationalism, citing the practice of Brazilian indigenous cannibalism feared by European colonizers. Reversing the colonial relationship between periphery and metropole, he argues that Brazil's greatest artistic strength is based on active devouring of all possible influences, including of international and metropolitan cultures, and digestion and transformation of them all into new Brazilian artistic products: "those who came here . . . were fugitives from a civilization we are eating, because we are strong and vindictive" (1991 [1928]). With a practice of "constant exchange between self and other" (Jackson 1994, 106), cannibalism has since been employed by poets, painters, and musicians working in popular, folkloric, and classical realms.

Far from recently globalized, Brazil has articulated, therefore, the conceptual framework of cannibalism that has promoted Brazilian artistic agency to engage with any and all influences throughout the world for the past century. These foundational modern discourses between rescue and cannibalism were not dialectically opposed but rather depended upon one another and have animated debates on Brazilian cultural production ever since.[8] These two poles could be understood as manifestations of "anxious" and "celebratory" narratives regarding musical hybridity, the former fueling a "kind of policing of the locations of musical authenticity and traditions" while the latter emphasize "fusion forms as rejections of bounded, fixed, or essentialized identities" (Feld 2000, 152).

The long-standing tension between anxious rescue and celebratory cannibalist narratives can be heard in examples throughout the history of Brazilian popular music in the twentieth century. The legacy of the Vargas-era construction of certain genres as authentic national expressions, such as samba and choro, pushed against Brazil's historically Eurocentric orientation. But interest in internationally influenced musical styles and exchanges, including bossa nova and 1950s Brazilian rock, arose in tension with the cultural nationalism of the previous decades. In response, leftist musicians articulated a protectionist discourse of nationalist rescue that they viewed as anti-imperialist in defining the genre of Brazilian Popular Music, or MPB. More than a particular style of music, MPB became a policing boundary of permissible genres that could "authentically" represent brasilidade. For Sean Stroud (2008), MPB was a "defense of tradition," is the musical expression of Brazil's leftist, Whiter middle classes, and has acted as its cultural icon because it is associated with notions of national "quality."

While MPB, by its very name, might seem to be a wholesale embrace of Brazilian popular music, notable Brazilian popular genres that are dismissed as commercial or too influenced by American music are outside of its realm because they supposedly promoted political alienation.[9] The restricted scope of MPB's cultural nationalism was famously challenged by the Tropicália movement in the late 1960s. The tropicalistas embraced international trends of the day, especially psychedelic rock, avant-garde classical music, electric guitars initially anathema to MPB, and theoretically anything else. They explicitly invoked Andrade's cannibalism in search of a "universal sound," forging an adventurous artistic counterculture. Rather than adhering to what the tropicalistas called MPB's "defensive nationalism," neofanfarristas embrace what Caetano Veloso described as Tropicália's more "aggressive" and "engaged kind of nationalism," which turned the colonial relationship with Europe on its head (1996, 123).

All these post-samba mid-century scenes were multiracial but trended toward the Whiter middle classes who have played an outsized role in defining Brazilian popular music genres despite being known for their Afro-Brazilian origins. By the 1980s, in the context of ascendant neoliberalism and embrace of international capitalism, Whiter middle-class urban youth were infatuated with international rock trends that, unlike Tropicália, dialogued little with local tradition (so-called "Brock"). The more racially diverse *mangue beat* movement of the 1990s, a musical movement that challenged the marginalized status of the city of Recife within the landscape of cultural production in Brazil, would critique 1980s Brock as overly imitative through invoking cannibalism and the Tropicália movement.

These musicians mixed local traditions in Recife and its state of Pernambuco, as well as rock, hip-hop, and electronic music.

In sum, invocations of nationalist rescue and internationalist cannibalism have occurred almost cyclically in a dialectical relationship for almost a century, as Brazilian artists have found dominant attitudes at times overly nationalist and at others too focused on international trends. While some have argued that this polemic is largely over in Brazilian cultural production,[10] I suggest that while cannibalism may have overtaken aspects of mediated popular music, these debates are far from resolved in other cultural spheres, including Rio's street carnival. Orquestra Voadora's trombonist and cofounder, Juliano Pires, who had before immersed himself in the world of the brass bloco revival, often makes the parallel between Tropicália's critique of MPB and neofanfarrismo's critique of blocos like Boitatá and Céu na Terra explicit:

> Tropicália is my biggest influence . . . The tropicalistas put rock 'n' roll guitar in Brazilian music and mix traditional folklore, MPB, and other genres from various places in the world—mambo, jazz, psychedelic rock, several different genres in the same song. They developed this movement when MPB people were holding marches against the electric guitar that was "polluting" Brazilian music . . . This was cannibalism because they created something new with Brazilian and global music. I think that musically this is also what neofanfarrismo is doing, a cannibalism of the format of horns and percussion . . . because of what we knew before of fanfarras that played only one type of genre, only frevo, only samba. You can create all kinds of sounds with a fanfarra. (Interview 2014)

Before exploring Orquestra Voadora and the movement of cannibalist brass bands that exploded by the 2010s, however, we need to return to the more nationalist musical world of Boitatá and Céu na Terra out of which Orquestra Voadora emerged in order to probe how this dialectic plays out in Rio's alternative brass movement.

THE DIVERSIFIED CULTURAL NATIONALISM
OF THE BRASS BLOCO REVIVAL

Under the encroaching but still blistering 7 a.m. sun in the hilly Santa Teresa neighborhood, I walk with my trumpet into the growing "concentration" of the Bloco do Céu na Terra (the "Heaven on Earth" bloco) for their precarnival procession, the Saturday before carnival officially begins. The musical director is dressed as a parrot, and he mingles among the other musicians dressed as pirates, flowers, and men in drag. More musicians slip under the cord held by strong men that separates them from the public growing larger by the minute and packing the street with bodies.

Mixing the sacred with the profane, as the band's name implies, the music of Céu na Terra is a kaleidoscope of Brazilian musical genres. A 12/8 beat from the Afro-Brazilian *Candomblé* religion sparks the beginning of the bloco. Next, we launch into the technically challenging maxixe genre, Rio's popular music of the turn of the twentieth century. The heart of Céu na Terra's repertoire is the marchinha, or the satirical carnival march. Almost all the foliões can, and do, sing along with the comical lyrics that celebrate, among other subjects, drinking, gender queerness, demands for money, and more drinking. The movement from one song and genre to the next, expected by the musicians and foliões alike, gives the event a ritualistic feeling. After playing a few "classic" sambas, the bloco goes into the "regional" Northeastern genres of *afoxé*, maracatu, and *ciranda*. We conclude with some beloved frevos, the fast-paced syncopated brass genre from Recife, before playing the final marchinha, "Cidade Maravilhosa," the famous anthem that celebrates the "marvelous city" of Rio.

The next day, I arrive at the morning parade of Cordão do Boitatá. Many of the same musicians from the day before are here, and we are expecting to play much of the same repertoire. But there are some important differences. There are horn players hired from the symphony orchestra, and the parts are more orchestrated. The master of the percussion section is also the master of percussion at the Vila Isabel samba school. There is sheet music hung around the backs of the musicians in front of me. But it is still fairly open—anyone with a horn can come under the cord, even not having gone to any of the four weekly rehearsals beforehand. The parade is led by an *ala* (section) of stilt walkers dressed in ornate gold performing elaborate choreographed movements. The name "Boitatá" references the mythical Amazonian serpent god, and a gigantic serpent doll is passed over the musicians and the crowd as we amble. A large doll of Pixinguinha, the Black Carioca musician who popularized instrumental music in the early twentieth century, rises above the musicians. The bloco parades with standards of a pantheon of Brazilian popular music icons, including Cartola (a *sambista*), Luiz Gonzaga (the icon of Northeastern forró), and the progressive "jazz" musician Hermeto Pascoal, who philosophized about a "universal music" based in Brazilian music (figure 2.2).

In chapter 1, I examined some of the performance practices of Céu na Terra

FIGURE 2.2 The annual carnival parade of Cordão do Boitatá.
Photo by author on January 31, 2016.

FIGURE 2.3 Pixinguinha alongside Gonzaga in the streets
of Rio de Janeiro. Photo by author on November 2, 2017.

(2001) and Cordão do Boitatá (1996), blocos that sparked a revival movement of Rio's carnival tradition of acoustic, participatory brass blocos. Musically, they aimed to defend, interpret, and disseminate the urban and folkloric musical traditions of Brazil, engaging a century-old debate discussed above on what constitutes "our music" (Hertzman 2013). As the years have passed since their founding, the music disseminated by these blocos became a canon of Rio's brass carnival world. Ethnomusicologist and former Céu na Terra musical director, Rafael Velloso, explains how the bloco embraced a notion of the "popular" that encompassed folkloric traditions of the Brazilian "people" and resonates with MPB's use of the term:

> The idea of the "popular" was very important to the group. They would say, we play popular music. We are a part of popular culture . . . We brought different kinds of music to the carnival, like samba, maracatu, and frevo to present a diverse show. We believed we should play all the rhythms of music of Brazil, and we pushed an idea of folk authenticity . . . It was an engagement with Brazilian traditions and a diversification of carnival music. (Interview 2015)

Though Vargas is remembered for his support for the samba schools in particular, these blocos were indebted to diverse constructions of cultural nationalism established during his regime. In the 1930s and '40s, a twofold distinction through which Brazilian subjects could culturally "belong" to the nation emerged, through the nationalist expressions of the cultural capital and conduit of Rio de Janeiro, as well as through regional expressions of the Blacker Northeast based on the foundational historical and cultural status of the region (McCann 2004).[11] The brass blocos drew on this heritage by "rescuing" and constructing a repertoire that reflected a preoccupation with diversified cultural nationalism beyond the unified samba paradigm. They mixed what I call *Carioca classicism*, or a preoccupation with music from the city's early twentieth-century "Golden Age," and *Northeastern regionalism*, leaving in place hallowed notions of which expressive practices and populations could constitute the nation during carnival. On the streets of Rio, I even encountered the enduring legacy of these distinct authenticating nationalisms in visual form upon finding a photo of Pixinguinha, icon of Carioca popular music, to the left of a photo of the voice of Northeastern regionalism, Luiz Gonzaga (figure 2.3). They were hung above a collection of objects in the streets, to be rescued and recycled.

While for many neofanfarristas, Boitatá and Céu na Terra are synonymous with the rebirth of street carnival, for neither group is carnival the sole focus in the year. Carnival was not even the primary mission of Boitatá when it was founded in 1996. Co-founder Pedro Pamplona explains that the group, formed by university music students, came together to study "a repertoire of 'folkloric' Brazilian music . . . We learned to play this music in our Carioca style, putting together a repertoire of *carimbó, boi, baião*. And when carnival arrived we thought, 'hell let's play carnival too, the old marches'" (interview 2015). Both groups developed a closed nucleus of members for presentational performances that would expand to include contracted, invited, and uninvited musicians in a participatory carnival bloco. Throughout the rest of the year, Boitatá and Céu na Terra perform for the cycle of Brazilian folkloric manifestations, with particular emphasis on carnival, the Northeastern June festivals, *folias de reis* (Kings' Day traditions), the Northeastern traditions of the boi (Brazil's famous ox drama), and the Christmas tradition of *pastoril*. Ethnomusicologist Dil Fonesco explained to me that both groups "have a profound link with Catholic rituals that form Brazilian traditions of popular culture. They call themselves research groups. They go inside Brazil and bring information that for urbanites is new" (interview 2014).

Carioca Classicism

What, then, was "rescued" by these groups? The repertoire ranges from 1869–1981, but the bulk is from the 1920s to the 1960s, the so-called Golden Age of Brazilian music (CW).[12] The aesthetic orientation of Carioca classicism and Brazilian regionalism (in this case Southeastern) of the brass blocos is clearly expressed in Boitatá's opening of its carnival parade with "O trenzinho do Caipira" (the "Little Train of the Caipira" from 1930) by Heitor Villa-Lobos, Rio de Janeiro's and Brazil's most famous classical music composer. The piece references the Brazilian *caipira* character, marked by straw hats and other characteristics of rurality, "a rustic man of mixed racial heritage whose homespun wisdom and virtues symbolized the 'authentic' national character" (Weinstein 2015, 33). In the original piece, the orchestra is used to simulate the sounds of a train passing in the wilderness over a repeated lyrical melody. When played in the streets during Boitatá's precarnival parade, the musicians play intentionally out-of-tune horn blasts to simulate the sound of a train horn (CW.Ch2.Ex2).[13]

Early in Boitatá's precarnival parade, the bloco launches into Pixinguinha's technically challenging maxixe "Cheguei," meaning "I've arrived" and declaring the arrival of the bloco itself. Maxixe is one of many genres that is today part of the broader umbrella of choro, which refers to the diverse instrumental music popular in Rio in the late nineteenth and early twentieth centuries before samba was declared the primary national expression. Indeed, the first song marketed as a carnival samba, "Pelo telefone" (1916), uses the maxixe rhythm rather than the more complex Estácio rhythms that would become characteristic of samba in the 1930s, and there was slippage in terminology between the two genres as samba was consolidated as a national genre. At the turn of the twentieth century, maxixe and choro were often played by wind ensembles and brass bands with the various complex counterpoints played by different horns, as can be heard on the recordings of Pixinguinha, who maintained a carnival bloco called Cabocla de Caxangá. The revival of interest in these older popular genres, or the "choro revival" in Rio de Janeiro, is part of a much larger revival of interest in "classic" Carioca genres that were commonly played in carnival before the samba schools' samba-enredo became the primary expression of the festivities (CW.Ch2.Ex3).[14]

This repertoire is taught at Uni-Rio's Escola Portátil de Música (Portable Music School, 2002) and the Casa do Choro (House of Choro, 2015), run by the same musicians and both offering accessible instruction in choro and related genres of early instrumental Brazilian music where many brass musicians seek training. Providing instruction on wind instruments as well as the instruments that became the standard instrumentation of choro, the school offers a space for Cariocas to learn or improve on their instruments at an affordable price. Students can take classes on the history of the genre, study associated instruments, and participate in the *bandão* (big band). This multilevel ensemble of up to two hundred musicians includes students and professors playing together elaborate arrangements of these older genres, mirroring the participatory formations of carnival blocos (CW.Ch2.Ex4).[15] Since 2017, Casa do Choro has offered an oficina specifically focused on playing in carnival. The reference to older Carioca instrumental styles associated with early styles of wind ensembles articulates a clear relationship with Rio's past within the alternative brass movement.

The genre that is at the heart of brass blocos is the marchinha, or "little carnival march." Before the rise of the marchinha at the beginning of the twentieth century, the city's carnival music was indistinguishable from music played in the rest of the year, and the marchinha became the first uniquely carnivalesque genre of Rio de Janeiro (Tinhorão 2013 [1974]). The diminutive "*inha*" suffix satirizes the military march genre and the "official culture" that the military emblematizes, and brass features prominently in these songs. "Zé Pereira," the first known song of Rio's carnival, is an old French march that had new words written in 1869. It celebrates one of the Carioca carnival's oldest identifiable characters, named after a mythologized Portuguese immigrant. He famously led popular-class carnival groups to parade around the city playing thunderous bass drums, offering a popular street carnival in distinction to the elite carnival of the mid-nineteenth century. The words of the song celebrate Zé Pereira as the personification of carnival, and Boitatá and Céu na Terra's renditions invite the foliões to sing the lyrics: "long live carnival" and "revel in its days of drunkenness."

The carnival march genre can be divided into the fast-paced and often comical marchinha that became popular in the 1920s and the older *marcha-rancho*, a slow and more somber version of the same rhythm. The first carnival song known as a Brazilian carnival march is a marcha-rancho, "Ó abre alas" (Open the Wings), composed in 1899 by the White composer Chiquinha Gonzaga, the first major female Brazilian composer. The song's opening lyrics demand the opening of the alas, or thematic sections within a parade, as the singer or musical group asks for passage: "Open the alas, for I want to pass." The lyrical focus of marchinhas is diverse, from satirizing contemporary politics to lambasting particular popular carnival characters. Some compositions, such as "Pierrô apaixonado" and "Máscara negra," reference the Italian *commedia dell'arte* theater tradition that maintains a hold on popular imagination in Rio's carnival and carnivals elsewhere. Others take an irreverent populist tone, such as "Me dá um dinheiro aí," which consists mostly of the narrator demanding, "Hey, you there, give me some money!" In "Cachaça não é água não" (Cachaça Isn't Water), the singer wisely advises about the sugarcane liquor, "You think that cachaça is water, but cachaça is not water, no."

In Céu na Terra and Boitatá, the order of marchinhas is somewhat set, and the musicians move through them as though they are suites of a larger piece. "Ó abre alas" is usually the first march played of many, underlining its historical importance in the development of the genre before the majority of songs that were popularized through the radio when competitions were sponsored for best marchinha. In Céu na Terra, "Ó abre alas" is followed by the introduction for "Turma do funil" (Drinking Team), after which all the musicians crouch on the ground intoning an "F" on accented quarter notes, quote an ominous line from the Star Wars "Imperial March," start the orientalist introduction to "Allah-la-ô," and jump up to start that marchinha's upbeat, major section. Céu na Terra's producer, Jean de Beyssac, describes playing marchinhas as an activation of Brazilian collective consciousness and a kind of ritual: "It was a genre that a grandfather sang to a father, a father to a son . . . It is an easy genre to sing in the street. People know the songs; even if they don't know all the words, they know the refrains. It's something that is very much in the consciousness of people in Rio de Janeiro, and of all Brazilians . . . Singing marchinhas is a ritual" (interview 2015). Despite their mass popularity, marchinhas' importance has been attributed by Roberto DaMatta to the aesthetic predilections of the Whiter middle classes as opposed to the Blacker samba and samba-enredo of poorer populations: "The march is the samba of the middle class, as it were" (1991 [1979], 110–11).

Of course, no genre is more associated with Rio de Janeiro or Brazil than the samba, and the brass bloco revival has not ignored this heritage. Former Céu na Terra director and ethnomusicologist Rafael Velloso suggests that the reduction of European horns in samba schools in 1934 was part of Vargas's nationalist campaign to frame Brazilian identity around Afro-Brazilian percussive practices (see also McCann 2004, 59). The choice to play samba in a brass and percussion format resounds within the memory, therefore, of what some samba sounded like before a particular form of the genre that excluded brass was normalized. As seen in chapter one, the brass bloco world of the street carnival often contrasts itself with the contemporary samba schools, but this disinheritance of the samba schools is not a dismissal of the genre itself. The range of sambas for Boitatá and Céu na Terra includes primarily older, "classic" sambas and samba-enredos from the 1930s to the 1970s, and, unlike the samba schools, composing an original yearly samba is not part of the brass blocos' project. Perhaps the most common samba in the brass bloco revival is "Tristeza" (1966), or "Sadness," by Nilton de Souza. It was released amid historic flooding in the beginning of 1966 that killed two hundred and left fifty thousand homeless in Rio de Janeiro. The words invite the singer to let sadness depart and exude the rebirth of happiness through singing.

The relationship of these blocos to samba represents an aesthetic positioning of the Carioca middle class that prizes "classic" sambas of "quality" and historical resonance. These older sambas are framed in opposition to what many Whiter middle-class Cariocas view as the "inauthentic," "low-quality," "commercial," and even "lower-class" predilections of the contemporary working-class and Blacker style of *pagode*. New samba-enredos, as well as plenty other forms of Carioca music, are not part of their hit parades. Like MPB, the aesthetics of these blocos reveal Whiter, middle-class anxieties over presumed quality and rescuing particular genres thought to represent Rio's "authentic" carnival, while largely eschewing related genres they view as commercialized. The fact that these supposedly commercialized genres are largely contemporary forms of local, popular

Black music reveals that such dismissals of "commercial expressions" can reflect a problematic racial and class bias.

Northeastern Regionalism

While marchinhas and classic sambas had also been played by older brass blocos such as Bola Preta (1918) and Banda de Ipanema (1965), the additions of regional genres marked a departure in the aesthetics of Rio's carnival in what Boitatá's publicity materials refer to as a more "multicultural" expression of Brazilian music. Given the vast territory of Brazil, regional identity has been important in any part of the country, often in contrast to the hegemonic cultural weight of Rio de Janeiro and São Paulo in the Southeast. McCann quips, however, that "not all regions were created equal . . . and in the process of national consolidation some regions would inevitably appear more 'Brazilian' than others" (101).[16] Indeed, while the serpent creature who protects the Amazon from those who would set fire to it for whom Boitatá is named in some ways represents the bloco's regionalist and protectionist aesthetic, Amazonian music is not part of the bloco's repertoire.

It is the Northeast, and in particular Pernambuco and Bahia, that figures as the primary reference for regional music. In the post-Vargas Brazilian imagination of "racial democracy," the Blacker Northeast represents a national cultural heartland and the birthplace of "authentic" forms of popular music and culture in contrast to the industrialized Southeast, what Barbara Weinstein calls Brazil's "internal orientalism" (2015). The region is the oldest colonized region of the country—Salvador da Bahia was the first capital of Brazil beginning in 1549 and remained so until the capital was ceded to Rio de Janeiro in 1763. As the two other cities most associated with Brazilian carnival, Salvador and Recife have produced well-known genres of carnival music and are primary carnival references for other parts of Brazil. The Northeast is also the heart of the Workers Party with President Lula da Silva hailing from Pernambuco, and the romanticizing of the Northeast can also reflect a leftist political alliance against the more politically conservative Southeast and South where the Northeast has long been derided as poor and backward with coded and explicit racism.

Recife's carnival, in particular, is known for its diversity of folkloric genres and has been a primary influence on the brass bloco revival. Recife's popular mangue beat movement, which fused regional forms with popular music in the 1990s, helped underline Pernambuco as a reference for Rio's street carnival revival. Céu na Terra's producer, Jean de Beyssac, explains that the carnival of Recife

> is very rich with diverse rhythms. Here it's samba, samba, samba, marchinha, marchinha. There you have frevo, ciranda, maracatu, *maracatu solto*. It's much richer than here. Here carnival was appropriated to sell the image of the city as the greatest carnival. For me the greatest carnival is the carnival that has the most possible diversity. And that is the carnival of Recife. (Interview 2015)

By contrast, the genre of *axé*, Salvador's commercialized carnival pop music originally based on the beat of samba-reggae, is often derided in Rio de Janeiro in ways that diminish the broader value of Salvador's carnival for many Cariocas. The opinion of Orquestra Voadora's producer, Renata Dias, was quite common: "Axé, I don't like it. I find it superficial. The marchinha sings of revelry and has a critical side, lyrics that make you think and that use analogies. Axé doesn't. It's very weak, no content" (interview 2016). There is widespread belief in Rio de Janeiro that the contemporary carnival of Salvador is highly commercialized and that the *camarotes* (private clubs along the parade routes) and the city's *trio eléctricos*, which charge admission to street carnival events, amount to the privatization of street carnival.

Still, the more folkloric musics of Bahia figure prominently in Rio's brass movement. They resonate with a long-held narrative of Bahian music as an African source of Carioca music, as many Blacker Bahians migrated to Rio de Janeiro following abolition and played important roles in the development of Carioca samba. One of the first pieces played by Céu na Terra and Boitatá in their precarnival parade is Moacir Santos's "Coisa número 4," based on a 12/8 candomblé rhythm. Candomblé is an Afro-Brazilian syncretic religion comparable to *santería* in Cuba and other Afro-diasporic religions. The genre acts as an important regional reference for the Northeast because of the importance of Afro-Brazilian religious expression in both Pernambuco and Bahia, particularly in the city of Salvador. The use of candomblé by these blocos is a reference to a regionalism that is at the heart of the Brazilian nation within the post-Vargas narrative that locates Afro-Brazilian culture as the authentic root of Brazilian culture. In homage to Salvador, Boitatá plays an arrangement of "Canto de Iemanjá" for the Candomblé goddess (*orixá*) of the sea, from Baden Powell's famous album *Os Afro-Sambas* (1966). In the original song, the singer invites the listener to come with her to Salvador to hear Iemanjá sing and see the sea covered with flowers, a traditional mode of honoring the orixá.

The brass bloco revival also drew on afoxé and maracatu, percussion traditions from Salvador and Recife respectively that are based in Candomblé practices and made their way into carnival in the late nineteenth century. Afoxé emerged in Salvador with the rise of Black parading groups that celebrated African themes and cultural expressions in the 1890s after the abolition of slavery. The song "Filhos de Gandhi" (Sons of Gandhi), played by Boitatá and composed by Tropicália artist Gilberto Gil, honors the first well-known afoxé group of the same name, founded in 1949 and inspired by the nonviolent campaigns of Mahatma Gandhi. Maracatu is a highly polyrhythmic percussion tradition from Recife that reconstructs lineage to the "nations" of African descent and has become popular in Rio's street carnival revival with several groups dedicated to the style. Céu na Terra's rendition of the maracatu song, "Verde mar de navegar," simulates the Afro-Brazilian call-and-response vocals of the original song between trumpets and trombones over dense syncopated polyrhythms.

Forró, the music of the dry interior lands of the Pernambucan *sertão* and not associated with carnival, also plays a role in these Carioca carnival parades, and Boitatá's version of Dominguinhos's "Eu só quero um xodó" is a perennial favorite. The selection of forró songs reveals class preferences based on the Whiter, middle-class movement *forró universitário* (university forró). The 1980s Southeastern movement expressed "middle-class nostalgia for the popular authenticity" of Luiz Gonzaga (Draper 2010, 3) and eschewed the more bombastic sounds of *forró estilizado* (stylized forró), popular with contemporary, poorer Northeastern migrants to the Southeast and featuring horns, synthesizer, and drum set. From Pernambuco, the blocos also draw on the frevo tradition, the principal brass reference for all of Brazil and the "official" carnival music of Recife. In Rio's brass blocos, Recife is worshipped for the high-quality performance level of the fast, technically demanding, and highly syncopated genre. Brass bands in Recife's carnival bring mass crowds to the street with loud renditions of street frevo standards. Both Céu na Terra and Boitatá usually conclude their parades with the well-known frevos "Cabelo de fogo" and "Vassourinhas," and the highly professional Bloco da Ansiedade has recreated the frevo tradition since 1997, providing a reference for the style in Rio during precarnival weekend (CW.Ch2.Ex5).[17]

A Restricted Nationalism

The brass bloco revival was not all encompassing in what it "rescued" in its diversified cultural nationalism. These regional references constitute a particular imagined national community (Anderson 1983) that privileges certain styles, regions, and populations as more Brazilian than others based on notions of quality and folkloric authenticity. Their selection of genres stands in contrast to Brazilian genres viewed as inauthentic and commodified manifestations, such as contemporary samba-enredo, axé, and others. Blackness is largely celebrated as a folkloric root of national origin, but contemporary Carioca and Bahian Blacker genres are distanced and marked as commercial. The blocos' strategies, aesthetics, and discourses can be understood within longer histories of leftist cultural nationalism and in particular MPB, a genre through which Whiter artists of the Southeastern middle classes have historically policed the "authenticity" and "quality" of Brazilian popular music in ways that might maintain unexamined racism.

These aesthetic preferences have also governed brass blocos inspired by Boitatá and Céu na Terra even in poorer and Blacker neighborhoods, as the case of the Blacker Prata Preta bloco demonstrates. Founded in 2004 by friends who had sought out the Boitatá parade but missed it (before cell phones) and resolved to start their own bloco, Prata Preta is a brass-and-percussion bloco that plays many of the same marchinhas and sambas popularized by Céu na Terra and Boitatá (CW.Ch2.Ex6).[18] The producers of Prata Preta drew inspiration from the early twentieth-century protests that took place in the central port neighborhood of Gamboa, where the bloco is based, against the federal government's obligatory pox vaccines led by Horácio José da Silva, better known as "Prata Preta." The Cordão do Prata Preta has developed a broader preoccupation with memorializing particular Brazilian leaders and movements of popular resistance, including the Pernambucan *cangaceiros*, populist rural bandits who challenged government rule in the Northeastern sertão, and Canudos, a racially diverse religious settlement in the Northeast that the federal government perceived as a threat to its legitimacy and destroyed in 1897.

Prata Preta's producers view their cultural mission as one of revitalization, not only of the "authentic" repertoire and ensembles of street carnival, but also of the neighborhood in which they live. Producer Fábio Sarol explains, "we try to maintain the root, the essence of carnival." Associating the prevalence of the Blacker *funk carioca* in the area with the violence and urban decadence of the 1990s, he recounts, "we suffered a lot. I grew up in the world of funk in the nineties, in the favelas, in dances with fights and gang conflicts. That was my culture. I came to know samba in Prata Preta. I came to know culture in Prata Preta. If it weren't for Prata Preta, I would be screwed today" (interview 2015). Such comments reveal the perception that the revitalization of "authentic" and "traditional" street carnival culture represents a disinheriting of "low-brow" manifestations of Brazilian popular music and culture, especially the Blacker funk carioca genre much maligned by many Whiter middle-class Cariocas. Prata Preta, according to Sarol, "brings culture here to Gamboa to present it for those who don't have it or don't have access." The repertoires of the brass bloco revival are presented as an acculturating force in ways that imply a kind of class superiority of certain genres over others in a locality that the producers see as disconnected from the cultural institutions and benefits of richer parts of the city.

In contrast to the alternative middle-class scene of Céu na Terra and Boitatá, the musicians of the core of Prata Preta are also more working class and Blacker, and some hail from military bands. But Prata Preta has become a well-known stop on the circuit of middle-class brass musicians, who are invited to play along, and it is frequented by many foliões of the "alternative" Whiter South Zone carnival scene. One of the challenges for the bloco has been to appeal to the neighborhood dwellers themselves when the brass bloco tradition has been so associated with the middle classes. Though a group like Prata Preta has provided important cultural resources for poorer neighborhoods of the city, its actions could also be likened to cultural gentrification, a theme we will often encounter in this book. In direct appeal to residents, one of the bloco's rituals is stopping the parade to play Pixinguinha's slow love song "Carinhoso" to couples in the balconies above the streets in an attempt to bridge the affective gap.

THE INTERNATIONALIST CANNIBALISM
OF NEOFANFARRISMO

After the organized rehearsal of Orquestra Voadora's bloco in the park around the Museum of Modern Art, the hierarchy of the band's leadership dissolves, and musicians from the bloco push around three hundred brass musicians into an extended, chaotic jam. Musical sources vary widely from the Romanian band Fanfare Ciocărlia to New Orleans' Rebirth Brass Band, Afrobeat legend Fela Kuti, Mario Brothers video games, Rage Against the Machine, and songs from Brazil's Tropicália and mangue beat movements. I play through some songs that I have played with brass bands in the United States. The rehearsal itself is a free performance and a mass event—sometimes up to two thousand people come for just the weekly rehearsal, known as "Woodstock carioca," in the months leading up to carnival.

After a couple hours, a trumpet player begins the opening of the marchinha "Ó abre alas" (Open the Wings), and the musicians begin to move, launching an unpermitted, two-hour parade to the nearby Lapa entertainment district. They start to scatter in the crowd, and separate bands develop as Brazilian marchinhas mix with brass repertoires from around the world. As we walk toward the pavilion of the museum, musicians take advantage of the concrete echo underneath the ceiling to play even louder with collective intensity. The act always reminds me of how in New Orleans second line bands often similarly play with the acoustics under the I-10 freeway (Sakakeeny 2010). Indeed, this sonic practice resounds from Rio de Janeiro to New Orleans and back, as some Carioca participants and many visiting foreign musicians have traveled between the cities and are aware of emergent translocalisms within the ever more connected international brass band community.

Brought together by Juliano Pires and others in 2008 to play diverse genres throughout the year beyond carnival, Orquestra Voadora (2008) plays an eclectic repertoire, much of which is relatively obscure except to those listening to brass repertoires throughout the world (CW).[19] Trombonist Gustavo Machado describes neofanfarrismo, the movement sparked by Voadora in contrast to the earlier brass blocos, as part of an "international subculture. These are people that have various affinities only separated by geography, such that you arrived from the United States and heard the same music as in your country" (interview 2014). Like what Jason Stanyek calls an "affinity interculture," Rio's *roda pequena* (small circle) of brass musicians, or the physical open circle of musical exchange, has expanded into a "transregional and planetary *roda grande*" of global encounters, one that has broadened repertoires beyond the local, national, and folkloric frames of the older blocos (2011, 113).

With Orquestra Voadora's name translating to the "Flying Orchestra," the band meant to evoke that they could play anywhere because of their mobile instrumentation, but equally important is its proposition that it could play any repertoire (*tocar qualquer coisa*), linking physical and aesthetic mobilities. Further broadening the boundaries opened by Boitatá and Céu na Terra, Orquestra Voadora and the bands it spawned have popularized the idea that any music could be carnivalesque and inspired a huge wave of experimentation. Beginning as a presentational band (figure 2.4), they quickly adopted the practice of Céu

FIGURE 2.4 Orquestra Voadora, the band. Photo by author on January 26, 2020.

na Terra and Boitatá of organizing a participatory bloco playing in their first
year in carnival of 2009. By later providing a space for amateurs to play in the
carnival bloco through their oficina by 2013 (chapter 3), the bloco opened the
door to anyone who wanted to learn a brass instrument, thereby doubling and
redoubling the number of brass bands and blocos with a voracious, cannibalistic
appetite for new musical references.

By the mid-2000s, the brass bloco revival had reached a point, precisely because of its success, at which the nationalist preoccupation for rescue had ceased
to be so pertinent. Bithell and Hill might call this a phase of "post-revival" in
which "the motivation behind the original revival impulse may in any case have
lost much of its potency as the core revivalists have either achieved their objec-
tives or moved on . . . Post-revival sows the seeds for new beginnings" (2016,
28). The campaign to raise Rio de Janeiro to the status of a "global city" with the
hosting of the World Cup and Olympics entailed situating the metropolis not only
as a cultural mediator of the nation, as the brass bloco revival may have viewed
it, but also as a mediation point of "global culture." Thiago Queiroz, director of
Boitatá, explains, "Rio has become much more cosmopolitan. There are more

foreigners here. We started to travel much more. Ten years ago, it was much more difficult. It became much more international on account of the boom of capitalism" (interview 2014). With increased funding available from numerous private and public sources, neofanfarrista bands started touring to international festivals, including in Serbia, Colombia, France, Portugal,[20] Scotland, and the HONK! festivals in the United States (chapter 6). Pedro Pamplona, a founder of Boitatá and the newer bands Songoro Cosongo and Fanfarrada (2009), underlines the role of the internet in this diversification: "We started to hear whatever kind of music from anywhere in the world with much more ease. Balkan music became closer. The universe of music of Latin America became closer. And I heard some things, and damn, I thought this music would be great in carnival!" (interview 2014). Orquestra Voadora trumpeter Daniel Paiva recounts how alternative brass musicians began to experiment with new repertoires in the mid-2000s:

> We came from Céu na Terra and Boitatá. We met each other in these blocos in the beginning of the band. We played marchinhas in various blocos, but we were also listening to American and European brass bands—Youngblood Brass Band and Fanfare Ciocărlia. Everyone loves the New Orleans bands—Rebirth, Dirty Dozen. Carnival links us with carnivals in other places. We have our carnival, but we hear the carnivals of New Orleans and of Colombia. We went looking for these kinds of sounds as much through carnival as through the [instrumental] formation of the brass band. (Interview 2014)

Neofanfarrista bands designated new "sites" of reference, both geographic and thematic, beyond the local and national frames of the earlier brass bloco revival.[21]

Orquestra Voadora's eclecticism owes much to its travels and meetings with other international bands—the band has toured through Western Europe, Brazil, and Colombia and hosted bands from France, the United States, Chile, Benin, and elsewhere. Voadora codified an instrumental formation that would become a standard for Carioca fanfarras, mixing trumpets, saxophones, trombones, and tubas with a particular formation of Brazilian percussion: *surdos* from samba, *alfaias* and *xekerés* from maracatu, and a rock-based snare/hi-hat/cowbell harness (figure 2.5). Musicians frequently noted the influence on this percussion format of Recife's mangue beat movement, which incorporated instruments from maracatu into a rock band format. The absence, or disinheritance, of most of the percussion instruments of the samba tradition, on the other hand, is notable in the city that is the birthplace of samba—*tamborim*, *agogô*, *ganzá*, and *repique* are almost nowhere to be found in neofanfarrismo. Percussionist Miguel Maron explains,

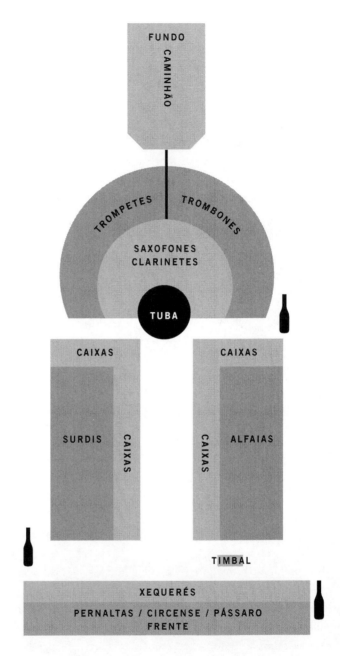

FIGURE 2.5 Schematic for arrangement of the 2015 carnival
performance of Orquestra Voadora's bloco showing sections by
instrument. Courtesy of André Ramos.

We took the foreign model of the fanfarra, but we adapted it with percussion of carnival. We don't use bass drum. We use the alfaia and surdo of carnival, and a huge amount [*porrada*] of percussion. But it's not just any kind of Brazilian percussion. Maybe an agogô is ok, but [samba] tamborim not really because there is a language here. We came to create these sections, of alfaia, surdos, snare, and xekeré. (Interview 2014)

With the rise of these newer brass bands, Cariocas began to distinguish between the terms "fanfarra" and "bloco" as a fanfarra movement arose distinct from carnival. The increased visiting of French *fanfares* and American brass bands to Rio provided examples of brass and drum presentational formations that were different from the city's participatory bloco tradition. "Fanfarra" is often used in the neofanfarrismo movement, but the term has some pejorative connotations because of its association with civic, military, and school band culture. Participants also use the English term "brass band" to refer to bands of the newer neofanfarrismo movement, in reference to the New Orleans style. Nevertheless, the boundaries between bloco and fanfarra are fluid and somewhat arbitrary, as Italian trumpeter and Rio resident Bruno de Nicola's comment suggests: "I can't say what the difference is in the division between fanfarra and bloco . . . I think it's more the repertoire really in peoples' heads because marchinha belongs to the history of Rio de Janeiro and the bloco. So in this sense you can see neofanfarrismo as an evolution of the fanfarra [that had before been] called 'bloco'" (interview 2016). In their effort to define these new ensembles, in other words, international models were at the forefront of neofanfarristas' minds as they compared them to local ones. In what follows, I discuss a few of their engagements with diverse new repertoires in order to show how neofanfarrismo, advancing the "alternative carnivalesque," critiqued and expanded the nationalist frame of the earlier movement by embracing cannibalism.

A Latin Movement

Like the United States, Brazil's massive territory, population, and language can make the country feel like a world unto itself having little to do with the rest of the Americas. In Brazil, the term *música latina* generally refers to Hispanic-American music and does not usually include *música brasileira*, which are instead two separate categories. "Gringo" refers to any non-Brazilian, including Hispanic Latin Americans, much to the chagrin of Hispanic-Americans who have made

Rio their home and bristle to be labeled as such. Neofanfarristas often criticize the provincialism of Brazilian musicians' disassociation of themselves from a larger sense of pan-Latin American identity, which they blame on the imperialist legacies of dividing Latin America.

The economic boom of the 2000s set the conditions for heightened immigration to Rio de Janeiro, particularly from other parts of Latin America. Bringing together musicians from Venezuela, Colombia, Argentina, and Brazil, such as Boitatá co-founder Pedro Pamplona, the bloco Songoro Cosongo (2005) resolved to play cumbia, *merengue*, *mambo*, and other Latin genres; they represented the first engagement in street carnival with eclectic international repertoires. The name of the band references the book of poetry by Cuban writer Nicolás Guillén (1931), which plays with Afro-Cuban musical expressions, as well as the *salsa* song by Héctor Lavoe of the same name (1978). Italian trumpeter Bruno de Nicola contrasts the internationalism of Songoro Cosongo with a kind of "autocannibalism" of nationalist culture that "feeds on itself":

> The influence [of international engagement] came from abroad with this bloco of gringos bringing Latin American inspiration from outside Brazil. I think that change never comes from the center. It comes always from the periphery, always from outside. In terms of the fanfarras of Rio, it came from outside, from people who came together and resolved that in carnival you could play other things . . . Really for a long time my foreign perception was that Carioca culture is very provincial. It feeds on itself . . . Songoro Cosongo was the match and Orquestra Voadora—boom—lit the fire. (Interview 2016)

Songoro Cosongo called itself the first band of a new style of "psicotropical musik," making reference to the psychedelic Tropicália movement and the many "tropical" origins of the musicians and styles used (CW.Ch2.Ex7).[22] Their original song "Maracuyá," for example, names multiple tropical fruits in Spanish and Portuguese over an extended *montuno* (an ostinato section in Cuban *son* and salsa). Songoro Cosongo grew into Pamplona's next project Fanfarrada (founded in 2009 soon after Voadora in 2008), a highly skilled fanfarra devoted to playing a variety of genres, mostly from Latin America, including *mambo*, cumbia, samba, *tango*, baião, Uruguayan *candombe*, as well as Afrobeat, jazz, and Balkan music. In cannibalistic, postmodern language, Fanfarrada bills itself as "the courageous Orquestra of strange rhythms and savage musics of the post-vanguardist tradition." In the carnival of 2015, I sat in with Songoro Cosongo and Fanfarrada during carnival when Pamplona united the groups to play a joint repertoire in carnival that he called a "Bolivarian repertoire."[23]

Today, Latin musical genres are references for Voadora and many other neo-fanfarrista bands. The bloco Besame Mucho, founded in 2012, carries on Songoro Cosongo's tradition of playing Latin music in carnival and brings together many immigrants from Hispanic America. In the carnival of 2014 and HONK! RiO of 2015, Rim Bam Bum, an excellent brass band from Santiago, Chile, was hosted by the neofanfarrismo community. The Chilean band has since formed a community "bloque" in Santiago based on Voadora's example, using a Spanishized version of the Portuguese word "bloco" rather than the Spanish "comparsa" (CW. Ch2.Ex8).[24] Neofanfarrismo articulates Rio de Janeiro not only as a global city, therefore, but also as a Latin American one.

Do You Know What it Means to Miss New Orleans?

When I began teaching in Orquestra Voadora's oficina, the band immediately asked me to teach a class on brass music of "my culture." When I asked what they were referring to, they said I could teach a New Orleans second line or a jazz funeral song. While it is problematic that I, as a White American, was seen as representing this Black American cultural manifestation from a city I have never lived in, it is telling that in the neofanfarrismo community to be associated with the United States is to be associated with the brass band music of New Orleans. I suggested teaching Rebirth Brass Band's famous Mardi Gras hit "Do Whatcha Wanna," and soon I would hear brass bands playing the call-and-response riffs of the song all over Rio de Janeiro.

Like the influence of Hispanic Latin Americans, an influx of American and English musician residents in Rio has helped propel the popularity of New Orleans brass music in Rio. Many neofanfarristas view the city as in many ways as akin to their own. Both Rio de Janeiro and New Orleans assume foundational narratives of national musical origins as the birthplaces of samba and jazz in their respective countries.[25] The city's second line brass parade tradition has become a primary reference for neofanfarrismo, and professional brass bands like Monte Alegre Hot Jazz brings trad jazz to the streets of Rio (CW.Ch2.Ex9).[26] Orquestra Voadora's original tuba player, Tim Malik, an American musician who had lived in New Orleans and moved to Rio with his Brazilian wife, helped popularize New Orleans music in the city. Malik's tuba playing is credited with bringing a strong sense of the harmonic function of an improvisatory and independent low bass line to Rio's brass bands. Orquestra Voadora's saxophonist André Ramos explains that in Rio's traditional brass blocos, "we often play the bass without tuba, but with trombone or saxophone . . . Samba schools don't have any bass. The bass is all percussive. [Due to Tim's influence] in Orquestra Voadora, we always were based in the tuba" (interview 2015). Indeed, a strong bass ostinato reminiscent of a New Orleans tuba line is present in Ramos's own original composition, "Elefante" from *Ferro Velho* (CW.Ch2.Ex10).[27] New Orleans influence brought not only new repertoires to the streets of Rio de Janeiro, but new conventions to the local instrumental formation of the brass band.

The French Connection

New Orleans music was transmitted to Rio de Janeiro not only by American jazz musicians, but also by musically eclectic French brass bands (fanfares) whose strong presence in the city has brought many such international genres to Rio's bands. Ramos recounts that "The French brass bands played a large role in our history. We started to have contact with French bands early in the beginning [of the band]. Voadora already existed—we didn't copy—but we exchanged a lot with them. It's even hard to say what we exchanged. It's something more conceptual than technical" (interview 2015). Many French brass bands are tied to particular schools and universities often distinguished by profession—such as the bands of architects, engineers, or doctors—an association that originates with the Fanfare des Beaux-Arts that mocked the military formation following World War II (Flanet 2015). Distinct from American university marching bands, this formation that is sometimes called in French "néofanfare" is closer to a New Orleans second line band with trumpets, sax, tuba, marching bass drum, and snare, numbering from about eight to twenty members (Boudjadja 2017).

As Rio de Janeiro became known internationally as a great city to show up and play in the streets in the 2000s, French brass bands started visiting as Voadora was just forming and have come frequently ever since. They were well received and struck a chord with a long history of Francophilia among the Carioca middle and upper classes. When the French band Ottokar arrived in Rio in 2015, one of its members described their reception as akin to entering a previously established channel of French musical "immigration," part of a larger musical network between Rio de Janeiro and France:

It really surprised me, obviously among a certain milieu, but that this milieu in Rio already knew us when we arrived. Two days later, we were programmed in a show. It made me think about the migration system and migratory fluxes. It works through this system of networks. In the migratory fluxes, you have migratory routes. Everyone goes to a place because there is the network of experience. From that, links are created. Globe Note met Orchestra Voadora. Then Orquestra Voadora went to France. Now we are here. (Interview 2015)

French trombonist Clément Mombereau's trajectory in the city has followed and fortified this network. An enthusiastic musician known for playing every line loudly an octave above the standard trombone range in carnival blocos, Mombereau first came to Rio with the band Octupus in 2011. That band was traveling around the world to do workshops with children in poor areas, including Rio's favelas, as part of the organization "Fanfares sans frontières," a play on Doctors without Borders (*Médecins sans frontières*), which was formed by Globe Note who had visited Rio in 2008 just as Voadora began playing together. Mombereau was struck by the musical similarities between neofanfarrismo and the brass bands in France, hearing songs he knew from France that had been passed on by Globe Note to Orquestra Voadora: "When I arrived here the first night I hallucinated a bit, because there was a Balkan brass band and Orquestra Voadora, which played French hits and was almost a fanfare Beaux-Arts. Well that's great, we already had returned to France! But then you see quickly that the Brazilian element [*jeito brasileiro*] is very present" (interview 2014). Returning to Rio as a foreign exchange student and eventually staying permanently, he arranged tours around Brazil for his French brass band Dumb and Brass, leading to the collboration of second line mashups with maracatu drummers in Recife (CW.Ch2.Ex11),[28] and tours in Europe of the Brazilian bands he founded, Bagunço and Technobrass, which have played important roles in the neofanfarrismo movement.

Balkan Fascination

Though few Balkan musicians themselves have visited the neofanfarrismo community, Balkan brass music became a primary reference for neofanfarristas through the increased visiting of French brass bands who regularly played the repertoire of Balkan brass bands. Eastern European bands and musicians—including Fanfare Ciocărlia, Kočani Orkestar, Taraf de Haïdouks, Boban Marković, and Goran Bregović—are admired by neofanfarristas. Rio's brass bands play direct covers of Balkan songs like "Miserlou" and also use musical modes associated with the Balkans, especially permutations of harmonic minor (*hijaz* and *nikriz*), to suggest a kind of musical otherness, such as Os Siderais' song, "Blues cigano" ("cigano" meaning "gypsy" in Portuguese). Since my fieldwork, klezmer songs such as "Bulgar from Odessa" have also entered the mix.

Balkan brass music has been disseminated through the Western world through the films of Serbian director Emir Kusturica and the soundtracks of the White Yugoslavian composer and arranger Goran Bregović, which focus on the musical cultures of Romani musicians. Much of the repertoire known in Rio de Janeiro—such as "Bubamara," "Mesečina," and "Kalashnikov"—was heard first through their films, including *Black Cat, White Cat* (1998) and *Underground* (1995), which became popular as Eastern Europe opened to the West after the end of the Cold War. Mirjana Laučević (2006) explores how Western "Balkan fascination" reaches back much further than the wave that began in the 1990s with the Balkanization of the International Folk Dance movements in the United States in the 1960s. She argues that participation in Balkan music in the US has formed as an "alternative music culture" that essentialized the Balkans as a place of folk authenticity uncorrupted by capitalism and "civilization." That is, Western infatuation with Balkan music, which neofanfarristas have adopted from the United States and Western Europe, has long been an articulation of alternative Whiteness.

Rio de Janeiro's professional Balkan brass band, Go East Orkestar (2010), was formed as the resident live music act of a preexistent series of electronic Balkan-themed dance parties called Go East Festas beginning in 2007, where scenes of Kusturica films were projected while Cariocas danced to remixed Balkan songs. The English name "Go East" at once shows the preoccupation with oriental otherness as well as the cosmopolitan origin of this orientalism. The Brazilian band even travelled to the famed Guča Balkan brass festival competition in Serbia in 2012. Go East was the first band from Latin America at the festival and won second place in the best foreign band competition. The band can be seen in videos of their performances on the main stage in Guča dressed in the national colors of yellow and green and playing mashups of the famous samba "Aquarela do Brasil" with Balkan standards (CW.Ch2.Ex12).[29]

The earlier brass bloco revival had articulated a preoccupation with "popular culture," but this formulation had been primarily based around a conception of the popular as folkloric and early mass culture. In contrast, neofanfarristas, like tropicalistas, celebrate the term "popular" as embracing contemporary mass culture, including its most commercialized manifestations, as they seek to move beyond the earlier groups' preoccupations with folk authenticity and MPB-like anxieties regarding the global cultural industries. Orquestra Voadora and other neofanfarrista bands have adapted a variety of American, Brazilian, and European pop songs to brass bands and mixed them with Brazilian rhythms. For example, neofanfarristas reach into the Whiter Brazilian middle classes' history of infatuation with American rock, off-limits within MPB's aesthetic boundaries. They identify with some of the most iconic and rebellious American and British rock bands of the 1960s to the 1990s, from Jimi Hendrix to Nirvana, and play brass covers of their songs. The name of the brass band Metais Pesados (literally "Heavy Metals"), a band formed in the Voadora oficina that plays rock covers, is a word play on the material heaviness of their brass instruments as well as the genre they adapt, and it evokes the "old iron" of Voadora's "Ferro velho."

FIGURE 2.6 Super Mario Bloco. Photo by author on February 4, 2016.

Neofanfarrismo's engagement with global popular music is not limited to "musics of resistance" and can range from the very "poppy" and apolitical, such as Britney Spears and Daft Punk, to the creative adaptations of techno music by Rio's TechnoBloco and TechnoBrass brought to the city by Mombereau and other French musicians (CW.Ch2.Ex13).[30] Since 2012, the brass band Cinebloco has adapted versions of well-known film music from mostly American films and mixed these songs with Brazilian percussion, reaching into the nostalgic memory of Cariocas who have been inundated by American media and films. The Super Mario Bloco (2012) has translated the affection of adults for the music of video games from their youth (figure 2.6, CW.Ch2.Ex14).[31] In neofanfarrismo, the global popular references of people who have grown up in a global city are voiced through the brass ensemble.[32]

African and Afro-Diasporic Romanticization

In their engagements with global pop culture, neofanfarristas also draw on a variety of African and Afro-diasporic styles. They are largely inspired by a construction of global Blackness as a culture of resistance within the racism of global imperialism, what Paul Gilroy (1993) calls the "counterculture of modernity" that is the Black Atlantic. This embrace of alternative Blackness stands in contrast to the hegemonic Blackness of the samba schools. Since the Tropicália movement promoted Black music genres from other parts of the world, many such genres have been celebrated in Brazil for their critical edge. Reggae has long denounced racism and unjust histories of the transnational Black experience, but the genre is equally well-known for musicians' use of marijuana considered by Rastafari to be sacred, and neofanfarristas too consume their share. Rio's Marofas Grass Band was formed by a group of musicians associated with Orquestra Voadora who first called themselves Orquestra Vegetal (Vegetable Orchestra) and played for the annual protest march for the legalization of marijuana. Afrobeat songs are also popular references celebrated for the Nigerian saxophonist Fela Kuti's pan-Africanist anticolonialism. Voadora medleys, for example, Fela's "My Lady Frustration" with one of Tom Jobim's more political songs, "O morro não tem vez" (1962, The Favela Has No Luck). Their version mixes the Black resistance politics of Afrobeat with a samba, the lyrics of which recount that if the favela were given a chance, the entire city would sing.

In the post-Vargas narrative of Brazilian identity, sub-Saharan Africa is romanticized as the fount of Brazilian music and as a place of origin, and even Whiter

FIGURE 2.7 Flag of Mozambique displayed during carnival march of Céu na Terra
with Mozambiquan musicians. Photo by author on January 30, 2016.

neofanfarristas have viewed encounters with African bands in the context of their
own country's Black heritage. International encounters with African brass bands
and musicians have brought particular songs and genres to Rio's brass movement, such as the visit of Benin's Gangbé Brass Band in 2009 (CW.Ch2.Ex15).[33] In
2016, even Céu na Terra, which had never before played non-Brazilian music in
carnival, crowdfunded to bring saxophonist and Professor Timóteo Cuche from
Mozambique to teach several songs of the Mozambican genre *marrabenta* (figure
2.7, CW.Ch2.Ex16).[34] Interest in global Black genres represents an "alternative"
cultural desire to affiliate with the cultural expressions of marginalized others
within the Whiter neofanfarrismo movement, especially with genres of African
and Afro-diasporic popular music viewed as rebellious.

Rescue of Contemporary Brazilian Popular Music

Like Tropicália and mangue beat, neofanfarrismo is not only a Brazilian cannibalization of what comes from outside Brazilian borders, but a conversation with
a much broader diversity of Brazilian genres. A cannibalist approach dispenses

with the aesthetic boundaries of the earlier rescue project and theoretically engages with any form of Brazilian popular music, including mass, "low-quality,"
and "kitsch" genres rejected by the MPB rationale, such as funk carioca, 1950s
Brazilian rock (*jovem guarda*), samba-reggae, and axé.[35] Cannibalism is not
only a transformation of the international but also a radical resignification of
the national.

The inclusion in neofanfarrismo of the repertoire known in Portuguese as
"Black music" is well represented by the Whiter band/bloco Fanfarra Black Clube
and the Blacker band Crispy Rio Brass Band. The infatuation with "Black music"
illustrates a distinctly different relation to Afro-diasporic music making than in
the brass bloco revival. "Black music" refers not to the various Afro-diasporic
traditional music genres of Brazil, which are generally known as "músicas negras,"
but rather to genres that dialogue with American Black popular music genres,
especially funk, soul, hip-hop, and Black pop musicians like Michael Jackson
and the Brazilian Tim Maia for whom neofanfarristas have particular affection.
While música negra is foundational to the MPB narrative of Brazilian music
and the leftist cultural nationalism of the brass bloco revival, "Black music"
represents a cannibalization of Black American popular music and is a primary
reference in neofanfarrismo.[36]

Samba-reggae and axé, the commercial carnival music from Salvador that
grew out of samba-reggae, had also been largely absent from the repertoire of
Céu na Terra and Boitatá, as recent manifestations of Salvador's carnival are often
viewed in Rio as bad taste. But songs of these genres now feature prominently in
neofanfarrista bands with the characteristic samba-reggae groove created by the
mixing of samba and candomblé instruments and rhythms with reggae's slower
tempo and upbeat skanks, playing an important role in bands and blocos such
as Amigos da Onça (CW.Ch2.Ex17).[37] Offering an alternative Blackness in the
1970s that contrasted with the racial democracy, samba-reggae affirmed pan-
African Black identity beyond the nation state, rejected the racial democracy's
masking of racism, and called attention through carnival to the suffering of Black
people around the world. Salvador's Afro-Brazilian bloco Olodum, the most
famous group associated with the style, makes transnational affiliations with
Afro-diasporic cultures, using the colors of Jamaican Rastafarianism, composing enredos that celebrate African nations, and bearing a name that refers to the
supreme deity of Candomblé, Olodumaré.

Lastly and also largely in contrast to the early brass blocos, the much maligned funk carioca genre popular in the favelas has also made its way into

neofanfarrismo (CW.Ch2.Ex18).[38] Also known as *baile funk*, the genre bears little relationship to American funk of the 1970s, and instead features a generally incessant electronic beat, reminiscent of 3-2 clave, that forms the rhythmic basis over which musicians rap. Lyrics are often noted for their portrayals of violence, drugs, life in the favela, social inequality, and pornographic sexuality. Associated with the rise in drug traffic and urban violence in the 1990s, funk has been constructed by the media as a moral panic and has been part of "legitimating" violent campaigns against the favelas, though it has also been consumed by Whiter middle-class Cariocas with many parallels to hip-hop in the United States. Critiquing the dismissal of this music by the earlier movement invested in middle-class notions of quality as an expression of racism and classism, neofanfarristas play funk songs in favelas and around the city in an attempt to forge solidarities with marginalized communities and for the pleasure of embracing the maligned genre. Despite their engagements with all these Blacker popular Brazilian genres largely deemed as too commercialized during the earlier brass bloco revival, I also heard problematic dismissals of them by neofanfarristas as lacking in taste, showing that neofanfarrismo is not free of bias.

Composing Carnival

While composition has long been a part of the Carioca carnival, it has mostly been limited to composing within a particular genre and often as part of a competition for the best song of that genre, within strict generic and formulaic guidelines, such as the competitions of marchinhas and samba-enredo. The brass bloco revival, seeking to "rescue tradition," had little use for composition, but neofanfarrista bands are increasingly writing their own material and propagating it by teaching it in their blocos. Original music composed by neofanfarrista bands draws on many of the musical references examined throughout this chapter that are fused into new musical experiments. The emerging interest in composing music will likely further revolutionize Rio de Janeiro's famous street carnival toward becoming a space in which original composition not bound by generic requirements becomes a stronger element of this gigantic musical festivity.

Along with Voadora, the neofanfarrista band that has recently led the movement toward promoting a repertoire of original music is Rio's Franco-Brazilian band Bagunço, in which I played as the band's trumpeter during my fieldwork. Founded by the French trombonist Clément Mombereau discussed above, the band's name plays on Mombereau's mispronunciation of the word *bagunça* (mess) by cannibalistically embracing the foreigner's mistake and placing it at the forefront of their musical identity. Bagunço creates sophisticated original compositions that draw on many of the musical influences of neofanfarrismo, including forró, samba, maracatu, American funk, Afrobeat, second line, and progressive jazz. Embracing an experimental aesthetic, in recent carnivals the band's bloco has drawn on the avant-garde techniques of Butch Morris's conduction method, with band members using signals to lead bloco participants in structured, collective, free improvisation.

Many of the band's songs move seamlessly through several different genres— "Gordona," for example, shifts between waltz, *rumba*, *ciranda*, and frevo. When Bagunço plays the song, the band always encourages audience members to join hands to participate in the traditional Brazilian ciranda circle dance before releasing into the frenetic frevo. When I toured with Bagunço in France for six weeks in 2016, we often attempted when playing "Gordona" to take the hands of bewildered French audience members to take part in the ciranda in their town squares. Hosted by bands around France, many of whom had visited Rio de Janeiro through the international brass circuit and influenced the development of neofanfarrismo in Rio, our tour was part of the wave of Carioca brass bands that have toured around Europe and North and South America and have in turn influenced bands outside of Brazil (CW.Ch2.Ex19).[39] With plenty of evidence that neofanfarristas are much more than passive consumers of global culture, I understood by this point why Voadora's trumpeter had strongly rejected the term "globalization!"

CANNIBALIZING CARNIVAL

In 2015, Rio de Janeiro hosted the first edition of the HONK! RiO Festival of Activist Brass Bands (chapter 6). The name was changed from its initial title, the HONK! RiO Festival of Cannibalist Brass Bands, which was discarded since it was acknowledged that few outside Brazil would understand the reference of cannibalism in what aimed to be an international festival. Despite the name change, the festival enshrined the experimental, cannibalist approach to cultural production as a primary element of the transformation of a movement that originated as a rescue of cultural nationalism into one theoretically hungry for anything. In its fourth edition in 2018, it would choose the fiftieth anniversary of the cannibalist Tropicália movement as its theme. But while the festival has showcased international brass bands, it also featured blocos like Céu na Terra as an homage to the origins of the city's brass movement. Boitatá, Céu na Terra, Voadora, and the neofanfarrista bands are indeed part of a shared musical world of the larger alternative brass movement, even if they manifest different aesthetic priorities. Musicians circulate between them, and Voadora's bloco often reverts to the marchinhas musicians learned playing with the older blocos, mixing them with their own eclectic repertoires. Similarly, while Tropicália was at first decried by MPB musicians, the cannibalist movement was not fundamentally opposed to MPB, but rather in dialogue with the musical nationalists, both part of what Caetano Veloso has called the "evolutionary line" of Brazilian popular music.

By embracing the alternative carnivalesque and disinheriting the city's official carnival, neofanfarristas have radically expanded the repertoires of carnival and pushed the popularity of the brass band scene beyond the festive season into a year-round movement.[40] At both stages, the brass movement forged novel affinities, relationships, and connections locally and around the world, using new technologies of circulation and benefitting from a boom in international migration and attention. Neofanfarristas created a carnival that is at once postnationalist and yet firmly concerned with the local context. But, as Fabiano Lacombe writes of Boitatá, the "proclaiming of plurality cannot be confused with totality" (2014, 105). The desire to "play anything" is still limited by particular references, cultural desires, and biases, reflecting an expression of Whiter, middle-class cosmopolitanism that manifests particular expressions of social distinction through repertoire choices. Approximations to and distancing from particular genres and communities have not been free of racism or classism, and neofanfarrismo, like the movement that preceded it, has its own aesthetic and social boundaries.

As we note the persistent importance of national references and local identity in neofanfarrismo as it moved beyond the brass bloco revival, Thomas Turino is surely correct in stating that "nationalism is neither increasingly irrelevant for cultural analysis nor at odds with cosmopolitanism and globalization" (2000, 12). But I have argued that these frames are best understood through the theoretical languages musicians themselves use, such as in this case the terms rescue and cannibalism. The fantastic diversity of Rio's contemporary street music movement may seem, and *is*, new, but these blocos are not simply expressing their contemporary "glocalized" existence. They call attention to longer Brazilian histories of exchange and self-discovery, and they aim for cultural dialogue to take place on their own terms. For these musicians, brasilidade remains connected to a strong sense of local and national roots while they voraciously explore, consume, and transform the musical diversity of the world.

THREE

Inclusion

Whose Rio?

"*Aaaaaaaaaaté a praça!*" Musicians and foliões sing "to the square" over a groovy bass line and thunderous percussion as they collectively wander, aggregating more musicians as they go, toward the large open spaces around the Lapa Arches, a central place of beginning and end for brass processions and jams. The refrain is a Portuguese adaptation of "Freedom" by New Orleans' Rebirth Brass Band, in which the Black brass band sings "Freeeeeeeee, free my people!" The song was popularized in Rio de Janeiro by Bagunço but quickly caught on as standard shared repertoire of the neofanfarrismo community, and many neofanfarristas don't know the original recording. For the musicians of Bagunço, the association between the original song of Black liberation with their version that directs paradors to occupy central public spaces was intentional. Brass musicians navigate a map of city spaces, some of which are to them sites of refuge for their practices. Singing "Até a praça" as they move toward Lapa encapsulates what could be called neofanfarristas' "acoustemology," or how they come to know city space through participatory music making.[1]

———

SOUNDSCAPES OF PUBLIC PARTICIPATION

For many neofanfarristas, the central practice of what I have called the movement's instrumental activism is the "liberation" of city space for "the people" by fostering what I call a "soundscape of public participation" that aims to be as inclusive as possible. Famed stilt walker Raquel Potí suggests that neofanfarristas aim to show that the street "is a public space. It shouldn't serve commercial interests. It shouldn't serve the interests of politicians. It should serve the interests of the population. We come here to the street because it is also our house" (interview 2016). Professional trombonist Marco Serragrande affectionately refers to the street as a privileged pedagogical and inclusive space for musicians: "My school was the street. The lesson [aula] was the street" (interview 2015). These affectionate depictions of the street as a home or school recall Brazilian sociologist Roberto DaMatta's belief in the capacity of rituals to mix the separate domains in Brazilian society of the street (rua)—the impersonal public universe—with the house (casa)—the intimate space of private domesticity: "The center of the city ceases to be the inhuman locale of impersonal decisions, and instead it becomes the meeting place of the whole population" (1991 [1979], 35–36).

Not all politics involves indignation and denunciation. As a sign at Rio's Festival of Public Art in 2015 read, "We are not a protest . . . We are a proposal," neofanfarristas have formed much of their critique of the privatization of urban space through performative example. Emphasizing the movement's nonsemantically based activism, Voadora's saxophonist André Ramos explains, "Our political transformation is much more about seeding and fomenting an alternative kind of thought and experience, not about discourse. People experiment" (interview 2015). As shown in the "Hino da Orquestra Voadora" (see introduction), in which the band's democratization of music making in public space is depicted as a form of social salvation, neofanfarristas argue that musical participation in the public commons can erode the senses of exclusion that characterize life in a neoliberal and profoundly unequal city. They aim to create a "horizontal" musical movement that levels distinctions between leader and follower, musician and spectator, and producer and consumer. These inclusive practices have allowed the movement to grow exponentially beyond the world of relatively more professional musicians, such as those who run Boitatá, Céu na Terra, and Orquestra Voadora, leading scores of Carioca adults to engage in music making in the streets for the first time.

The ubiquitous graffiti and street art tag "Rio pra quem?" (Whose Rio?) that appeared around the city in the mid-2000s put at stake the question of what populations should benefit from Olympic Rio de Janeiro's economic rise. Neofanfarristas answer that the city should be for "the people" (o povo). But as Judith Butler reminds us, naming the people is inherently inclusive as well as exclusive and we must examine "what we mean by 'the people' and what various people mean when they invoke that term" (2015, 7). In the case of neofanfarrismo, who are "the people?" What kinds of participation are fostered in these musical happenings in public space between diverse groups with differing privileges? Whom is neofanfarrismo's activism ultimately for? In this chapter, I explore the efforts to create a soundscape of public participation by examining diverse cases, including a "radically open" brass bloco, Rio de Janeiro's unofficial carnival movement, Orquestra Voadora's brass band oficina (class), and brass jam sessions in the streets. By examining one of Voadora's most popular songs as it circulates between these scenarios, I show how the community's shared musical knowledge enables the participatory taking of public spaces around the city. I argue that the movement's fostering of a soundscape of public participation has forged tangible possibilities for inclusion and diversification, but meets many limits and contradictions in its realization especially because of its dominant Whiter, middle-class profile.

Public Space and Social Inclusion

For neofanfarristas, social inclusion and the occupation of public space cannot be conceptually divorced from each other. Public space is where the social Other can be included and horizontal social relationships can be constructed. For trombonist Juliano Pires, the inclusive nature of the brass ensemble is an element of the instrumental formation itself:

> Wind instruments congregate differently from electronic instruments. If you have several guitars, it doesn't work—you don't need them. But with horns, you have sections and can bring together many trumpets or trombones. Fanfarras are different from other musical formations because of the physical element that makes it possible to be in the street and make a live, horizontal, and mobile intervention. (Interview 2014)

Likewise, in her consideration of the activist brass HONK! movement in the United States, Meghan Kallman argues that "HONK! does three things simultaneously: it reclaims physical space in cities, it organizes decision-making processes based on participation and inclusion, and in doing the first two things, it (re)defines publics. The three process are interdependent" (2020, 118). This chapter builds on a growing literature that regards sound, space, and participation as dynamically interrelated.[2] Standing in contrast to the loneliness and alienation of the "civilized," neoliberal city, neofanfarristas understand acoustic music making to have the capacity to produce intimate and public sociality that can remake the public commons.

Much of the work on participatory music making and community music has generally not taken into account the spatial contexts in which this music making occurs (Keil 1987; Turino 2008). It generally relies on a Marxist frame similar to the neofanfarrista imagination of a participatory, populist movement against a commodified, presentational musical culture: capitalist society promotes specialized labor tasks, resulting in the production of an alienating art of spectacle for consumers, and musical participation is proposed as the moral antidote.[3] But beyond the lack of attention to space in these analyses, the binary between an uncommodified participatory field of music making and a capitalist presentational field cannot account for the existence of a participatory movement like neofanfarrismo that is predicated on financial exchange for its existence (see also Snyder 2019b). An analysis of one of Voadora's most well-known songs, moreover, shows how the song circulates between presentational and participatory, private and public, hierarchical and horizontal manifestations, complicating any simple binaries. Nevertheless, much of neofanfarrismo's ethics about fostering a soundscape of public participation also promotes beliefs similar to Keil's and Turino's, and they provide an ethical inspiration to action even if actual manifestations may be more complicated.

In staking a claim on public space, neofanfarristas' participatory music precariously finds itself at the heart of a debate about what Rio de Janeiro should sound like, as brass bands "redefine the soundscape" and its "territoriality," as Reily and Brucher write of brass bands the world over (2013, 17–18).[4] In transforming the city's places, the movement has both been appropriated and commodified as a cultural expedient, as well as repressed and silenced as a threat to urban order. The debate over creating and managing a city's soundscapes between groups with diverse interests is an example of what Leonardo Cardoso calls "sound-politics."[5] Of course, not all street music artists face the same risks and opportunities when engaging with a city's sound-politics. Matt Sakakeeny shows, for example how working-class Black brass bands contest New Orleans' public spaces by staking a vulnerable claim on the soundscape of New Orleans through public cultural expression: "Making public sounds in public spaces is, quite literally, a practice of being heard" (2010, 25). Because of neofanfarrismo's prevailing Whiteness and relative privilege, however, the Carioca case is not parallel to Sakakeeny's.

As one could reasonably argue that Bagunço's interpretation of Rebirth's "Freedom," a song of Black liberation, is an act of cultural appropriation, one could similarly ask if a soundscape of public participation forged by Whiter middle-class musicians constitutes anything more than a spatial appropriation, or a form of gentrification. Can these musicians tangibly erode the social barriers between themselves and marginalized urban populations in an intensely unequal city such as Olympic Rio de Janeiro?

To Play in the Street

Cariocas often refer to the "street" (rua) as an all-encompassing signifier of public space, including the city's streets, squares, beaches, parks, Lapa's Arches, as well as a mythology of space that encompasses, according to DaMatta, "everything relating to the public, uncontrolled aspects of the urban world" (1991 [1979], 67). Racialized, marginalized, and associated with the universe of rogues (malandros), the street might represent for DaMatta an alternative set of values and identifications for the Whiter middle classes raised to identify with the domesticity of the home. In Rio, simply "to be in the street" (estar na rua) is conceived by some as militating against a city trending toward privatization and militarization in elites' effort to bring the city further under hegemonic control. "To play in the street" (tocar na rua) is viewed as an act of cultural resistance to that rationale, and it is not just the sounds created that are contentious but the physical presence of bodies in public space. Trombonist Rodrigo Daniel claims, "if you go to the street to make music you are already being political. The very act of occupying the street with culture and art is already political because there exists another political tendency contrary to this—to transform this, the arches of Lapa, into a shopping center" (interview 2015).

Such claims of the inherent political character of participatory playing in the street are manifestations of a conflict between what Theresa Williamson portrays as "two opposing visions of [Rio de Janeiro] that can be observed in more subtle conflicts in cities around the world today," between the commercial city wholly based around the interests of profit and "the city as fulfilling a human need for connection and social interaction . . . The freedom to make and remake our cities and ourselves is . . . one of the most precious yet most neglected of our human rights" (2016, 145).[6] Much of this activist discourse is framed around what

David Harvey (2012), drawing on Henri Lefebvre (1968), calls the "right to the city," or the staking of claim to city spaces against the interests of capitalism.[7] Neofanfarristas contest the hegemonic governance of a global city motivated by the interests of multinational capital, including institutions like FIFA and the IOC that sought to enforce militarized neoliberalization of the city.

Neofanfarristas believe central spaces for brass band gatherings like Lapa in particular are at risk of becoming commodified "societies of spectacle" (Debord 1995 [1970]). As central areas of Olympic Rio de Janeiro gentrified, special forces such as Lapa Presente and *choque de ordem* (shock of order)[8] police have focused their efforts on regulating public spaces and soundscapes in order to facilitate private interests and impose a hegemonic sound-politics. Orquestra Voadora trombonist Márcio Sobrosa argues that "the hygienization of Lapa expels street dwellers and locals to create something for tourists . . . Inside this Disneyland script of Rio de Janeiro, those who will be able to stay are only those who live off of this process" (interview 2015). The "process" is not unidirectional, however, and neofanfarristas view themselves as part of disrupting these developments by contesting public spaces. Trombonist Rodrigo Daniel argues that "At the same time . . . that public spaces are being privatized, I think that we are able to shift this logic by showing that the street can also have good things . . . The street is the place where the people should be. It's kind of a battle for space. We are occupying and reoccupying" (*Aprendendo a Voar* 2015). Playing music in the street is often referred as an *ataque* (attack), an intervention in the hegemonic ordering of city space—Daniel's former brass band Ataque Brasil references this idea in its name.

For the average tourist understandably impressed by the city's vibrant public musical culture, the notion that playing in Rio's streets could be controversial might be surprising, as performances in the street with permitted public consumption of alcohol are ubiquitous in the city. Such performances are permitted with a considerable degree of freedom unknown to a North American, but they are not without repression. Street musicians won a considerable degree of freedom with the 2012 passage of the "Street Artist Law," which significantly limited police intervention at musical events in the streets.[9] Some street musicians keep copies of the law with them when they perform in order to protect themselves from police who may claim not to know it. Holding an unofficial event beyond the confines of the Street Artist Law will likely not cause problems, but the police will be found in the right if they decide to interfere with the event. Obtaining official permission, however, can involve negotiating a Byzantine bureaucratic system, and, even when musicians attain permission, police can cancel events for vague reasons. Renata Dias, agent for Bagunço and Orquestra Voadora, explains her exasperation with the system and the rationale for choosing to hold events illegally:

> It's not enough just to have this law because if you don't communicate with the administrative bodies, the police, the municipal guard, and you just present the law of the artist, they will cancel your event and say it can't happen. Ok then we will do it nice and legally. I will go speak with the administrative body. I say that I want to do the event. They give me a response that is always the same: your event is inconvenient. Why? They don't give authorization . . . You are at an impasse. Should you do the event legally and run the risk of the event being banned when you could run the same risk without asking for anything? . . . We have to prepare the entire year for carnival, and it's ridiculous that the city government believes that the "city of carnival" doesn't need to prepare for carnival. (Interview 2016)

Indeed, such experiences of arbitrary power produce deep cynicism toward the city administration, and, in this context, the notion that playing music in the street is itself a resistant act becomes more palpable.

Boi Tolo and Unofficial Street Carnival

I heard the police sirens before I saw what was happening. The Boi Tolo bloco started to entrain the beat of the marchinha rhythm to the whining of the siren in sonic defiance as foliões entered a large building. As I approached the building trumpet in hand and carnival mask on face, I realized it was the Santos-Dumont airport, the secondary domestic airport in the Center of the city. Police cars had blocked the doors to the airport, but foliões and musicians simply went around and over them. This was the "Official Opening of Unofficial Carnival" in January 2015. There was little interest in respecting any formal boundaries; the bloco aimed to provide carnival cheer to airport workers and weary travelers whether they wanted it or not.

This wasn't a protest—there was no particular cause beyond the act itself or attempt to shut down the airport and prevent people from working, though the massive crowd of thousands that filled the airport lobby can't have facilitated the functioning of the airport. Eventually after thirty minutes of playing marchinhas inside the terminal, reports started to filter through the crowd that the military

FIGURE 3.1 Boi Tolo musically occupying the Santos-Dumont domestic airport. Photo by author on January 3, 2015.

police had been called, and the crowd decided to take its roaming carnival parade elsewhere. Having started at 1:00 in the afternoon, the parade would not end until around 11:00 at night. But ten hours of parading pales in comparison to the endurance of Boi Tolo's parade during carnival itself, which can last from 7:00 in the morning to the dwindling hours of the night (figure 3.1).

Boi Tolo, which can mobilize tens of thousands of foliões, is a brass bloco often described as "anarchist." With a spirit of radical inclusion and defiance of authority and officialdom, Boi Tolo has no official musical or tactical leadership, there is no cord that separates musicians from foliões, and absolutely anyone can play. Musicians cycle in and out playing through marchinhas, neofanfarrista repertoire, and theoretically anything else on repeat (CW.Ch3.Ex1).[10] Its parades have no defined direction, and social media inquiries of "Where is Boi Tolo?" (Cadê o Boi Tolo?) can be the only way to find the bloco. On January 6, 2021, Cariocas comically speculated that the bizarrely dressed invaders of the US capitol might be the Boi Tolo bloco before the bloco's Facebook page avowed that they did not support coups.

The origin story of Boi Tolo is an outgrowth of the brass bloco revival. On February 26, 2006, foliões of Boitatá gathered for the "concentration" (meeting point) of the bloco, but Boitatá did not and would not appear. After ten years of existence, Boitatá's parades had become so crowded that the bloco's leadership decided to inform only friends who would spread the location of the parade by word of mouth. As street carnival became increasingly popular and worries about overcrowding grew more pressing, some blocos chose to spread misinformation about the start point and would "spontaneously" start somewhere else in the city. While social media has made keeping these kinds of secrets more difficult, street musicians in Rio worry much more that too many people will show up rather than too few, and this tactic of reducing crowding is still used today.

On this carnival day in 2006, as the foliões realized Boitatá would not appear, some in the crowd took out their own instruments and began to play, with future Voadora trumpeter Tiago Rodrigues initially the only horn. Friends called other friends, more musicians appeared, someone wrote "Boi Tolo" on a large piece of paper creating a standard, and a new bloco was born. "Boi Tolo" played on the similar sound of the name of "Boitatá," but the meaning is completely different. While "Boitatá" is the name of a mythical Amazonian serpent, "Boi Tolo" translates to "silly bull," underlining the ludic and far less stately nature of the new bloco's parades[11] (see bloco standard on page 61, figure 1.4). Boi Tolo and Prata Preta (chapter 2) were both founded by fans who went to find Boitatá and, in failing, started their own blocos. They both view Boitatá as a parental bloco and each other as "brother blocos," often holding parades together.

I showed in chapter 2 that Boitatá and Céu na Terra established a participatory musical structure that was relatively free and open to brass musicians. They were animated by what Pires called "the principles of carnival," in opposition to samba schools and other blocos, that carnival be spontaneous, open, free, anti-commercial, and authentic. Boitatá and Céu na Terra, however, are organized hierarchically and use a cord to separate the musicians from spectators. There is a musical director in both groups, some musicians are paid ringers while others receive no financial compensation, and they require the ability to read music to participate properly. They receive sponsorship and request authorization for their parades. They are now very much a part of an official city-controlled street carnival despite their discourses of being an alternative to its dominant practices.

By contrast, some neofanfarristas view Boi Tolo as extending the principles of equality, participation, spontaneity, and rebellion to their furthest possible conclusions, making it the most "authentic" bloco of carnival according to the "principles of carnival." Boi Tolo receives no sponsorship, and there are thus no limitations on what kinds of beer or other products can be sold. Because it has no sponsorship, it makes no money and pays no official musicians. Recalling the unruly and spontaneous blocos de sujo of old, the bloco pushes the boundaries on where music can be played, carnivalizing airports, traffic tunnels, and public spaces, and imposing its soundscape where it pleases. Boi Tolo roams where it wants with generally no planned route, recalling DaMatta's portrait of the ideal carnival march, which "simply walks without destination or direction, intensely enjoying the act of the walking, occupying the streets of the commercial center of the city" (1991 [1979], 89). Sometimes when the crowd numbers into the thousands, the bloco can accidentally separate into mini-Boi Tolos with separate bands that follow their own routes and may or may not meet again.[12]

Even if Boi Tolo appears not to be openly combative toward the government or engaging in specific protests, trombonist Juliano Pires argues that the bloco's positioning is political in its denial of state legitimacy:

> Boi Tolo has a political proposal and it's the most political of all of them. Boi Tolo parades without authorization wherever it wants . . . Nobody should come bureaucratize and buy space, which is what they have started to do—lots of sponsorship, everything [owned by] Antarctica [beer sponsor]. The mayor and the state governor are creating a business to make money and privatize space that doesn't belong them. It belongs to the people—public space! (Interview 2014)

While initially tolerated, Boi Tolo and other unofficial blocos have met with increasing police repression, including a violent attack on the unofficial carnival parade in the year of the Olympics, 2016 (chapter 6), making their practices more markedly political in opposition to regulation. In 2018, RioTur created a more rigid penalization system for what they called "pirate blocos," and these events are increasingly under threat (Sézérat 2020).

Boi Tolo is the figurehead of a movement of blocos called "Desliga," meaning "disconnect," which plays on the officialdom of the carnival ligas (leagues, or official groupings of blocos such as Sebastiana). Participants make clear that Desliga, founded in 2009 in response to encroaching regulations of street carnival, is a movement, not a league. Desliga organizes the "Official Opening of Unofficial Carnival," which brings together the musicians and foliões of Boi Tolo and several other blocos that embrace the spirit of unofficialdom. This opening is generally held on the first Sunday of the year close to January 6, or Kings' Day, a day that in many places marks the "official" opening of carnival and the end of the Christmas season. Desliga's manifesto, published on Brazilian Independence Day in 2010, expounds on the principles of carnivalesque resistance to officialdom:

Street carnival is the party of the people. It is made by and for the people. A manifestation of spontaneity, genuine creativity, and free spirit. The praça is the people's as the sky is the condor's . . . After many years of dictatorship, our representatives guaranteed in the Brazilian Constitution the right to free expression . . . independently of authorization. The mayor's decree . . . deepens the attack on the creative freedom and spontaneity of Rio's carnival and the process of "Bahianization" of the festivities. Its essence is being suffocated by money. (Desliga website)

Along with familiar alternative carnivalesque references to the will of "the people," their inalienable ownership of public space under threat by moneyed interests, the "essence" of the festivities, and the opposition to the commercialized carnival of Bahia, the justification through the 1988 postdictatorship Constitution grounds the movement in an appeal to the foundation of Brazilian democracy. By citing these various "higher authorities," Desliga argues that it is the mayor who is in violation of various laws, not the unofficial carnival movement.

By "anarchist," participants do not only mean that Boi Tolo, and Desliga more broadly, resist the prescribed order of rules, routes, or repertoire. Trumpeter Gert Wimmer explains, "I see it as an anarchist bloco because, beyond the political proposal of street occupation, its form of organization is a collective construction, and whoever wants calls tunes" (interview 2015). With no cord separating musicians from foliões, in Boi Tolo anyone can be a musician and anyone can start a song and lead, creating a collective and "horizontal" experience of equality. The expandable and variable size of the musical organization that can bring thousands of people together at the "same level" in the streets makes it difficult for any one person to emerge as a director or leader. They seek to eliminate the hierarchical distinction between "core and elaboration" (Turino 2008) in the directed participatory music making of Boitatá and Céu na Terra.

Some amateur musicians find Boi Tolo to be a liberating space to experiment on an instrument where one may learn by osmosis and imitation rather than formal or hierarchical music education. Wimmer, a psychologist who learned to play trumpet in such spaces, recounts that he

went to Boi Tolo despite not knowing how to play almost a single note correctly. It's a bloco that welcomes people who are just learning to play . . . It was liberating . . . a catharsis. We look for references from each other—that's what gives organization to the bloco so that everything comes out together. There is no one [person] who coordinates the thing. (Interview 2015)

The inevitable "errors" that result in such a space are examples of what ethno-musicologist Charles Keil calls "participatory discrepancies" (1987) that for him are the sonic markers of democratic musical participation. For professional musicians who play in Boi Tolo, the spontaneous construction of a multilevel ensemble presents difficulties, but saxophonist Mathias Mafort suggest that these encounters are necessary to open access to musical production: "When you converse with a child, they don't speak as well as you. They don't have as rich a vocabulary, and they have fewer resources . . . But still you converse with them. Just the same in music. We are not always speaking with people at the same level, but the conversation has to happen . . . It's a necessary challenge for the sake of integrating people" (interview 2015).

Not criticizing others for engaging in an artistic practice as beginners is strongly valued in Rio and is taken to its extreme conclusions in Boi Tolo. For many neofanfarristas, the positive response of peers toward engaging in music produces an encouraging atmosphere for experimentation in which typical anxieties around music making and performance are diminished. Orquestra Voadora's American former tuba player, Tim Malik, reflects that in Rio,

if someone takes up an instrument everybody thinks it's great. Any artistic endeavor is awesome. To my New York ears, I'm like, "that's not excellent, that sucks, that's ridiculous. Why aren't you being more critical?" But the answer is that there's no point or value in being that critical. It's so much better for creation when you don't have this sense of "let's see what you can do—let me find how this sucks." Cariocas think, "let me find how this is good. I'll give a really positive response cause we're all in this together." That attitude makes it a really fertile environment for exploring new things. (Interview 2015)

Former Orquestra Voadora trombonist Márcio Sobrosa theorizes such horizontal practices as instantiations of radical Brazilian pedadogue Paulo Freire's theory of the "pedagogy of the oppressed" (1970).[13] Sobrosa favors practices like Boi Tolo as fertile spaces for dialogic education:

I created a practice based on the pedagogy of Paulo Freire and the theme of horizontality, which transforms the relation between the oppressor teacher and the oppressed students. This horizontal pedagogy of the street introduces a person to a universe. Where that person goes to search for things is for them to decide. It's not you who is going to give the entire path. (Interview 2015)

The experience of playing in "democratic," "horizontal," and "anarchist" spaces like Boi Tolo was frequently cited as a foundation for the tendency in many neofanfarrista bands to resist a "leader" figure and organize instead through consensus or voting. Orquestra Voadora saxophonist André Ramos explains how the band's collective decision-making process grew out of the experiences of playing in blocos like Boi Tolo:

> Where there exists a strong leadership . . . people have to resolve fewer problems. The problems stay with the leader. The musicians of Voadora got to know each other in many blocos that didn't have this structure. In this anarchy, you have the same problems or even more, and how are you going to resolve them? You will have to communicate, watch, and resolve the problems that arise the entire time. (Interview 2015)

Boi Tolo presented a space where amateurs could try their hands at leadership and musical production rather than submitting to a maestro. As neofanfarrismo has expanded since the founding of Orquestra Voadora in 2008, Boi Tolo has also continued to grow, representing a moment of chaotic union between the various brass musicians of the city. Its ethics of radical inclusion and occupation of public space have permeated the larger movement in fostering a soundscape of public participation.

Formalizing Horizontal Education
at Orquestra Voadora's Oficina

While Boi Tolo represents an anarchic way to freely join the neofanfarrismo movement, Orquestra Voadora has organized its bloco since 2009 with a clear distinction between musical leaders (mostly musicians in the official band) and bloco musicians more based on the "core and elaboration model" of Céu na Terra and Boitatá's approach to participatory music (Turino 2008). In the park of the Museum of Modern Art (MAM) every Sunday afternoon for five months before carnival, the band's musicians teach the parts of their songs by instrument before running larger bloco rehearsals. These events were until recently open for participation with no experience on a musical instrument explicitly required. Nevertheless, the rehearsals presumed some ability on one's instrument, since the bloco was not intended to teach the mechanics of the instruments but rather to spread the band's repertoire and prepare for the bloco's carnival performance.

Still, people would show up with little to no musical training and attempt to play along as the bloco became increasingly popular.

In 2013, the band decided to focus on musical education by offering a year-round oficina (class), an institutionalized setting for learning brass and drum instruments and spreading the band's repertoire. Managed by established bands, oficinas run throughout the year and provide instruction often with the ultimate goal of playing in the band's carnival bloco, and their popularity has exploded along with the street carnival revival. Every night in Rio de Janeiro, one has a huge variety of oficina options to study a new instrument, folkloric tradition, or dance practice at a relatively low (*popular*) price at various institutions, schools, and venues. By all accounts, musical education is sorely lacking in schools, but many middle-class adults have started to learn a variety of musical traditions through these institutions.

Voadora's oficina takes place in the large open-air venue of Circo Voador ("Flying Circus") in Lapa, a venue with its own alternative history in relation to the relative prominence of samba in Lapa (Herschmann 2007) and described by those involved with Orquestra Voadora as a cultural home.[14] Circo Voador helps organize many events for Orquestra Voadora and has taken an active role in promoting the neofanfarrismo movement. The oficina is taught by members of the band and professional musician friends, and I became an official trumpet teacher in the oficina during the duration of my fieldwork, which paid me 200 USD/month, or two thirds of my rent. During the oficina, the band divides the students into sections by instrument, and instructors begin by warming up and teaching basic technique. The students are then divided by ability and sent with individual instructors who might teach twenty beginners at a time. Subjects vary and include music theory, technique, repertoire, and improvisation, and the ultimate goal is to bring all of the sections to play together and participate in the band's carnival bloco. Students are encouraged to collaborate, play together in different formations, and ultimately form their own bands.[15]

Commenting on her experience of learning trombone in the oficina, Cristiana Campanha relates with delight, "It was a revolution in my life that an instrument of which I didn't even know the name some years past entered my life. But this same revolution is happening in the lives of many people. Orquestra Voadora is creating a revolution in Rio de Janeiro" (interview 2014). An engineer by training, Campanha began learning the trombone in 2013 at forty-three years of age with no previous musical experience outside of a few recent lessons on percussion in other oficinas. One day, she found herself at the MAM rehearsal of the Voadora

FIGURE 3.2 Trombone teacher Márcio Sobrosa on left in "horizontal" pedagogical engagement with student Cristiana Campanha in Orquestra Voadora's oficina in Circo Voador. Photo by author on December 9, 2014.

bloco, and she was enthralled but didn't know how to become involved. When the oficina was announced, she eagerly signed up for the chance to "play with [her] idols." Though she began on percussion, she found herself at the oficina with a trombone in her hand, the slide seemed intuitive to her, and she never looked back, enthusiastically joining a series of brass blocos and bands and becoming a familiar fixture of the scene. Her story of joining the movement with little to no musical experience is far from unique (figure 3.2).

Anyone who wants to learn a brass instrument, has the financial wherewithal to buy one, and can pay the oficina's relatively low monthly price of 140 reais may sign up (in 2016, about 40$ USD). The band organizes much of its student community through social media, and the oficina administers a student Facebook page (ASSOPRA) on which events are announced, the community discusses issues of relevance, and participants organize new musical projects. During my fieldwork, the oficina counted approximately three hundred students, and it has expanded exponentially the number of new brass musicians and launched new bands. Some oficina students have eventually become subs and even members in Voadora's band. By consuming musical education in oficinas, students can eventually become musical producers, complicating boundaries between musician and audience, professional and amateur, leader and follower, core and elaboration, artist and spectator.

Closing the first full year of the oficina before the culmination of the 2015 carnival, the students created an auto-documentary about the experience of learning a new musical instrument and engaging with the world of neofanfarrismo, entitled *Learning to Fly* (Aprendendo a voar) in reference to the "Flying Orchestra" (Orquestra Voadora). In the film, musicians speak of the knowledge gained in the oficina as an exchange, a horizontal passing of knowledge between teachers to students. Some students describe the oficina as a form of therapy in which they sought a "cure" to life's problems through engaging in music. Gaining access to musical education outside of the formalism and academic setting of much musical education was profoundly liberating for many students.

Despite the inherent hierarchy involved in the oficina, students often spoke of the "horizontal" relationships they developed with the teachers who would play and drink with them after the oficina and encourage them to lead songs and take on new roles. Voadora trombonist Márcio Sobrosa, who espoused Freirean pedagogy above, suggests in the film that

> We are in a way creating something new. We don't know what it is. There is no specific model that we are presenting to the students. There is desire and pedagogic space, and we work with horizontality. I am not the holder of knowledge. Everyone has knowledge, and we are creating a pedagogic environment to exchange it. (Interview 2014)

Voadora's oficina and newer oficinas founded on its model have provided institutionalized space for musical training and participation that has multiplied the ranks of neofanfarristas in a short time. In subsequent trips since fieldwork, I have been impressed by their efficacy in producing new musicians, some of whom are now professionals, as well as growing the numbers of dedicated amateurs who can read music and improvise competently. Voadora's monopoly on brass band oficinas has been challenged by a proliferation of new oficinas, many of them spawned by Voadora's students, including an "Oficina do Neo-fanfarrismo."

Inter-Class Collaborations at Cracudagem

Voadora's oficina is run in the closed space of a major venue that cannot be considered public, though teachers have attempted to keep the price of participation low and accessible. It leads however to a weekly public event when the students of Orquestra Voadora spill into the streets after the Tuesday night oficina for hours of street music, filling the praça around the nearby arches of Lapa with music sometimes until 3:00 or 4:00 in the morning. Hundreds of musicians, some of whom have just picked up a horn or percussion instrument for the first time, form a circle (roda), as more experienced musicians and Voadora band members gather around the wings. They play through the tunes they have learned from Orquestra Voadora, the broader neofanfarrismo movement, and, as carnival approaches, the repertoire passed on from Céu na Terra, Boitatá, and Boi Tolo. No firmly established rules on calling tunes apply, as they anarchically move from one song to another. Beer and caipirinha sellers gather on the periphery of the circle, fueling the musical happening as it goes on into the morning. Sometimes Lapa Presente, the police force that somewhat arbitrarily manages Lapa, attempts an arrest of an unlicensed beer seller only to be met by an army of trombonists who chase the police away with horn blasts.

Bystanders show up to watch, dancers emerge in the circle, and fire spinners light up the center. Instruments are shared with strangers who may become future participants, and musicians sometimes pass around flammable powder and breathe fire through their horns. While the overall effect of the jam is certainly musical from a distance, standing and playing among the musicians is to hear the wide diversities of tuning, rhythmic precision, and tone quality of this open, multilevel, and student-led ensemble. Playing trumpet among them, I am reminded of ethnomusicologist Charles Keil's belief that "music, to be personally valuable and socially valuable, must be 'out-of-time' and 'out-of-tune'" (1987, 275). The stationary weekly jam in Lapa is chaotically managed in many ways similar to a Boi Tolo parade. Trombonist Rodrigo Daniel, who joined Voadora's oficina in its first year and is now a professional touring musician, explains,

> It's really good for people who are learning to play because you lose shame. You can be more daring. This helps in your learning. It doesn't matter if you're playing badly. It's a school: playing without knowing how to play, which always happened a lot in carnival. It is this experience that gave me the interest to learn

more. It's possible to play even though I know I will make mistakes. Fuck it. The next note will be good. Or not. (Interview 2015)

Among the participants of this weekly jam are the homeless and marginalized of central Rio de Janeiro. They often enter the circle to dance, chant, and rap. Sometimes musicians share their instruments with these folks and let them try a concert B♭ for the first time in their lives. One night, a poor Blacker man entered the circle in a wheelchair, and a trombonist set aside her instrument to dance with him, wheeling him around the circle. Sometimes it seems that the scene could easily get out of hand. On another occasion, an unknown, clearly inebriated man picked up a female trombonist to dance with her. I expected her to run, but instead she trusted that the larger group had her back and let herself be taken by the man in the ecstasy of the music. We are still in the Center of Rio in the middle of the night, however; sometimes knives are pulled and phones stolen, and participants question whether their lack of caution creates an unsafe environment. They pile their instrument cases in the center of the roda to prevent robberies.

Musicians call this event "cracudagem," which loosely translates to the act of using crack or being "cracked out," for two widely accepted reasons. The students are themselves "addicted" to music and to the process of learning in this chaotic environment: "this addiction to play for hours—the drug of music" (Cristiana Campanha interview 2014). The term also plays with the fact that musicians play in the Center of the city late at night in contact with marginalized populations, those most likely to be actually affected by street drugs. These musicians often jokingly refer to themselves as "cracudos," or "crack heads," identifying with the street dwellers who wander into the circle. Rodrigo Daniel, credited for coining the term, explains,

We started using the word "crack" because everyone would leave after the oficina, and the only people who stayed were very crazy and drunk and wanted to keep playing with street dwellers—some really drugged-out people—who would dance with us. We played badly and everyone else had left. Only the cracudos stayed . . . It has a lot to do with what it is to play in the street and to see oneself as a person of the street. Some of these people don't have anywhere to live, are addicted to drugs, have plenty of problems, but they can enjoy music. We used this term ironically, but it has a certain value as well that helps to resignify things a bit—what it is to be in the street. (Interview 2015)[16]

By identifying as cracudos, neofanfarristas involve the most vulnerable populations of the city center in creating a soundscape of public participation, seeking to create what DaMatta might call the domestic intimacy of the realm of the house in the uncontrolled, marginalized universe of the street (figure 3.3, CW.Ch3.Ex2).[17]

Flying with Fela

"Éééé Voadooooor!" In homage to the band's name and the sense of freedom it symbolizes, tens of thousands of musicians and foliões sing "Oh Flying" during a performance of Fela Kuti's song "Expensive Shit" at Orquestra Voador's annual bloco on carnival Tuesday. Uniting the various manifestations of musical participation in public space chronicled thus far is an impressive, informal cataologue of songs shared by neofanfarristas and played in variety of settings, of which Voadora's repertoire plays an important role. "Expensive Shit," arranged and covered by the band, was Voadora's most popular song among neofanfarristas during my fieldwork. Analysis of the song across several manifestations reveals the diverse range of performative interpretations within the movement, troubling any neat distinction between presentational and participatory performance, leader and follower, core and elaboration, or public and private in the construction of soundscapes of public participation.

The Nigerian saxophonist Fela Kuti is known for his cultural and political activism during the 1960s and '70s in postcolonial Nigeria, his fierce critiques of the Eurocentric ruling elite, and his unique mix of Afrocentrism and global counterculture. His Afrobeat musical style brought together diverse influences, including West African highlife, American funk, and modal jazz. Released in 1975, "Expensive Shit" playfully relates his run-ins with the Lagos police through the perhaps apocryphal story of an instance in which the police arrested and planted a joint on the artist. Fela purportedly ate the joint so that it couldn't be used against him, but the police brought him into custody at the Alagbon prison to test his excrement, which he managed to substitute with that of another inmate, again outsmarting the police.

Like other Fela songs of the same period, the "high-fidelity" recording[18] of the song is long at 13:13 minutes, reflecting the band's lengthy performances at Fela's Kalakuta Compound. The drums, horns, and strings create a dense polyrhythmic texture that is sustained as a prolonged, mid-tempo groove over a single minor chord in the dorian mode with little dramatic change in texture or dynamic throughout the song. At the beginning, each instrument enters into the groove

FIGURE 3.3 Spontaneous breakdancing at cracudagem.
Photo by author on May 13, 2015.

progressively when finally, at the end of the second minute, the horn section enters with a confident head melody. Musical diversity is sustained over the perpetual groove by a series of repeated riffs, instrumental solos, Fela's characteristic solo singing (which only enters in the seventh minute of the track), and call and response between the singer and backup vocals. A climax of sorts begins in the ninth minute with the male back-up singers' repetition of the prison name: "En! Alagbon o," which Voadora substitutes in their version with "Éééé Voadooooor." The horns come back in with the head, and the groove progressively loses energy until it finally stops and only the keyboard is left (CW.Ch3.Ex3).[19]

The story of creatively escaping prison appealed to Voadora's countercultural musicians, and Fela's Afrobeat style has been widely interpreted by alternative brass bands around the world. Voadora included their arrangement of the song on the band's first album *Ferro Velho* (2013), with a high-fidelity recording played almost exactly as during presentational performances.[20] In contrast to Fela's original, Voadora's cover is shorter, more dramatic, and more aggressive at 5:27 minutes, as it is geared toward the high-intensity brass party energy they market (CW.Ch3.Ex4).

Energetic polyrhythmic percussion is heard immediately, as the trumpets loudly play the backing ostinato riff that is played softly by guitar in Fela's version (figure 3.4).

Other brass instruments loudly proclaim the short melodic statement that was originally played by an understated keyboard (figure 3.5).

The song begins to gather even more intense energy by the end of the first minute with the addition of more percussion and tuba. The texture builds to a short dramatic break of all instruments, something that Fela's original never does, that leads to a statement of the head punctuated by snare hits (figure 3.6).

Band member André Ramos then begins a short baritone solo over a riff played by the other horns before the band enters into the call and response between the sung line, "Éééé Voadooooor" (figure 3.7).

Throughout this section, the band breaks down to a softer and more simplified texture before energetically building back up into a loud restating of the head and a punctuated collective end to the song.[21]

In the first presentational performance of the band I witnessed at a paid show at Circo Voador in 2014, as soon as the percussion launched into this groove well into their stage show, the audience knowingly responded with excited cheers. As the groove built with the tuba's propulsive entrance, the crammed fans began

FIGURE 3.4 Trumpet riff of Voadora's version of "Expensive Shit."

FIGURE 3.5 Melody 1 of Voadora's version of "Expensive Shit."

FIGURE 3.6 Melody 2 of "Expensive Shit."

FIGURE 3.7 Call and Response of "Expensive Shit."

moshing, crashing into each other until the break that leads to the head provided a pregnant instrumental pause for the fans to scream. As in the recording, Ramos's saxophone began the solo section as band and audience members crouched down, but trombonist Márcio Sobrosa, with his characteristic pirate flag hanging from his slide, descended into the crowd, finding audience members to play during the solo.

I would later learn that some of these chosen musicians in the audience were other neofanfarristas known to the trombonist, some professionals and some students, but others were not expecting to have a trombone offered to them in the middle of the show. As then a novice to neofanfarrismo, I was surprised to hear unpracticed solos that were far from conventionally competent at this presentational, professional show. In contrast, Turino characterizes presentational performances as maintaining a distinction between artists and spectator in order to sustain a consumable performance of high artistic quality. But the other audience members responded with gratification at the participatory inclusion of spectators. They began to sing along with the band, "Éééé Voadooooor," before jumping up to mosh again during the final buildup. Voadora expanded their version's recorded length in order to foment participation, but they retained their dramatic interpretation of Fela's original in this live rendering (CW.Ch3.Ex5).[22]

I soon learned that part of the reason the fans responded with such enthusiastic recognition to "Expensive Shit" is that many of them are students of Voadora's oficina, where they learn this song and others in the very same space of Circo Voador every Tuesday. Broken into instrumental sections during the oficina, they learn each riff, groove, and melody of the song before joining all together to practice the form of the entire song together with the band in a core-and-elaboration format. Distinct from Turino's view that participatory performances generally use open, cyclical forms rather than the closed, linear forms of presentational performances, however, Voadora's three hundred oficina students learn the exact same linear performance form played by the presentational band, as they do with all of Voadora's material.

The cyclical, open form comes during the solo section, as it does during the band's presentational performance, when everyone crouches down as the band members walk through the students offering a microphone for those interested to try their hand at soloing over the dorian groove. Some are better than others and who decides to participate is certainly influenced by other race, class, and gender privileges, but all are welcome and encouraged in the oficina. As I frequented the oficina and began to teach in it, I witnessed how the band introduced improvisation for this song with an activity that involves color-coded circles chalked on the ground representing the notes of a C minor pentatonic scale. The teacher would jump from circle to circle as the students followed what note to play in what rhythm, and student volunteers would then try leading the other students (CW.Ch3.Ex6).[23]

This participatory rehearsal performance lacks the crisp preciseness of the professional band. The student horn players play along with a wide variety of tuning and articulation, but the percussion holds together the energy, with the end result being exciting and musically gratifying for all involved, if far from "perfect" from a presentational standpoint. The oficina is every Tuesday, but for the five months before carnival on Sundays they also repeat this rehearsal ritual in the gardens of the Modern Art Museum as the bloco, composed of oficina students and other musician friends of Voadora, practices weekly to prepare for their carnival performance.

After the Tuesday oficina, the students scatter out of Circo Voadora into the public square of Lapa while many of the oficina teachers of the band take their leave, and cracudagem begins. A student trumpeter initiates the guitar riff of "Expensive Shit," as percussionists gather around to play the groove. The other instrumentalists join in as they form a roda and interested bystanders gather at the edges. Without the "core" of the band members, this student rendition is even more ragged, but the enthusiasm is even greater as the students assert their musical independence from the band. During the solo section, student instrumentalists pass the solo around as they crouch down to watch the soloists come to the center, largely sounding more confident. Some audience members are given instruments to take a try at a solo, whether they have ever played the instrument or not. As they then sing "Éééé Voadooooor," the students encourage everyone around them to crouch and sing with them before jumping up, moshing, and ending the song with shouts of satisfaction. This same musical ritual repeats itself at Boi Tolo parades, after bloco rehearsals, at protests, and in unplanned parades that run through the night, played by a rotating cast of characters, independently of whether a Voadora band member is present or not.

The annual culmination of the song is, of course, Voadora's carnival bloco, which for musicians in Voadora's scene is a participatory performance but for the tens of thousands in attendance is musically a largely presentational experience. The bloco and foliões are dressed in a wide variety of colorful and imaginative fantasias as a section of stilt walkers leads the foliões in dance. The bloco follows the same song form, bringing the tens of thousands down to crouch for solos and participatory singing of "Éééé Voadooooor," but, since this is also presentational performance in Turino's conception, the band chooses ringers to solo rather than opening it to any participant. As the postsolo buildup begins again, the tens of thousands leap up to energetically mosh and dance along. With the final hits, mass cheering ensues (CW.Ch3.Ex7).[24]

Voadora's version of Fela's "Expensive Shit" is only one example of how songs circulate within the neofanfarrismo movement through what Turino would call multiple fields, from high-fidelity recording to presentational and participatory performance. But the fact that the same song is adaptable in so many settings that blur the lines between presentational and participatory performance complicates any characterization of Voadora's musical universe as either presentational or participatory based on Turino's delineations or even the movement's own participatory rhetoric. Rather, it is more useful to understand the repertoire of the neofanfarrismo movement as embodied knowledge deployed in a range of scenarios (Taylor 2003) for a variety of purposes, in which both presentational and participatory manifestations play fundamental roles in the propagation of the movement. Leaders play crucial roles in fomenting horizontal musical experiences, and the "private" experiences of listening to the band's recordings, watching the band perform in a venue that can only be entered at cost, and paying to learn from the band in the same venue are fundamental to the creation of the public, participatory manifestations of the neofanfarrismo. Flying isn't free.

PARADOXES OF INSTRUMENTAL ACTIVISM

These tensions between discourse and practice also point to deeper schisms in neofanfarrismo's construction of a soundscape of public participation, leading some Cariocas to view the self-congratulatory populism of a middle-class musical movement as a contradiction in terms. In exploring these paradoxes of instrumental activism, I call attention to the limits, challenges, and contradictions involved in the construction of a soundscape of public participation fomented by the city's Whiter middle class.

Professionalism and Musical Quality

According to conservatory-trained trumpeter and Voadora oficina teacher Leandro Joaquim, neofanfarrismo went through three stages in its expansion throughout Rio de Janeiro. Initiated by professional-level blocos like Boitatá, the movement in the early 2000s was largely confined to carnival and limited to musicians who had already attained a high degree of training on their instruments, many of whom lived only from music. In their blocos, they opened spaces for participatory music making to amateur musicians who could "keep up" with the professionals but were not of the same musical level. Beginning a second stage associated with the birth of neofanfarrismo, these less professional musicians participated in increasing numbers, formed their own blocos and bands, and began playing throughout the year. Some of these groups passed into the professional circuit and became income-generating professional musical projects that allowed some members to live off the bands' success, which was the case of Orquestra Voadora itself. Joaquim suggests that since the opening of Orquestra Voadora's oficina, the alternative brass movement had entered a third stage, one in which anyone who can buy a horn can learn and be part of the movement, regardless of whether they have any musical experience: "The positive part is that everyone is included, everyone occupying the street, everyone having fun in a different way than they did before. I love it—it's very praiseworthy. You see people with horns everywhere, playing in whatever way they know how" (interview 2015).

But for Joaquim, neofanfarrismo had also become a Frankensteinian monster in which a mass of new musicians with little training is taught by the musicians of Voadora, some of whom had not trained in conservatory but by playing in carnival initially as amateurs. While some students have sought out disciplined training, others regularly invade the streets playing out of tune with bad technique and passing on limited knowledge to their friends. A weakening chain of musical training has been created in which musical knowledge has dissipated so much from its professional "origin" of Boitatá and Céu na Terra that quality standards have become major concerns. Some complain that bringing in so many people with no clear leadership results in low-quality music, general disorder, and bad training for learning an instrument and repertoire. Bruno de Nicola explains, "I'm not a great trumpet player and when someone comes playing incorrectly in my ear it pushes me to play incorrectly as well. I prefer to have more confident people around . . . How can you really integrate so many people?" (interview 2016). The derogatory term "fanfarrão" is often used to refer to what some see as pleasure-seeking and unserious musicians.

While the oficina students tend to view themselves as involved in an important social and political project that is revolutionizing city street life in Rio de Janeiro by a creating free, public musical culture, others view the logic of "free music" as threatening to the livelihood of professional musicians. As a performing musician in Rio, I found it far easier to organize people to come to a free musical event in the streets than inviting them to pay to enter a club. Some neofanfarrista bands eschew clubs because they limit the audience to those who can pay, and, because many of the new musicians are not playing for money, lack of remuneration is not a concern. The accessibility of learning music in the alternative brass movement, of which the oficina is only a recent manifestation, is, for some, cause for concern regarding the value of music, how it should be compensated, and what financial reward one should expect to receive from training. Other professional musicians disagree. Bassist Chico Oliveira of BlocAto observes that "there are professional musicians that don't love this lower quality of music of the new generation. Not me, I think that these people wouldn't be doing anything related to music if it weren't for Orquestra Voadora, and so I think what Voadora is doing is very important" (interview 2014).

Ironically, a musical movement that has come to espouse the participation of all people has limited the inclusion of professional musicians to some extent, including even some brass bands who share the movement's instrumental formation, leftist politics, and musical eclecticism but are devoted to a higher degree of professionalism. Pedro Pamplona, founder of Boitatá and Fanfarrada, distances himself from neofanfarrismo for this reason:

> Fanfarrada is a friend of neofanfarrismo, but I don't know if we are neofanfarrismo. Juba [Juliano Pires, trombonist in Orquestra Voadora] believes that neofanfarrismo upholds a communitarian philosophy, democratic decisions, and the participation of all. I don't think that is Fanfarrada. We have all experienced this in other groups, but in Fanfarrada I am the director. I do the production and artistic direction. The musicians accept it. (Interview 2014)

The Façade of Open Horizontalism

While maestros like Pamplona reject horizontalism to uphold musical professionalism, some musicians view the idea that institutions like Boi Tolo and cracudagem are horizontal, anarchist, and structureless as a façade. Trombonist Clément Mombereau dismisses the belief that there are no leaders in such spaces and argues that leaders arise by force of assertion and knowledge: "It's those that want to play the most and know the songs the best that will succeed at being a leader. There are always people who lead" (interview 2014). Likewise, trumpeter Ana Martins argues that "Cracudagem isn't so open. It has a subtle elite" (interview 2015). Jo Freeman, in an article written for anarchist feminist groups, critiques what she calls the "tyranny of structurelessness" (1972), arguing that the idea of "structurelessness" had become a "goddess in its own right," but that "there is no such thing as a 'structureless' group." For her, the presumption of structurelessness in a group creates unaccountable leaders who become an invisible elite:

> A "laisser-faire" group is about as realistic as a "laisser-faire" society; the idea becomes a smoke screen for the strong or the lucky to establish unquestioned

hegemony over others. This hegemony can easily be established because the idea of "structurelessness" does not prevent the formation of informal structures, but only formal ones . . . power is curtailed to those who know the rules, as long as the structure of the group is informal . . . If the movement continues to deliberately not select who shall exercise power, it does not thereby abolish power. All it does is abdicate the right to demand that those who do exercise power and influence be responsible for it.

While Orquestra Voadora saxophonist André Ramos credits the development of a horizontally run band structure to the experience of playing in blocos like Boi Tolo, he also admits that "structurelessness" in Orquestra Voadora is a result of lack of process and order. In reality, no one person had enough power to actually lead the band:

We come with this experience and interest in anarchism. But there's another side that is just merely practical. The band has no leader because no one will manage to be a leader and no one will let this person be a leader . . . Our experience in these blocos has a big role, but these concepts of horizontality and consensus would not be sufficient in practice. Practice speaks louder than concepts. It is not just that we believe that we should be anarchic. In practice, it functions like this because everyone wants to lead. (Interview 2015)

Invisible authority arises not only from musical experience but from the privileges of particular socializations. In the context of American "leaderless" HONK! bands, Kallman argues that "people with voice in other parts of their lives (whether it derives from musical ability, gender, experience, race, or personality) often also have voice within their bands" (2020, 124). Female musicians were more likely to criticize the supposition that spaces like cracudagem and Boi Tolo were horizontal spaces, as they experienced familiar patterns of male privilege playing out in supposedly anarchist and horizontal spaces. Arguing that these spaces are marked by social inequality, trombonist and community organizer Claire Haas reflects,

In Boi Tolo there are specific men who play leadership roles and who take up a lot of space. I see them being the ones to lead songs, I see them taking a lot of solos, I see them not leaving blank space . . . In movement spaces when we are trying to create horizontal leadership . . . the goal is to make sure that everyone's voice is heard and break down the paradigm that those who are loudest make the decisions. In the bands here in Rio, people who are the loudest and making the decisions are also the people who are the most likely to talk about how horizontal the movement is . . . I would much rather play with a clear director than in a situation of horizontal leadership where there's a secret leadership structure that no one acknowledges or where they deny its existence. (Interview 2016)

Similarly, Kallman argues that without collectively agreed-upon structures to ensure participation, leaderless groups risk simply reproducing social inequality.[25]

One often hears that Boi Tolo, cracudagem, and Voadora's oficina and bloco are "open for whomever wants to come." But more precisely, they are open for those who *can* come. For marginalized populations in the North Zone and favelas, events in the Center are off limits due to geographical, class, and racial segregations built into the city's fabric. Unhoused people and the poor who do wander into these spaces play secondary roles and are transient participants. They are unlikely to purchase trumpets, chaotically learn to play amid a middle-class carnival parade or jam session, or register for a paying oficina. Neofanfarrismo's particular cultural caché and stances may also exclude those who do not share participants' cultural capital, what Naomi Podber refers to as a tension between "wide and provisional inclusion" in activist scenes (2020). The desire to "widely include" all people conflicts with "provisional inclusion," or the urge to create a community of like minds, which can lead to demographic homogenization.

These celebratory interclass musical encounters in the streets, where middle-class musicians go as far as identifying with the plights of cracudos and the unhoused, create fleeting senses of solidarity that likely do little to shift patterns of privilege beyond a few hours of entertainment. The soundscape of public participation dissolves when the musicians go home to comfortable apartments and remove their cracudo masks, while the unhoused stay in the streets. A more pessimistic view of neofanfarrismo's stated horizontalism might even see this momentary celebration and unity of "the people" in the streets as a typical farce of Brazilian culture and carnival practices in which celebratory mixing conceals real inequalities.[26]

The Reality of Money

Neofanfarristas have not only the leisure but the monetary capacity to participate. Due to high import taxes and lack of local manufacturing, brass instruments are two to three times more expensive than in the United States. The discourse of musical participation as somehow outside of the capitalist production system of commodified products is compromised by the roles financial transaction plays in fomenting this soundscape of public participation. The oficinas, for example, may be at a "popular" price, but the middle-class profile of the classes clearly shows that they are inaccessible to poorer Cariocas. While cracudagem may be a relatively open space, the oficina that precedes it is far more limited to those with the resources and leisure time to procure and study an expensive instrument. Generally held inside the open-air venue of Circo Voador with entrances guarded by security, the students of Voadora drop the vigilance they maintain in the street, leaving their instruments unattended while they fraternize with friends.

Ironically, it is for-profit oficinas that have played a fundamental role in expanding this public, participatory, "anticapitalist" movement (Snyder 2019b). Until opening their oficina in 2013, Voadora's "open" bloco was much smaller and really only "open" to those who already had some chops on their instruments. Voadora saw an economic opportunity on which many other street carnival performance groups had already capitalized. The oficina would offer the opportunity for the band to derive income from teaching a musical style to interested fans and prepare them to perform alongside them in the bloco. These students would magnify the band's own fan base and the popularity of their shows by blurring the distinction between participant and fan. But the widespread discourse of horizontalism occludes the pedagogical labor of those who run the oficinas, cloaking the very real precarity of the teachers' lives, many of whom live only from music, while many amateur students have middle-class professional careers. In other words, the movement's feelings of communitas is produced by people with distinct roles and financial incentives and is an experience that can be bought by those with means.

Voadora trombonist and teacher Márcio Sobrosa, who would later leave Voadora entirely, suggests that the oficina's introduction of instruction for profit compromises the idea of neofanfarrismo as a social movement that destabilizes hegemonic relations:

FIGURE 3.8 Orquestra Voadora bloco rehearsal at MAM
(Museum of Modern Art). Photo by author on January 12, 2020.

Voadora is turning into a product captured by capitalism. The oficina creates a new relation that wasn't there before. Before we taught in the bloco for
whomever wanted to come. There was no obligation or relation to a product
to be consumed . . . and suddenly they pay and want a return, the relation of
consumer and product. This is something that is eating our work even though
we come from a movement. (Interview 2015)

By 2019, the once open bloco had become "too large," and for the 2020 carnival,
Voadora closed the bloco to only those who paid to receive training in the oficina,
focusing their participatory efforts on compensated teaching and eliminating
the previously free participatory bloco experience. Trombonist Clément Mombereau, jokingly pointing to the entanglement of leftist movements in capitalist
cultural production, reflects, "to start a musical movement, you have to make
people pay" (interview 2014).

Gentrification

Orquestra Voadora is credited for having "revitalized" the park spaces around the Museum of Modern Art (MAM) where the band holds its carnival bloco rehearsals for five months preceding the event, making a "place" through its spatial practices (Reily and Brucher 2013). The area was and is still known as abandoned and dangerous, and the entire Aterro do Flamengo of which it is a part, the grassy park that extends along much of the bay from the Center to South Zone Urca, is often described as a beautiful place to get robbed. But on Sunday afternoon, a mass of middle-class musicians and foliões arrives to rehearse, jam, and parade back to Lapa for hours (figure 3.8). Often the ground is left littered with beer bottles by the end of the event, though many neofanfarristas are conscientious about picking up litter and reminding others to do so.

Musicians arrive guardedly in fear of being assaulted in the area before entering the security of the largely middle-class crowd. They leave in a large parade to Lapa partly to provide a safe means of helping participants get back to "secure" locations in the center of the city. For many neofanfarristas, the "secured" environment offered by this "Woodstock Carioca" and other brass band occupations of the street are an intrinsic element of what is meant by activism: the reclaiming, or "rescue," of abandoned and dangerous spaces for art makes them safe, habitable, and useable for the population. When I asked about the band's political commitments despite its reticence to participate in protest, Voadora's trumpeter Daniel Paiva responded,

> What we have done in MAM for free for seven years, this is pure politics. We influenced many people to play in the street and multiplied the size of the movement. That park around the MAM, seven years ago there was no one going there for leisure. It was all abandoned. You would get mugged if you went there at whatever time of day. Today it is a space occupied with culture and art. Now it is full of people learning stilts, music, whatever, even when Voadora is not there. For me, this is politics. (Interview 2014)

The purpose of these occupations of public space for Paiva is to break out of cycles of abandonment and segregation, for public spaces to be used by the public. But the question is which public? Whose Rio? Whose soundscape? Saxophonist Michel Moreau questions the supposed politics of the MAM rehearsals: "This activism here in Rio is very linked to the university, to the youth of the middle class—playboy activism. Playing in MAM on Sunday afternoon is activism? I don't know, it's a lot of leisure also" (interview 2015). Voadora participated in making the MAM gardens a safer place for largely *middle-class* bodies to frequent. The mass occupations of the streets they accomplish would not be acceptable to city elites if it were favelados occupying them.[27]

Artists are, of course, often viewed as the "foot soldiers" of gentrification, as they move into poorer neighborhoods, buy property, and make spaces more comfortable and exciting for richer communities, who drive up prices and make an area unaffordable. Since, in this case, we are not dealing with property speculation or fixed places of cultural capital, such as art galleries or music venues, these temporary musical occupations could be called practices of *itinerant gentrification*. Privileged bodies enter "abandoned" squares and poorer areas of the city to create "accessible" and participatory parties for several hours and then leave. Garofalo, Allen, and I note a similar connection between the original HONK! festival and the gentrification of Somerville, Massachusetts: "HONK! is perceived as 'hip,' white, and middle class and can contribute to the kinds of development that lead to gentrification and, ultimately, displacement. The challenge for HONK! bands and festivals is how to reclaim public space in a way that protects the existing populations from displacement and promotes their own agency" (2020, 6).

Many neofanfarristas relate that they had gone with the brass bands to places in the city they would never go alone but that these experiences had increased the likelihood of frequenting those places in the future. As the center of the city gentrified during the Olympic process, with the middle classes moving into some of these areas, it is impossible to separate the cultural events that have a growing presence in these areas from the increasing economic capital of the areas themselves. The bloco of Prata Preta (chapter 2) in the poorer but gentrifying central port area of Gamboa is a good example of this dynamic. The producers of the bloco view Prata Preta as a practice of cultural resistance within a neighborhood that became more expensive due to real estate speculation. But estimating that four thousand foliões come to the bloco during carnival, producer Fábio Sarol laments that, because of the middle-class aesthetics of the brass bloco revival, "The majority of the public of Prata Preta, unfortunately, isn't from the neighborhood. Lots of people from the South Zone started to frequent the bloco. The crowd from outside embraced the bloco in a way that we wanted people here to embrace it" (interview 2015).

For trombonist Cristiana Campanha, neofanfarrismo's left-wing and alternative credentials are based on its willingness to play in the streets and to go to the peripheral neighborhoods of blocos like Prata Preta. In contrast, Rio de Janeiro's right-wing and mainstream middle classes shelter themselves in the privileged South Zone or Barra de Tijuca:

> It's not everyone that can stand to be in a place that has poor people. Those rich people pay a lot of money to go to expensive places where poor people will not go. They are in an isolated world, not in the street. They have no desire to mix and preoccupy themselves with others. Those who are in the street have to have a minimal acceptance [for poor people]. (Interview 2014)

While neofanfarristas may indeed have more openness to such experiences, they still bring privileged bodies to marginalized spaces and help make them more alluring for other privileged people to follow.

Rio de Janeiro is one of the most dangerous militarized metropolises in the world, and for the political right the answer to urban violence and insecurity is increasing police presence. By contrast, a seeming truism of neofanfarrismo's activism is that free musical occupations make an unsafe city safer and more livable. Brass band events are widely viewed as "securing" urban territory, transforming the city's "culture of fear," and offering alternative models of public safety. Trumpeter Gert Wimmer argues that, "A street occupied with art is a more secure street because people are there to fraternize. It's not more secure because of force" (interview 2015). A trumpeter describes this as a process of transformation of dangerous urban spaces into useable ones:

> We can transform a place that people believe is dangerous into a place that people use . . . the more people in the street, the less people are afraid; more people in the street, less violence, you feel more secure. It's a cycle. This is something great about the fanfarras and cracudagem—with bands playing in the street and attracting people, you feel more secure to go out also. It's important not to leave the city deserted. (Anonymous interview 2015)[28]

This is no doubt true. But coming back to the question of "Whose Rio?" it is also important for neofanfarristas to ask themselves: for whom are these spaces becoming more secure? Certainly, I felt more secure in a crowd of middle-class Cariocas. Having been violently mugged twice in Rio de Janeiro late at night with few people around, the idea that there is safety in numbers is intuitive. But when robberies did occur at neofanfarrista events, heightened police presence observing middle-class crowds produced vigilant and sometimes violent responses. On one occasion, I witnessed a theft at a Voadora rehearsal in MAM in which a young Black boy ran off with a middle-class woman's purse. He was pursued by the police and beaten unnecessarily before being arrested. The police supervision that may result from middle-class bodies putting themselves in spaces of contact with marginalized populations does not necessarily make those marginalized populations safer or less at risk of being removed from them. The influx of partiers to a public space can also create a chaotic environment in which other insecure situations can arise. After the precarnival parade in Santa Teresa of Céu na Terra in 2016, for example, gang violence broke out as the bloco crowds dwindled, leading to a man's death.

Conflicts also arise between musicians occupying what they view as "their" streets and residents who complain of loud and disorderly soundscapes in the middle of the night, long after the protections of the street musician law have expired. Voadora saxophonist André Ramos argues that musicians need to maintain awareness of how they interact with urban others to avoid wholesale appropriation of public space for musicians and their foliões alone: "Playing music in the streets requires responsibility. The street is owned by no one, not by musicians, not by old women, and not by the police. The street is everyone's. We have to find a way to collectively use the space. The musician who believes that the street is theirs alone is just as anti-inclusive as the people who speculate on it" (interview 2015).

WHOSE RIO?

This chapter has examined discourses and practices of instrumental activism in relation to the movement's aim to foster an inclusive soundscape of public participation, an extension of the "principles of carnival" espoused in earlier periods of the alternative brass movement. In Boi Tolo, unofficial carnival, and cracudagem, neofanfarristas play collectively known songs like "Expensive Shit" to create open musical spaces in which participation and experimentation are possible, even by people with little musical training and including marginalized communities. The oficinas have multiplied the ranks of new musicians, some of whom have over the years become professional performers and teachers. For them, these events offer an alternative city to the divided city of Olympic Rio, as they aim to make Rio's many beautiful open spaces more public and combat the logics of exclusion and privatization through intercultural engagement. The street is understood as offering an alternative space for inclusive practices and educational models that are viewed as incompatible with the consumptive practices of private concert spaces, the privacy of which is well captured, in accord with DaMatta's opposition of street and house, in the Portuguese term for music clubs: "casas de show."

Though neofanfarrismo has indeed created many new possibilities for public participatory music in Rio de Janeiro, I have also pointed to limitations and contradictions in these practices that can lead some Cariocas to roll their eyes at the purported activism of neofanfarrismo. Like the street carnival revival, these alternative practices are embedded in the dominant systems that make their existence possible. Free public events like Boi Tolo and cracudagem are fueled by musicians who have the capacity to pay for musical instruction, while professional musicians eke out a living from presentational performance as well as fomenting musical participation through the oficinas. The important roles of leaders and presentational performances problematize the movement's pretension to participatory horizontalism. The liberation of public spaces could be viewed as practices of gentrification that can put marginalized Cariocas at risk, and, though neofanfarristas do suffer repression, the soundscapes they produce are tolerated much more than those of poorer and Blacker communities.

Unsurprisingly, building a soundscape of public participation led by a privileged vanguard is a fraught process. The inclusion of the "public" has limits based on the social barriers of class, gender, and race that order the "people's" lives, and persistent inequalities within the movement reflect inequalities in society more broadly that remain unexamined by many participants. Chapter 5 shows, however, how varied new projects such as feminist bands and bands in the favelas have sought to address these limits and contradictions in order to bring a more diverse soundscape of public participation closer to reality. Before we evaluate those projects, the next chapter considers a more unambiguous expression of instrumental activism: musical engagement in protest during a period of growing political crisis and polarization in Brazil.

FOUR

Resistance

Nothing Should Seem
Impossible to Change

Soon after the carnival of 2017, Technobloco invades the sambódromo late at night, filling it with thousands of bodies lit up with LEDs. Over the melodic backdrop of Robert Miles's "Children" (1996), a huge crowd crouches in the sambódromo lambasting the conservative mayor and rhythmically shouting, "Fora Crivella" (Down with Crivella). As the snare roll crescendos, they ready themselves to jump up at the "beat drop" when the bateria will enter. When it does, mass euphoria ensues—thousands of people run through the sambódromo as acoustic "boom-kat" beats resound through the structure. The invasion of the sambódromo in this way with acoustic techno music is a grotesque appropriation of the most symbolic site of Brazil. In taking over the parade route with this sonic vandalism, the alternative carnivalesque performs the triumph of street carnival over the city's official carnival, briefly taking the opportunity to criticize the city's mayor at the time who was hostile to Rio's carnival in all its forms (CW.Ch4.Ex1).[1]

———

Not all politics involves indignation, denunciation, and expressions of resistance, as shown in the last chapter. But, as this episode illustrates in the easy adoption of a chant condemning Mayor Crivella, such politics are never far away in neofanfarrismo. The taking of city spaces for participatory music may be in itself political, but it also offers an opportunity for a much more explicit and targeted form of politics, what I call *instrumental protest*.

In more official protests, musicians strategically deploy their repertoires in ostensibly nonfestive scenarios. According to trombonist Clément Mombereau, musicians playing in Rio de Janeiro during the momentous Brazilian protests of June 2013 adapted musical repertoires associated with carnival, often changing the words to themes of protest to suit more militant occasions. But he also relates that there was a concern to restrain carnivalesque elements in a city well accustomed to large festive crowds in the streets:

> There was a good bit of discussion about what songs we should play in the 2013 protests, because if you play too much carnival music it creates too much of a party. There were lots of carnival songs that were reprised with changed words to create political slogans. But once I launched into "Carinhoso" and the shaker player told me "quiet, we can't play that!" (Interview 2014)

Pixinguinha's "Carinhoso" (1918), a classic choro love song commonly played by the brass band community in Rio's carnival (chapter 2), was heard by some to be inappropriate, generating the wrong mood, during the indignant protests that criticized the governing Workers Party for having prioritized the demands of the World Cup and the Olympics over its leftist agenda. Nevertheless, the story of trumpeter Leo Adler shows that "Carinhoso" might not always be remiss in a protest. He relates a moment in a June 2013 protest in which "The police arrived unnecessarily, rather brutish and ignorant. They took my ID . . . and it came into my head this idea of playing 'Carinhoso,' which is a love song . . . The police left looking ashamed" (interview 2014, CW.Ch4.Ex2).[2] On another occasion, Mombereau played "Carinhoso" for the police at five in the morning at the end of a long procession shortly after the 2016 carnival, to which police responded with gas bombs that dispersed the crowd (CW.Ch4.Ex3).[3]

These three stories of "Carinhoso" used in protests and confrontations with the police show that brass musicians strategize, sometimes unsuccessfully, about the political roles and effectiveness of particular songs. While it is important for protest musicians to underline a distinction between a street protest and a street party, the appropriateness of certain festive songs in a protest may vary substantially, and the police response may differ also. "Carinhoso," a slow love song, might be used to pacify a situation in an intense confrontation with the police, but, if the desired effect is militancy, it may not be the favored choice. In another case, the police might hear it as mocking and an invitation for attack. Evoking the militant uses of brass and drum instruments, Leo Adler aspires for Rio's brass musicians to gain "the consciousness that an instrument is a weapon. Music has the capacity to change the dynamic of whatever social space" (interview 2014). In framing music as a tactic, a nimble source of musical support for political change, rather than as a performance that is the ultimate object of engagement, neofanfarrismo offers innovative practical and theoretical modes of musicking rarely accounted for by scholars.

Why have the carnival repertoires and practices of neofanfarrismo gained prominence as modes of resistance in contemporary Rio de Janeiro? How have neofanfarristas responded musically and politically to the crises that engulfed Brazil beginning in the early 2010s, and how has this engagement changed the movement? More broadly, how might the repurposing of carnivalesque repertoires to political scenarios broaden our understanding of the concept of repertoire?

Social movement scholar Charles Tilly (2010) has used the term "repertoire of contention" to refer to a given set of protest tools available to social movement actors. But despite the musical resonance of the term "repertoire," the musical choices of protesters have rarely been interpreted as repertoires of contention. Here, I expand on Tilly's concept by examining neofanfarristas' strategic musical choices in public street protests, what I call the movement's "musical repertoires of contention." Scholars of music in social movements have often implicitly relied on a functionalist model in which social movements "mobilize" music as a resource for political ends.[4] But in a musical social movement such as neofanfarrismo, public festivity is also a generative source of social and political mobilization, as the story of the invasion of the sambódromo demonstrates. Diana Taylor's notion of repertoire as comprising enactments of "embodied memory" in a variety of scenarios helps us move past a functionalist understanding of repertoires in social movements (2003, 20, see introduction). Her model also upsets a generic understanding of repertoire, in which "carnival repertoires" are designated as such by their uses in carnival, "political repertoires" for their uses in protest. In neofanfarrismo, the circulation of repertoires between festive and protest scenarios complicates any useful distinction between festive and political repertoires and encourages us to examine how they are deployed for diverse ends.

In this chapter, I examine how many of the repertoires considered in preceding chapters have made their way into protests and back into carnival as well as other festive spaces. I argue that an examination of musical protest in relation to the sonic force of instrumental ensembles and their strategic musical choices enriches the ways we can understand music to express political power beyond semantic critique. Lastly, I examine the roles of these musical actions in consolidating this street-based instrumental musical community as a self-defined activist movement in the context of sustained political crisis in the Olympic City of Rio de Janeiro. Indeed, the 2010s witnessed the mega-events of the World Cup and Olympics, the epochal leftist June 2013 protests, the downfall of the Workers Party by impeachment in 2016, and the election of right-wing populist Jair Bolsonaro to the presidency in 2018. As explicit appeals to White supremacy, authoritarianism, and violence against minorities have grown mainstream, neofanfarristas have affirmed alternative political visions by more explicitly aligning themselves with the left and acting in musical solidarity with those most threatened by these emergent realities. The commitment to political action is far from universally embraced among neofanfarristas, however, and has been a subject of controversy as the movement has debated what it stands for.

INSTRUMENTAL PROTEST

Public demonstrations are moments of confrontation in which the senses of belonging and control of urban space that loud, mobile, instrumental ensembles can engender are paramount. Trombonist Juliano Pires likens the tactical roles of a brass band to other groups that organize to enable the success of a protest: "In protests, there are various groups that help in the street: the groups overseeing the security of the people, the activist media, the lawyers, the Red Cross, and the street artists who do the ludic part. Each one has a function of protecting the people" (interview 2014). In the neofanfarrismo community, participating in a protest (*protesto* or *manifestação*) is generally understood to be a distinct form of musical action within the more ample meaning of the word activism (*ativismo*). When instrumental musicians use music strategically to achieve an explicit political change and confront state and corporate regimes, they engage in instrumental protest, only one element of the community's larger debate about instrumental activism, both of which I contrast with a predominant academic focus on lyrics to understand political engagement. While lyrics are not irrelevant in considering instrumental protest, as many bands play songs with well-known melodies that invite protesters to sing politicized lyrics, an analysis of instrumental protest

FIGURE 4.1 Musicians helping to keep crowds mobilized to prevent the confiscation of working-class ambulatory drink vendors' equipment. Photo by author on January 3, 2016.

focuses materially and affectively on how sound mobilizes protesters in public space, as seen in figure 4.1, which shows Clément Mombereau attempting to prevent the arrest of beer sellers with his trombone.[5]

These sounds that neofanfarrista bands produce help create senses of cohesion among the urban left in its resistance to political repression and (at times literal) civil war against Brazil's right wing. The repurposing of carnival repertoires for protest scenarios might be understood as elements of what Martin Daughtry calls "the belliphonic," encompassing "the spectrum of sounds produced by armed combat" (2015, 3). Perhaps Jennifer Whitney, writing about her experience playing in Seattle's brass and percussion ensemble the Infernal Noise Brigade, portrays something like instrumental protest best: "Because humans have too long bleated slogans and carried signs, the aesthetic of the INB is entirely post-textual; we provide tactical psychological support through a 'propaganda of sound.' The street is the venue for action and symbology, the domain of emotion and intuition; ideology is homework" (2003: 221–22).

Protest and Carnival

"In Brazil, everything turns into a party" trombonist Gustavo Machado told me as he explained the role of music in protests, and, indeed, a street protest and a carnival bloco in contemporary Rio de Janeiro share much in common (interview 2014). In both, people crowd the city streets with subversive and topical fantasias while mobile vendors sell beer to protesters and carnival audiences alike. Both use erected and mobile visual signs, such as standards and flags, that proclaim the identity of the crowd, and sound trucks lead marches and processions. And, of course, there is music and a consistent rhythmic pulse that drive the crowd forward in street carnival and street protest. Protests in Brazil are a kaleidoscopic cacophony with varying levels of coordination of syncopated chants, whistles, percussive beats, and, increasingly in Rio, brass bands. That is to say, the lines between protest and parades are less distinct in Rio de Janeiro than is often depicted, such as in Matt Sakakeeny's portrait of New Orleans second line bands: "Organized marches tend to be associated with 'official' displays of authority . . . or oppositional social movements . . . but the messages of the second line and jazz funeral parades are sung and played in another key; theirs is a politics of pleasure and festivity articulated through musical instruments and moving bodies as well as voices" (2010, 13).

Famed street carnival stilt walker Raquel Potí suggests instead that the diverse street manifestations of Rio constitute a subversive continuum between disciplined street protests, street carnival events, and divisive street chaos:

When we are in a protest, we have a single established discourse and go deeply into it . . . When we are in carnival, we have millions of discourses. These are discourses that are always latent—the discourse of diversity, equality, respect for difference, sexual diversity, feminism, social relations, and disparities . . . In carnival, when there are so many voices, it turns into a party . . . Even when we have discourses that seem apparently different, we are together and strengthening each other. It turns into a party when we support each other. If we don't support each other, it turns into chaos [confusão]. A protest can turn into chaos when people are limited in their own discourse and don't accept the diversity of discourses of others. (Interview 2016)

For Potí, the difference between a protest and carnival is based on the varying levels of monologism and dialogism. In situations of antagonism, either between movement actors, foliões, or the police, a party or a protest in public space can become chaotic "confusion."

Neofanfarristas' employment of the repertoires of carnival in protest can be understood as expressions of what Larry Bogad calls "tactical performance," or the "use of performance techniques, tactics, and aesthetics in social-movement campaigns" (2016, 2). Like Potí, Bogad makes the distinction between political actions that "occupy" public space with a single defined discourse and those that "open" them to a carnivalesque multivocality. He suggests that leftist protest models have trended internationally since the 1990s, with the fall of institutional leftist governments and their "occupying" models, to increasingly open models that promote horizontalism, dialogism, and the aesthetics and ethics of carnival. Many of the leftist movements that neofanfarristas mobilize broadly dialogue with larger frames of the "global justice movement," which Bogad describes as "a 'movement of movements' due to its great diversity in geography, identity, and ideology" (100). He suggests that

> The idea of carnival helped to inspire and galvanize the theory and action of a global, antiauthoritarian, and anti-capitalist movement. This global movement was determined to build and sustain its own cultures, in defiance of the homogenizing corporate monoculture that is spreading so rapidly. This concept, influenced by older ideas but moving beyond Bakhtin, developed new parameters and tactics through activist praxis. The movement aimed to reclaim the carnival for its own purposes and agendas . . . in pursuit of sustained, deeply oppositional, creative, and egalitarian activism. (108)

Likewise, writing about the Reclaim the Streets direct action collectives and "Carnivals against Capitalism" in Britain, Graham St. John views contemporary protests as often strategically taking the form of a "protestival," which appropriates the carnivalesque as a "critical tool in the activist repertoire" (2008, 171). Collectively, these global movements signal "a turn away from the oppositional politics of indignation toward a new politics of festivity" (Abe 2018, 160). However, as all this research on the carnivalesque in protest is primarily focused in the Global North, in these cases the notion of carnival is mostly imagined and not based in local practices. Neofanfarristas also describe a shift away from institutionalized and hierarchical leftist movements toward more carnivalesque, horizontal, and "open" modes of engagement, or a shift from an "old" to a "new" left. But they draw on their own local carnival practices rather than on an imagined festive Other. What these authors argue in relation to the uses of carnival in protests in the Global North is all the more true in places where communities have a vibrant history of carnival traditions on which to draw.

The Tactical Capacities of the Brass Band

Due to its mobility and loudness, few musical ensembles are made for marching and mobilizing large crowds as well as the brass band. While baterias, which are ubiquitous in Rio, are also loud and mobile, neofanfarristas argue that without amplification of vocals they cannot project melodies that compel protesters to sing. For snare player Miguel Maron, the brass band "cries and calls people. It congregates them around something . . . It has power, a sonorous potential" (interview 2014). Many other neofanfarristas speak of the capacity of the brass ensemble to create audibility and visibility for an action, calling attention to a given cause. Protest music throughout the Americas may be more associated with folk singers, but it is much more difficult for folk songs, especially without amplification, to mobilize a protest march. As Saxophonist Gabriel Fomm notes, "you can go to an occupation to play guitar and five people will sing along. But they won't be heard by all the movement" (interview 2015).

By contrast, brass bands have the capacity to "open" protests in Bogad's sense by creating an inviting, experimental atmosphere for protesters and bystanders alike. In Rio, their performances in protests are generally inclusive for other musicians to participate spontaneously on a horn, drum, or other instruments, as musicians translate their experiences of playing in open blocos to political settings. Saxophonist and activist Tomás Ramos argues that the emergence of brass ensembles in protests represents the ascendance of a more horizontal new left that Bogad (2016) has observed worldwide. For him, the traditional sound car, used in carnival as well as in protests to lead crowds through the streets, represents a hierarchical model of the old left. While it allows a social movement to amplify its rhetoric and musical choices, the march leaders are high above the protesters proclaiming a monologic discourse and not responsive to changing conditions on the ground. The brass band, on the other hand, is more agile, responsive, and horizontal—"open" for those around it who want to engage. Ramos explains,

> We saw that we filled a role of education, security, and direction, the roles that the sound cars always filled. But the sound car is huge and has many limits.

Someone tells the people what they must do from up high. It's very vertical and I think we have come to surpass the sound car . . . Just like Occupy Wall Street, the actions of June 2013 put in question the various forms of classical organization and representation on the left . . . [that] the sound car represented. (Interview 2014)

For these musicians, the brass band has the capacity to "open," or decenter, music making in a protest in the ways that Occupy Wall Street's mic check[6] could decenter the discursive hierarchy of those who amplify a monologic left-wing discourse from a sound car. The opposition to sound cars in protests parallels the original brass bloco revival's prizing of acoustic music making in the streets instead of sound cars in street carnival (chapter 1).

By creating a carnivalesque ambience, or "carnivalizing protest," neofanfarristas suggest that brass ensembles have the capacity to "break" the logic of violence that typifies encounters with the police and alter the outcome. Gabriel Fomm recounts, "From the moment that a brass band arrives, it's much harder for the police to confront because the climate is not confrontational. It's celebratory" (interview 2015). Suggesting that a brass band can dignify and legitimize a protest, Fomm recounts that the 2011 tent occupation of Ocupa Rio (Occupy Rio), in solidarity with Occupy Wall Street, was viewed

from the beginning as heavy and violent. There was a huge police presence, so keeping it light was fundamental. The arts had the function of giving equilibrium to the movement and a lightness for those who saw it from outside as a "favelization" of Cinelândia [square] . . . The brass band transforms outsiders who cast a prejudiced look and gives credibility to the movement. (Interview 2015)

While many neofanfarristas likewise stress the role of security and pacification a brass band can play in spaces of contention, in other cases it can heighten the militant intents of protesters. Trumpeter Leo Adler, who frequently played in the June 2013 protests, stresses the militaristic aspect of brass bands in protest:

Protesters would tell me that they had gotten sick from the tear gas. They wanted to leave, but they heard me playing and felt the force to continue holding back the police. The police were dispersing people and throwing gas bombs all around, and I would start a song. The protesters would group up again and start to sing over the police. Music helps in the resistance. Every army has a trumpeter to play the call to advance, the call to retreat. (Interview 2014)

Saxophonist Mathias Mafort similarly argues that pacification is only one strategic choice of many that brass bands have available: "Protests are a bit like war . . . The brass band always has a function in this context. In some cases, the brass band is pacifying. In others, it is the heart of the movement as if it were its motor force. It can have many faces . . . It depends on the intention" (interview 2015).

When engaging in protests, Rio's brass bands reinterpret carnival marches, punk music, funk carioca, Brazilian protest songs, and much more to tactically frame and support a given protest. Below, I examine the repertoire choices of the bands BlocAto do Nada and Os Siderais, as well as spontaneous musical engagements in protests. The first band draws especially on Brazilian musical repertoires of protest and the oppressed, or "radical nationalism" (Klubock 1998), whereas the second band dialogues with international repertoires of protest and is influenced by the cannibalist discourse of Orquestra Voadora. The distinction somewhat parallels the difference between the nationalist stage of the brass blocos and the internationalist stage of neofanfarrismo (chapter 2).

Though I have shown that there is considerable overlap between participatory and presentational modes (Turino 2008) of music making in neofanfarrismo (see chapters 1 and 3), I distinguish between BlocAto do Nada's participatory style of musical protest and Os Siderais' presentational style. By participatory musical protest, I mean that musicians strategically choose repertoires in order to involve the audience in the musical performance of protest. By presentational musical protest I mean that the transgression involved in musicians' performance is primarily an object of emotive spectacle that maintains a distinction between performer and audience. The prioritization of one or the other has strategic implications for the choice of musical repertoires of contention and ultimately the tactical political goal of an action.

BlocAto do Nada and Participatory Musical Repertoires of Contention

BlocAto do Nada (Action Bloco of Nothing) was founded in 2012 and was during my fieldwork the only brass band of the neofanfarrismo movement that played exclusively for protests. The band name was taken from a line of a Bertolt Brecht poem, "Nothing must seem impossible to change," a phrase that adorns the bloco's standard (*Nada deve parecer impossível de mudar*). The line presents an invitation to actively imagine the construction of an alternative world. Saxophonist and activist Tomás Ramos, who worked closely with Rio de Janeiro's 2016 PSoL mayoral candidate Marcelo Freixo, founded the brass bloco to play throughout the year for social movements. He organized within the neofanfarrismo movement and its major moment of mobilization in carnival, putting together the carnival ensemble word "bloco" with "*ato*," or political action. The use of carnival resources was not intended, Ramos relates,

> to just stay in carnival, but to strengthen social movements . . . Carnival would only be an excuse to bring together musicians and organize the bloco . . . The traditional aesthetic of the left [no longer] has the same effect that other aesthetics can have. [The question was] what is there in Rio de Janeiro that mobilizes so many people in the streets? The brass bloco . . . I put my faith in this—in art as a method of action, in carnival as a strategy of struggle. (Interview 2014)

On November 11, 2014, I went with BlocAto do Nada to nearby São Gonçalo, a poor city near Niterói across the bay from Rio de Janeiro. The Homeless Workers Movement (MTST) had helped workers stage an occupation in a peripheral area of São Gonçalo that had already lasted ten days to demand formal housing. Shabbily constructed huts had been set up with tarps held up by sticks—seven hundred barracks for seven hundred families. They were calling it Ocupação Zumbi dos Palmares in homage to the Black king Zumbi of the free runaway slave community Palmares that lasted for almost a century in the 1600s. The musicians handed out percussion instruments to children and let them experiment on horns. A box of carnival costumes had been brought for the parade, and occupiers dressed themselves in clothes and masks, celebrating the occupation through expressions of carnival. The carnivalesque practice of the poor taking on the identity of a king took on a much more subversive signification than simply a temporary inversion. Ultimately, the action was part of an effective direct action strategy of occupation. The next day, Rio's city government signed an accord through the Workers Party program Minha Casa, Minha Vida (My House, My Life) for the construction of one thousand houses for the occupiers.

We marched through the community encampment, supporting the occupiers with Brazilian protest songs from the 1960s, funk carioca songs, carnival marches, and syncopated chants. Protesters enthusiastically sang along to BlocAto's instrumental renditions of especially known funk carioca songs of Rio's favelas like "Rap da felicidade" (1995):

I just want to be happy,
To walk freely in the favela where I was born
To be able to take pride
And know that the poor have a place.

BlocAto strategically employs an instrumental repertoire that merges arrangements of Brazilian protests songs from the 1960s and 1970s with Rio's contemporary funk carioca style of the favelas, fusing two divergent Brazilian musical
repertoires of resistance. These repertoire choices facilitate the mobilization and
musical participation of middle-class and poorer populations in Rio de Janeiro
respectively, though many songs are appreciated by both. Just as I experienced in
the occupation of São Gonçalo, the band's percussionist Chico Oliveira explains,

> When we play "Rap da felicidade," which has very politicized lyrics, people
> always sing naturally. The choice of repertoire and songs is based in the imagi-
> nary of the people. We take care to propose things that make sense for others
> and not just for those who already think about politics. The choice of repertoire
> makes people come closer and feel something in common with us. The principal
> idea is that anyone can sing in the street. For this, BlocAto's repertoire is based
> mostly on the Carioca aesthetic. (Interview 2014)

In protests that have a more middle-class profile, the band plays songs based in
the middle-class Brazilian protest tradition of the 1960s, such as Chico Buarque's
"Apesar de você" (1970), to which protesters sing along (figure 4.2). To get past
the military censors, Buarque's subtle lyrics were couched in the language of a
breakup song, but fans perceptively viewed it as a stringent critique of the regime:
"In spite of you, tomorrow must be another day." BlocAto mixes a 12/8 candomblé
beat with perhaps the most iconic Brazilian protest song of the 1960s, Geraldo
Vandré's "Caminhando:"

Marching and singing
And following the song,
We are all equal . . .

Beyond repertoire choices, Ramos explains that BlocAto "was preoccupied
with creating beats for the street chants. If someone yells 'tarifa zero' [no fees],
we would do a beat for 'tarifa zero.' More important than us simply playing our

FIGURE 4.2 Photo of author (center) playing at protest with BlocAto do Nada.
Courtesy of Breno Lima in 2015.

music is that we be a great microphone for everyone." When MTST organizers in São Gonçalo, for example, led the occupiers in call-and-response chants like "Zumbi presente agora e sempre" (Zumbi is present now and always), the horn players stopped while the drummers provided a rhythmic backbone that further energized the chants, such as

Call: "MTST"
Response: "a luta é pra valer" (the fight is for our worth)
Call: "pra criar, pra criar" (to create, to create)
Response: "o poder popular" (the people's power)

In mostly using well-known national musical references, the strategic employment of musical repertoires of contention by BlocAto is primarily participatory, oriented to mobilizing the musical and political involvement of the protesters. Oliveira views the band's diverse repertoires as the "accumulation of leftist social movements of various authors and cultures that have been involved in political struggles in our tradition here in Brazil. These are songs that marked the fight against the dictatorship and many other struggles for rights" (interview 2014). Together, these songs tell a musical story of the Brazilian urban left since the emergence of politicized MPB and are employed to mobilize the "masses." It is clearly easier to mobilize people after all through the repertoires they know. Ramos explains, "A challenge for neofanfarrismo, just like radical politics, is to construct bridges with places marginalized by capital, in the favelas, in distant places. To this end, it is very important that BlocAto be aligned with these movements . . . to construct politics with those who suffer the most from capitalism" (interview 2014, CW.Ch4.Ex4).[7]

Os Siderais and Presentational Musical Repertoires of Contention

In contrast to BlocAto, Os Siderais, founded in 2011 when no band in the neofanfarrismo community had yet adopted an explicitly political stance, has brought an internationalist, presentational, and musically eclectic repertoire to protests throughout the city. Juliano Pires, who had played a role in founding Orquestra Voadora, had grown frustrated with that band's lack of desire to participate in protest and clearly emphasize its political positions in favor of maintaining a low political profile as a commercial act. He later left Voadora due to such discords. He gathered the members of Os Siderais with the explicit intention of creating a performance band that was also committed to political engagement. Many of the band's members consider themselves "militants" within their chosen profession, and they use their links to radical sectors within these fields to organize the band to play at particular actions. The band's snare player, Miguel Maron, who is also a public school teacher, explains that, "We have a militant proposal within social movements and our own careers, so this priority emerged in the band around supporting social movements. We believe that the brass band . . . is an element of politics, of political transformation, and it can make an intervention" (interview 2014).

Os Siderais's repertoire includes punk songs, Afrobeat, and covers of Tropicália and mangue beat songs, as well as songs from diverse international brass movements. With original songs entitled "Palmares in the Streets" (Palmares nas ruas) and "Liberty Square" (Praça da liberdade), the band's repertoire is less well known to the Brazilian "masses" than that of BlocAto. Like Voadora, Os Siderais has travelled extensively and exchanged with international bands, including in France and Scotland in 2012, HONK! in Boston in 2013, and HONK!TX in Austin in 2017. Its internationalist aesthetic has been well suited for engaging in protests that are either explicitly internationally oriented or for generally middle-class audiences with awareness and interest in international protest movements and traditions. The band's internationalist orientation can be understood as part of

FIGURE 4.3 Os Siderais playing at the original protests in defense of teachers on
September 27, 2013. Photo by Gabriel Seibt, courtesy of Juliano Pires.

the increasing translocalism of leftist protest culture globally. Given the more
obscure references in their musical repertoires of contention for local Cariocas,
they generally practice a more presentational form of musical protest intended to
provide senses of legitimacy and enthusiasm to protesters rather than mobilizing
them to engage in music making or collective singing as part of the act of protest.

On October 1, 2014, teachers in Rio de Janeiro held an anniversary commemoration for a repressed teachers' strike, one of the bloodiest days in the
protest movement in 2013 (figure 4.3). Miguel Maron, a high school teacher and
union member as well as the band's snare player, organized the band to play at
the action in Cinelândia, a well-trod central square for protests. When I arrived
at the scene to play one of my first "shows" with the band, the entire square
was already surrounded by armed riot cops, looking like they could close in at
any point. Many young and mostly Whiter protesters were dressed all in black
as the internationally recognizable Black Bloc,[8] waving giant black flags and
ready for a police attack. Amid the menacing police presence, the mood was
tense and subdued before we began to play, but Os Siderais would transform a
lackluster protest into an exuberant street party in defiance of the police. Brass
band renditions of punk songs triggered a mosh pit, and the Black Bloc yelled

the English words "Hey Ho, Let's Go" from the Ramones song "Blitzkrieg Pop" (1976) in recognition of Os Siderais' rendition.

The band ended the protest performance with the Italian leftist anthem, "Bella ciao," a partisan song of uncertain origin that is most associated with the leftist Italian Resistance against fascism during World War II and spread across the world (Bagini 2014). After singing the lyrics in Italian, Os Siderais began playing the song repeatedly at increasing speeds, again triggering a mosh pit. I knew the song from playing in the HONK! circuit in the United States, but I hadn't known it before joining the protest-focused Brass Liberation Orchestra of San Francisco. Trombonist Gustavo Machado explains about "Bella ciao," "it's not known by the public in general, only to those who have studied a bit to know that this is a resistance song from the second World War" (interview 2014). The use of this song stands in direct contrast to BlocAto's strategy of playing music to mobilize those who may not be fluent in the history of international leftist repertoires. Unlike the participatory and mass-oriented repertoire and tactics of BlocAto, Os Siderais' engagement in this protest was presentational and invited a middle-class audience to create a politicized street party, diffusing confrontational energy with the police (CW.Ch4.Ex5).[9]

Os Siderais has engaged in translating elements to Rio de Janeiro of the international Occupy movement, which was also widely depicted as predominantly middle class. Many of the tactics that were developed in New York, including mic check, general assemblies, and tent-city occupations of public space, were practiced in Rio and in cities around the world (Holston 2014). In 2011, early in its history, Os Siderais played at the Ocupa Rio tent occupation of the central square of Cinelândia. The band incorporated particular symbols and practices from the protests, including the Guy Fawkes[10] mask worn by the band's standard bearer. The iconic mask became an internationally recognized anticapitalist symbol of the Occupy Movement and became a common carnival costume in Rio. According to neofanfarristas, although *ocupar* (to occupy) had been used previously by local anarchist squat movements as well as by MST and MTST, the word's increasing prevalence in Rio de Janeiro was a direct result of the American Occupy movement and the Ocupa Rio protests inspired by it. The word ocupar is now extremely prevalent in the vocabulary of the social and music movements that stake claims on public space in Rio. Os Siderais' associations with protest scenes that were internationally oriented and more middle class led it to make different strategic choices, largely presentational ones, in selecting its repertoires of contention, than BlocAto.

Spontaneous Musical Repertoires of Contention

While some bands prepare repertoires specifically intended to provide musical support within a protest, Rio's brass musicians are also well accustomed to playing with one another spontaneously in a participatory mode of musical protest by resorting to a vast collective repertoire available from street carnival and neofanfarrismo. The strategic impact of repertoire selection, however, is no less important than more planned actions, as, for example, they often launch into the Star Wars "Imperial March" during any police encroachment to dramatize the confrontation and assign moral culpability to the police.

Carnival marches (marchinhas) are often adapted for protests because they are so well known among the carnival brass community and act as a kind of musical default repertoire (chapter 2). "Ó abre alas" (Open the wings), for example, is a famous marchinha that during carnival is often played first as a bloco sets off. At protests, musicians can use this song to compel crowds to transgress barriers set by the police. Ramos relates that on June 20, the day of the largest of the June 2013 protests, a slow marcha-rancho helped calm a situation that might have otherwise ended in stampede:

> With a million people in the streets, the police started to fight with a group that was trying to advance . . . There were a lot of people. The police arrived and everyone started running from gas bombs . . . A trombonist started to play "Bandeira branca" [White Flag], which is a song that pleas for peace. It's very slow and when people heard the song they stopped running and went more slowly. Everyone started to play the song very slowly and people followed the standard. And we saw that we provide an incredible security role. (Interview 2014)

At times, spontaneous decisions about protest repertoires taken from carnival are reactive rather than strategic. Trumpet player Leo Adler recounts that in the 2013 protests,

> There is a video of a policeman shooting and someone else shooting back and I am playing "Allah-la-ô," which is a marchinha. But it's not the song that I would have liked to play at that moment. I think that there are songs that would be better suited, but in the moment of tear gas on all sides, the last thing you think about is what song you will play. Whatever comes out helps the people. (Interview 2014)

Beyond these stock songs, musicians who assemble together also make particular contextual choices on the spot in order to animate a given protest. I attended a protest in September 2014 calling for the release of Rafael Braga, a Black man and the only arrestee imprisoned during the 2013 protests. Musicians and protesters assembled outside of the city's legislative assembly as speakers denounced disparity in the justice system against Blacker people. The march that followed was headed by a theatrical procession in which four Black women were roped together acting as a chain of enslaved people, while a man ceremoniously whipped them as he walked alongside. This theatrical enactment of slavery drew a performative link from legacies of slavery to contemporary Black incarceration.

The brass musicians, reacting to the performance, launched into Baden Powell's "Berimbau" (1963). The song refers to the power of the Afro-Brazilian musical instrument *berimbau* that accompanies *capoeira*, the Afro-Brazilian martial arts form disguised as dance that is widely considered to have been a method of training to fight, particularly against slave masters and police. Protesters sang as they recognized the song: "Capoeira has sent me to say that it has come—it has come to fight." While the image of whipping the Black women certainly created an acerbic critique of Braga's imprisonment, the brass musicians sonically reinterpreted this reference to slavery through reprising a song that memorialized the cultural traditions of struggle during slavery in Brazil, prompting the protesters to sing.

POLITICIZING NEOFANFARRISMO

These musicians and bands' strategic employment of musical repertoires for spaces of contention have played an important role in shifting the political priorities of the larger, previously more politically ambivalent neofanfarrismo movement by providing opportunities for instrumental protest. But the shifting contexts of political polarization and crisis have also politicized musicians and influenced the growing consolidation of neofanfarrismo around the frame of activism. Orquestra Voadora saxophonist André Ramos explained in early 2015 that

> In the past seven years, we have lived through a time in which crisis has intensified a lot . . . and this certainly influenced the work of Orquestra Voadora. These questions of privatization and of appropriation of public space became

increasingly more intense, especially with the World Cup and the Olympics, which caused a speculative boom . . . The issues brought by the [2013] protests changed people's thinking, and we started to see Orquestra Voadora as a way of thinking about alternatives . . . With the intensification of the crisis, we saw that we had a political role. (Interview 2015)

Indeed, early on in the movement's history before the intensification of the political climate and the founding of explicitly political bands, some musicians complained that it was impossible to unify a single band around engaging in political action. Voadora trumpeter Daniel Paiva recounts, "I go to many protests but Voadora wouldn't go [as the band] because we have become an institution. We have a huge carnival event. We have sponsorship from the government. Some people in the group don't get along politically . . . As a band and institution in Rio, we cannot be out there with a [partisan] flag" (interview 2014). Voadora's former tubist Tim Malik explains that "taking a public political stance in Brazil is not necessarily the thing to do. It can be hard core. There's people watching you. There's a complete lack of accountability. People can tend to appear complacent but there's just no protection. You get on someone's bad side and if they have power, they can make your life terrible" (interview 2015).

Moreover, despite the prevalence of the word "activism" in the neofanfarrismo movement, there has never existed an absolute mission statement regarding the politics of the movement. Most musicians voted for Workers Party President Dilma Rousseff and have supported the party (Partido dos Trabalhadores or PT) in some way, but many express political views far left of the institutional PT. Some support the PSoL, eschew party politics altogether, or may furtively support the center-right or right (though I never met any). Politicized musicians within neofanfarrismo, such as those of BlocAto do Nada or Os Siderais, complain that much of the carnivalesque movement consists of fanfarrões, or partiers with little sense of social responsibility.

In Portuguese, politicized leftists often distinguish between the politically engaged (*engajados*) and alienated (*alienados*), pointing to a supposed divide between those preoccupied with the concerns of "the people" (*o povo*) and those who are "alienated" from them, more attentive to material comforts, international trends, and festive "distractions" such as carnival—the fanfarrões. A further distinction in Portuguese between "activism" (*ativismo*) and "militancy" (*militância*) stakes the level of one's political engagement. The Anarchist Federation of Rio de Janeiro (FARJ) argues that militancy presupposes a degree of seriousness and devotion that generally is not present in activism. It is the development of regular work that seeks to involve in the revolutionary fight [*luta*] the most diverse, exploited, and oppressed sectors of society . . . In [militancy], personal life is adapted to the fight. In [activism], militancy must fit into the personal life of the individual.

The distinction between militancy and activism illustrates how so many neofanfarrista bands can define themselves as activist without engaging in protests or social movements as a first priority by pointing to, for example, their efforts at inclusive musical education, such as Voadora's oficina. Other bands view themselves as militant alternatives in relation to what they see as the "soft" activism, or outright hedonism, of others. Engaging in instrumental protest is to take part in a debate that puts at stake the fundamental priorities of this alternative community, as well as the meaning of the widespread term "alternative."

The Days of June

June 2013, however, provided a tipping point for political and musical engagement that fundamentally transformed the movement's focus on carnival and parties into a broader preoccupation with politics. Petra Costa, in her Oscar-nominated documentary *Democracia em Vertigem* (2019) about the political breakdown of the 2010s, marks the 2013 protests as the beginning of a growing political divide that tore open the consensus politics of the 2000s. As John Street writes, the question of music's political potential becomes especially relevant when music "forms as a site of public deliberation" and presents people with a choice of engagement (2012, 8). While political action may have been controversial in a band like Orquestra Voadora before, tubist Malik relates that by June 2013, "that discussion was out the window . . . we had to participate, obviously" (interview 2014).

Initiated by the Free Pass Movement (*Movimento Passe Livre*), the explosive June 2013 protests captured global attention, and observers suggested that the supposedly apolitical "sleeping giant" of Brazil had awakened. The Free Pass Movement has demanded free access to public transportation (*tarifa zero*) since 2005, but it ignited a series of nationwide protests in 2013 when it launched a campaign against the raising of bus fares in São Paulo by twenty *centavos*. Idelber Avelar notes the "affective multiplicity" of the diverse protests that followed and their refusal to be reduced to a singular demand, expressing a wholesale rejection of the Brazilian State's governance worthy of the term "uprising." As the protests grew exponentially, culminating with two million people in the streets in over one hundred Brazilian cities on June 20, they proved a tipping point for the disenchantment of the urban left with the until then mostly popular governing Workers Party, whose conciliatory relationships to neoliberal policies and institutions reached a breaking point for frustrated leftists. The protests ended up "divorcing" the Workers Party infrastructure from the social movements that had been before so closely linked, irrevocably weakening the party and opening a space for the right to eventually take over (Avelar 2017).

Protesters challenged the Workers Party's prioritizing of spending for the World Cup and the Olympics and their neoliberal trickle-down rationale. They claimed they wanted education, health care, housing, and transportation for the people in the "padrão FIFA" (the FIFA standard) because, as BlocAto organizer Tomás Ramos explains, "the mega-events were sold as something that could bring benefits to the cities" (interview 2014). Indeed, Rio de Janeiro and other major urban centers bore the brunt of hosting the mega-events, including heightened militarization, housing speculation, rising costs of living, and the construction of massive stadiums, some of which stand today largely unused. Ramos credits the particularly urban character of the June 2013 protests as a response to the perfect storm of deprioritizing public services, the demands of mega-events, and the militarization of the police.[11]

Earlier in 2013, Os Siderais had already been bringing protesters and neo-fanfarristas to musical protests in defense of the Aldeia Maracanã, an urban indigenous settlement that would be expelled during construction projects for the World Cup on the city's famous Maracanã soccer stadium. By June, Orquestra Voadora and other bands joined the protests against the World Cup that were gathering strength, using social media to support the protests and organize musicians to come to them "armed" with instruments. The police repression that met protesters was extreme, with gas bombs, rubber bullets, and other measures used to disperse the crowd, and this response ignited even larger protests framed against police repression. Musicians describe playing in intense and violent situations. Juliano Pires relates that June 20, the largest day of protest, was "the biggest repression of all time. They managed to explode gas bombs in five neighborhoods at the same time . . . Bombs, bombs, smoke, smoke . . . And I was there playing trombone" (interview 2014). Brass bands supported chants of thousands: "It hasn't stopped. It has to stop. I want the end of the military police." Protestors adapted carnival lyrics to the occasion, and musicians covered their instruments with stickers produced by social movements that used well-known slogans, like

"Whose Cup?" (*Copa pra quem?*) and "There will be no World Cup" (*Não vai ter copa*). The latter chant became the inspiration for an original song by the Chilean brass band Rim Bam Bum in solidarity with their Brazilian compatriots.

Many commentators and neofanfarristas saw the Brazilian protests as part of an international wave of protests including the Arab Spring and Occupy Wall Street that were internationally oriented and antipartisan and shared many new repertoires of contention across borders as they broadly rejected global neoliberalism (Castells 2012). Some neofanfarristas saw the enormous protests of June 2013 as a watershed moment of rejecting the "old left," or what Bogad refers to as "occupying practices," toward more democratic and "open" practices. BlocAto organizer Tomás Ramos believed optimistically in 2014 that,

> In the future, they will analyze June 2013 for Brazil as having an importance as big as what happened in May of 1968 in France. I think that this is a turning point. A new political generation has been created since then. This is a generation coming after twelve years of government by the Workers Party that managed to enter into power after twenty or thirty years of popular mobilization. And all the disenchantment with the limits of this project that the party represented made a new stage of politics emerge. June represents the disenchantment with traditional forms of political representation and with the limits that the Workers Party promoted. (Interview 2014)

Ocupa Carnaval

By July 2013, police repression had produced effective results, and protest energies on a mass scale diminished, but although these mass protests were short-lived, they were influential in shifting the orientations of many neofanfarristas, as Ramos predicted. Social movement groups increasingly began to organize occupations of public space with cultural programming, such as Ocupa Lapa and Ocupa Escola focusing around particular campaigns, and neofanfarrista bands and other musical groups would play in support. The desire to maintain the activist energies of June and translate them into the city's largest popular mobilization, the annual carnival, led to the Ocupa Carnaval movement. Ocupa Carnaval fused the vocabulary of the Occupy Movement with street carnival. Saxophonist Tomás Ramos, who also organized BlocAto, describes the Ocupa Carnaval movement as "an attempt to construct a common campaign, a politics of communication with all these collectives and militants that were participating in this idea of using carnival as an opportunity to strengthen the platforms of social movements, principally those that were in the street during the protests" (interview 2014).

Just as protesters had adopted the musical repertoires of carnival during the protests, musical activists primarily from BlocAto aimed to politicize the street carnival itself around contemporary issues. They rewrote carnival marches with new satirical lyrics, professionally recorded them, and broadcast them on YouTube. In Ocupa Carnaval's bloco parade during carnival, brass musicians play through the marchinhas, while the public sings the well-known lyrics with new lyrics handed out in leaflets. Ocupa Carnaval's practice of changing the words of popular carnival tunes to suit protests drew on a practice that emerged in the 2013 protests. Percussionist Emerson Guerra observes about the movement that, "As the protest had become carnival, the carnival became protest as well" (interview 2014, CW.Ch4.Ex6).[12]

In an effort to popularize Ocupa Carnaval in order to politicize carnival and other street music events, the organizers passed out movement stickers of the group's logo that appeared all over the standards and instruments of their bands (figure 4.4). They produced a manifesto of the movement that overtly contests what many on the left see as the privatization, spectacle, and militarization of Olympic Rio de Janeiro at the expense of the public:

Carnival is the most beautiful cry of the people. We occupy the streets with banners, confetti, and coils to show that Rio is ours . . . Down with the ratchets that transform the city into a huge business, where profit matters more than life, where money is freer than people. While they capitalize reality, we socialize the dream. Long live the energy of rebellion. Long live the creativity of the carnival costumes. Long live Zé Pereira . . . The city is not for sale and our rights are not merchandise. (Ocupa carnaval's Facebook page, 2015)

In the 2014 carnival, Ocupa Carnaval created a large puppet of Fuleco, the official mascot of the 2014 World Cup and a Brazilian armadillo (*tatu-bola* in Portuguese). Lambasting the image, Ocupa Carnaval portrayed him as a rich aristocrat and called him "Tatu derrado," a play on the Portuguese " 'tá tudo errado," or "it's all wrong." In 2016, Ocupa Carnaval billed the parade as "Olim piada," a play on the word *Olimpíadas* (Olympics). "Piada" means joke in Portuguese, and musicians intended to highlight, as Ramos explains, the "joke that is all this debate of the mega-events, of the sold city" (interview 2014).

FIGURE 4.4 Ocupa Carnaval image with commedia dell'arte/carnival figure of Colombina reimagined as a Black Bloc protester. Courtesy of Tomás Ramos, art by André Mantelli.

The songs of Ocupa Carnaval lambasted the political pretensions of Olympic Rio de Janeiro and called attention to the corruption and inequalities of daily life in the city. For example, Ocupa Carnaval rewrote the lyrics of "Cidade Maravilhosa," a beloved marchinha written by André Filho in 1935 that is often played at the end of carnival brass blocos like Boitatá and Céu na Terra (CW.Ch4.Ex7).[13] "Cidade maravilhosa" (the marvelous city) is a common nickname for Rio, and the lyrics sing of an enchanting city full of spectacular sights and sounds, the heart of Brazil and the cradle of samba. Below are the original lyrics of the song on the left and Ocupa Carnaval's satirical rewrite on the right:

Marvelous city	Marvelous city
Full of a thousand enchantments.	Full of a thousand enchantments.
Marvelous city	Greedy city
Heart of my Brazil.	Removed 40,000!
Marvelous city	Marvelous city
Full of a thousand enchantments	Full of a thousand enchantments
Marvelous city	Mafia-run city
Heart of my Brazil.	Where Amarildo disappeared.

Cradle of samba and of pretty songs	Cradle of bullets and of tanks
That live in the soul of the people	Stealing the souls of people
You are the altar of our hearts	You are the altar of great scorn
That sing cheerfully.	Made violently.
Flourishing garden of love and nostalgia	It is Brazil's most expensive city
Land that seduces everyone	Expelling its people.
May God bring you happiness	Prices only the rich can pay,
Nest of dream and light.	The gringo sways contentedly.

The video of Ocupa Carnaval's version shows the famous Christ the Redeemer statue reimagined as a choque de ordem officer. Scenes of violent police operations in destitute favelas contrast with rich city elites, while pacification police tanks roll through favelas. Police brutally repress protesters, and homes are destroyed to make way for golf courses. The lyrics refer to the 2013 protests and to the disappearance amid pacification operations of Amarildo, who never returned to his residence in Rio's largest favela Rocinha after being detained by the pacification police. The phrase "We must resist" (Resistir é preciso) is spray painted on a wall as the video closes on a dissonant chord, visually and aurally implying a lack of closure to the song.

Impeachment and Realignment

Amid such critiques of the Olympic City that resounded beginning in June 2013, the Workers Party had become increasingly unpopular among the left, which widely viewed it as having overly compromised with the forces of neoliberal capitalism and political enemies in Brasília. In the wake of the 2013 protests, economic recession, and a vulnerable situation epitomized by the catastrophic embarrassment for Brazil in the 2014 World Cup with its 7–1 loss to Germany, the 2014 presidential campaign produced schisms within the neofanfarrismo community about whether to align with the party at all. Almost all neofanfarristas were united in their opposition to the right's candidate Aécio Neves, but some moderate participants did not feel that political content should be a part of neofanfarrista events outside of protests. Those who wanted to openly support the Workers Party faced disagreement from those further left as well as from the apolitical flanks of the movement.

These tensions mounted on the day of Dilma Rousseff's reelection, October 26, 2014, when the Boi Tolo bloco, which expresses no party affiliations or political goals outside its resistance to official carnival (chapter 3), held its first march of the carnival season. Though the parade was not intended as a celebration for Rousseff, street revelers with red party banners nonetheless flooded the march in celebration once her reelection had been announced. To the consternation of many musicians, the visual appearance of the parade seemed to become a Rousseff celebration. A counterdemonstration soon emerged when leftist Black Blocs arrived chanting "Dilma is a fascist," and skirmishes arose between the anarchist and institutional lefts in a march originally intended to have no political platform.

When the process of impeaching Rousseff mounted just one year after her reelection, many neofanfarristas not particularly keen on the Workers Party chose to realign themselves in defense of democracy and the electoral right of the party to rule, ambivalently coming to its defense after the schisms of June 2013. In 2015 and 2016, right-wing reaction had reached a fever pitch with mass demonstrations selectively charging the party with responsibility for the Operation Carwash Petrobras scandal that had engulfed the entire political system. The right developed its own repertoires of contention with inflatable dolls viciously caricaturing Lula and Rousseff as criminals and appropriating the green and yellow of the Brazilian flag and the national anthem as the prerogative of the right. The vague antipartisanship of 2013 was being transformed into a more polarized and fractured political landscape in which disavowing the Workers Party was increasingly seen less as a credible leftist stance than one that played into the hands of a right wing that wanted to see the left fragmented. Neofanfarristas mobilized in defense of democracy, and, deploying the repertoires of street carnival and neofanfarrismo, brass bands marched together in events they called "Carnivals for Democracy" (Carnavais pela democracia). Once Rousseff was successfully ousted and replaced by Michel Temer, "Fora Temer" (down with Temer) became a rallying call for leftists fighting what they viewed as an illegitimate presidency.

A flashpoint in the establishment of this new defensive leftist position that made common cause with the Workers Party took place early in Temer's presidency when he attempted to abolish the Ministry of Culture by folding it into the Ministry of Education. Founded in 1985 with redemocratization, the initially neoliberal and elitist ministry had been transformed by Workers Party rule, especially with the tenure of Gilberto Gil, to foment cultural production in marginalized communities and in regions outside the privileged Southeast, making it a source of right-wing ire. A swift response to the announced closure came in mass occupations of ministry buildings throughout Brazil in the movement Ocupa MinC. The occupation in Rio de Janeiro was frequented by a wide variety of artists, including performances by Orquestra Voadora and other neofanfarrista bands as well as stars such as Caetano Veloso and Chico Buarque. Orchestral musicians organized under the collective Music for Democracy (Música pela Democracia) played at the occupation, where they adapted an orchestral repertoire to the politicized occasion, such as a widely circulated rendition of "O Fortuna" from Carl Orff's *Carmina Burana* with the sung text of "Fora Temer" (CW.Ch4. Ex8).[14] Juliano Pires played the melody at protests on the trombone, and it soon became a part of neofanfarrismo's repertoires of contention (Martins 2016). The seventy-day occupation succeeded at preventing the Ministry of Culture from closure and demonstrated the left's willingness to collectively push back.

In yet another bleak development for the left, former President Lula, the favorite for the 2018 presidential election, was sentenced to prison on dubious charges of a money laundering scheme. His imprisonment, which lasted from April 7, 2018, to November 8, 2019, was widely viewed as motivated by the right's desire to bar the presidential frontrunner from qualifying for the election. Supporting the emerging Lula Livre (Free Lula) campaign, neofanfarrista Ju Storino, organizer of the feminist collective Todas por Todas, began a daily protest ritual two days after his imprisonment. She played on her trombone the short song chant, "Olê, olê, olê, olá, Lula, Lula," every day at 1 p.m., or 13h in Brazil, because 13 is the voting number for the Workers Party. She also played it daily at 8:30 p.m. during the "Jornal Nacional" news show on Globo, the dominant Brazilian network that broadly supported the impeachment campaign against Rousseff and the demonization of the Workers Party. The "Lula-lá" song is based on the well-known chant originally associated with Spanish bullfighting and popular in sporting events. It has long been associated with Lula since his first presidential campaign in 1989, when the jingle was recorded by MPB stars Chico Buarque, Gilberto Gil, and Djavan (CW.Ch4.Ex9).[15] In the tense political moment of 2018, the song became a cry for his freedom and the opposition of the left.

Videos shared of Storino's daily ritual show supportive neighbors singing along and cheering from the streets. Based on her example, other videos appeared on social media of horn players playing the song around Brazil. On June 15, 2018, Lula himself shared a video on his Facebook page of Storino playing from her window, mistakenly calling her a "young trumpeter." Storino wrote on Facebook, "If Lula says I am a trumpeter, who am I to disagree?" On July 28, 2018, Storino opened the Lula Livre festival, held in Lapa, by playing the tune.

FIGURE 4.5
Ju Storino with Lula
at Ato Lula Abraça a
Cultura on December
18, 2019. Courtesy of
Ju Storino.

The festival drew 60,000 people, and Orquestra Voadora played on a program with famous Brazilian musicians. Chico Buarque and Gilberto Gil reprised the famous protest song against the dictatorship's censorship "Cálice" (1973), which had cleverly played on the Portuguese word for "chalice" that also sounds like "shut up" (cale-se). Shortly after Lula's release, Storino was called to play at an event in Circo Voador on December 18, 2019, in which Lula publicly thanked the support of artists. She informed the audience that her instrument was in fact a trombone, which Lula, Gil, Buarque, and Beth Carvalho all signed. Storino no longer uses that trombone, which has become a valuable museum piece, and a documentary was made about her daily protest (figure 4.5, CW.Ch4.Ex10).[16]

Continuing to fight on what increasingly began to seem like vanishing ground, musicians have musically supported public mourning for the political assassination of PSoL councilwoman Marielle Franco in 2018 and helped mobilize the protests against Bolsonaro's candidacy, most notably in the women-led protests #EleNão (Not him). After the first round of the 2018 elections when Bolsonaro's candidacy appeared likely to succeed, acts of violence against the left spiked and my interlocutors described a climate of fear. Even wearing red, the color associated with the Workers Party and the left in general, might result in attack. During a trip I took to Rio de Janeiro in January 2020, protests and brass band participation in them had died down. Neofanfarristas related that under Bolsonaro, whose government has casually threatened retaliation comparable to the dictatorship's tactics, they feared protests could result in intense repression. The pandemic further clamped down on possibilities for instrumental protest, though energies have gathered against Bolsonaro as his position weakened due to his mismanagement of the public health health emergency. Musical mobilization depends not only on clear targets and choices of engagement but also on collective perception of possible success and personal safety. When such moments of possibility arise in the future, I have little doubt that neofanfarrista bands will be creatively manifesting their repertoires on the front lines of protest.

A MOVEMENT TRANSFORMED

Neofanfarrismo emerged from alternative carnival movements that were loosely allied with the city's left and earlier causes such as the redemocratization movement, which was supported by the earlier street carnival revival blocos in the 1980s and '90s. But until the 2010s, a clear political commitment to explicitly allying with leftist social movements was not necessarily a given for a participant in the alternative side of Rio's carnival. True right-wingers were unlikely to be involved, but the debate until 2013 was generally between those who thought it important to use neofanfarrismo's instrumental capacities to support left-wing causes and those who preferred to be inclusive by maintaining an "apolitical" stance. With the extreme polarization and imminent sense of threat to the left that emerged by 2016, neofanfarristas grew far less sympathetic to apolitical stances, and neofanfarrismo became a more self-consciously left-wing movement. This shift made neofanfarrismo simultaneously a less inviting space for those without such tendencies but more capable of coherently defining its politics. The consolidation of the movement around activism was made somewhat official in the city's inaugural HONK! RiO Festival of Activist Brass Bands in 2015 (see chapter 6).

In these engagements, neofanfarristas have theorized and acted upon the potentials that instrumental street ensembles can manifest to contest power. Employing both participatory and presentational musical strategies, they creatively and strategically draw on familiar and unfamiliar repertoires to mobilize protesters toward engaging in different kinds of political actions. These modes of musical engagement reflect, in large part, a desire for horizontal and "open" modes of political engagement that are shared by many contemporary leftist social movements around the world, are often based on an idealized Bakhtinian carnival, and form a direct extension of Pires's "principles of carnival" into the political sphere. Participation in protests that support Brazil's radical tradition of insurgent citizenship (Holston 2014) in search of a more genuine democracy forms one of the clearest ways one can see the movement's alternative Whiteness in stark contrast to the country's hegemonic Whiteness. It is in this sense that neofanfarrismo has definitively emerged as a musical social movement.

Even with its increased ideological cohesion, however, the movement's political commitments are still ambivalent and open to debate, paralleling various factions within the broader left. While there are many political disputes within the movement, there is no clear priority given to apolitical festivity over political engagement or vice versa. Instead, repertoires circulate between political and festive scenarios with heightened expression during the yearly carnival and major protest mobilizations.

Employing the instrumental force, volume, and mobility of the brass band as a "tactical performance" of protest, these musicians' activities offer a model of musical protest beyond semantic critique that puts at stake how music enables popular control of city space. In neofanfarrismo, the vocabulary, repertoires, and ethics of carnival have been translated into political action, while political action and thought have also come in turn to permeate street carnival. It is not only the cultural politics of the carnival season, therefore, that is at stake in understanding the politics of carnival. It is how carnival's theories and repertoires are enacted for other political priorities that also reveals its political importance.

FIVE

Diversification

Neofanfarrismo of the Excluded

At 6:00 p.m. three nights a week during my fieldwork, residents of the favela Pereira da Silva in central Rio de Janeiro heard the triadic call of Tom Ashe's trumpet, as the British jazz musician summoned the favela's children to his house. In the free music classes he organizes for the project he calls Favela Brass, founded in 2013, Ashe aims to fill a hole in music education in the poorer parts of the city and build a model of social inclusion for children of the favelas, areas of the city renowned for their poverty, violence, and drug trafficking. He organizes the students to play in a brass band format that integrates samba percussion, New Orleans jazz, and a variety of musical traditions from around Brazil and the world. By performing daily in the central Olympic boulevard during the Olympics, the children gained access to the international spotlight that descended upon the city in August 2016, which Ashe hoped would help challenge dominant representations of favelas in the local and global imaginaries (CW.Ch5.Ex1).[1]

In early December 2014, Rio's first all-women brass band Damas de Ferro (the Iron Ladies), formed just the year before, was set to play a packed show on the stage of Lapa's popular Bola Preta club, named after the famed brass bloco founded in 1918 (figure 5.1). With neofanfarrismo's traditions of international exchange and hospitality, my wife Claire Haas was invited to play trombone with them during her first visit and later recounted of the experience, "It was one of their biggest shows at the time. We were talking backstage and there was a group hug where someone was saying something to the effect of, 'they said it couldn't be done but here we are and we are doing it'" (interview 2016). By early 2017, the

FIGURE 5.1 Damas de Ferro at Circo Voador on February 19, 2016.
Courtesy of Carol Schavarosk.

band had come a long way from these beginnings, setting off to tour in Brazil and Cuba and later that year to the HONK! festival in Boston (CW.Ch5.Ex2).[2]

Damas de Ferro and Favela Brass are brass projects that in very different ways initiated a process of diversification of neofanfarrismo. In chapter 3, I showed how neofanfarrismo's instrumental activism aims to foster a soundscape of public participation, engendering social inclusion in public space. But I called attention to the limitations of such practices as long as they are primarily enacted by Whiter, predominantly male, middle-class South Zone Cariocas. These newer, critical movements have argued that neofanfarrismo can hardly be an expression of the alternative carnivalesque if it manifests familiar forms of exclusion. They argue that the movement needs not only to include but be led by a more diverse representation of the public. In other words, if Voadora's initial aim at fostering a soundscape of public participation has been an unfinished project, excluded populations have creatively responded with new projects that seek to bring it further into realization.

Of course, gender, class, and racial exclusions by no means represent parallel cases, and the intersectionality of identities makes exclusion different in each case. The historical lack of middle-class women playing brass instruments in Rio de Janeiro is a fundamentally different form of exclusion than that experienced by young girls deprived of musical education in favelas. While these diverse projects that challenge the gender, class, and racial orders of neofanfarrismo are quite distinct, they all form a "neofanfarrismo of the excluded" that widens the possibilities of participation in the movement and contests the "capability deprivation" faced by marginalized groups (Perlman 2010).

Just as the brass blocos emerged as alternatives to the samba schools and neo-fanfarrismo later arose as an alternative to the cultural nationalism of the brass blocos, these newer projects emerged as alternatives to the dominant identities of the movement led by Orquestra Voadora. But the growth of these projects did not take place independently from the movement's structures of privilege. Favela Brass is managed by a British trumpeter who teaches music based in the aesthetics and traditions of Rio's middle-class alternative brass movement, and the largely middle-class and Whiter band Damas de Ferro grew out of Voadora's oficina and initially relied on male mentors for some aspects of musical devel-opment. Rather, they are what Raymond Williams (1977) might call "emergent alternatives" within neofanfarrismo, inextricably connected to and conditioned by the structures of privilege and authority of the larger alternative brass band movement, yet with real power to transform them. Here, I explore these move-ments of the excluded as relational and destabilizing alternatives within the hierarchies of the broader movement.

What kinds of limitations and difficulties have marginalized communities experienced as they take part in a movement that initially emerged as primarily middle class, Whiter, and male? How does a musical social movement change when it diversifies? In this chapter, I examine the all-women's band Damas de Ferro, the feminist bloco Mulheres Rodadas, neofanfarrista events in favelas, and the Favela Brass project. I also explore emergent critiques regarding the repre-sentation of excluded racial and gendered communities in the repertoires of the alternative brass movement that were launched by these diverse new musicians' participation. I argue that processes of genuine inclusion and diversification bring in excluded Others not only at the tolerated margins but also invite them to contest the center.

WOMEN IN NEOFANFARRISMO

Despite its purported equality, freedom, and security, street carnival can present dangerous spaces for anyone, but especially for women, and threats of sexual assault are ever pervasive. Many women recounted that playing an instrument allowed them not only to play a more active role in a bloco, but that this also helped protect them from harassment. In blocos that enclose musicians inside a cord, playing a musical instrument allows women to enter the relatively vetted space of the musicians physically separated from the foliões. Increasing numbers of women have participated as percussionists since the revival of street carnival, but the newspaper *O Dia* reports in "Women throw themselves into carnival" that, "Today, women are in the directorship, in the instrumental sections, in the composer teams, and even in the human *corda*," or the circle of people holding hands to protect musicians, a job that requires strength and physical assertion (Monnerat 2017). This growing musical participation parallels a broader movement of increasingly militant feminism in Brazil. In late 2015, a series of mobilizations known as the "Women's Spring" (Primavera das mulheres) challenged various forms of gender inequality, including the illegality of abortions, economic inequality, domestic violence, and *machishmo* in general. Protesters directed their anger especially at the conservative politician Eduardo Cunha, who would lead the charge to impeach Dilma Rousseff. They would later lead the #EleNão protests against the candidacy of Jair Bolsonaro in 2018.

These women's musical engagements counter long-established normalized gender roles in Brazil, especially those tied to carnival's performativity. In hegemonic Brazilian carnival culture as mediated by samba schools, men learn masculinities primarily through playing instruments, while women learn sexualized femininities through dance.[3] In the international world of brass bands, the engagement of female musicians in a generally male world has also contested gendered notions of performance and genre.[4] Though today the prominence of women playing brass and percussion in the streets of Rio is striking, this is a recent phenomenon. In 2012, when Carol Schavarosk started playing trombone, she reports that there were no female trombonist models. She followed the neofanfarrismo movement in the early 2010s, attending the shows of Orquestra Voadora, Go East, and Songoro Cosongo. She began to participate on percussion, though she had her eye on the trombone, but she points out that she "had never seen a woman playing trombone . . . Still I had the crazy desire to do this and the next year I resolved to learn. I bought one and went to MAM in October of 2012. I got addicted and I have only thought of trombone since then" (interview 2014).

Voadora's open bloco presented a space to start experimenting with the instrument because ostensibly anyone could show up. Schavarosk did not expect to immediately play in Voadora's carnival bloco, but she found her peers encouraging, and she became a familiar character in the bloco. Teaming up with two other female musicians learning saxophone and euphonium, they began to talk of an all-women band in 2013, but there were still very few women playing brass. With the announcement that Voadora would start an oficina to provide a more disciplined space to learn brass instruments and brass band music than that afforded at the MAM, the three enrolled and encountered many other female musicians eager to start participating. The Voadora oficina played the primary role of impetus for the dramatic increase in women learning brass instruments, despite the all-male makeup of the Voadora band. Schavarosk recounts, "When I started it was just me playing trombone. Now there are many women. It transformed in less than a year" (interview 2014). Indeed, during my fieldwork Voadora's oficina and bloco were approximately half female, and while some sections are notably gendered (xekeré being dominated by women), women are present in all sections. Since 2019, the tubist of Voadora's professional once all-male band is a woman who was trained in the band's oficina.

Damas de Ferro: Rio's First All-Female Brass Band

With hopes of creating an all-women brass band, Schavarosk and her friends began floating the name "Damas de Ferro," or the Iron Ladies (though they were worried that an unintentional reference to Margaret Thatcher might turn a few off from the group). Initially with help from male mentors, they started arranging a repertoire similar to many other neofanfarrista bands, mixing global pop music, Afro-Brazilian rhythms, MPB covers, and other genres. Though they were supported by their peers, they also encountered sexism from the beginning. As the band was preparing to play officially in the 2014 carnival, *Jornal do Dia* wrote a story on the band that undermined the seriousness of their endeavor:

> They manage to squeeze free time for Damas de Ferro between time for family and boyfriends. But sometimes there's stress. "My husband complains a lot that I don't have time for anything. I try to have rehearsals on the days of his meetings," recounts the trumpeter (and biologist) Maysa Salles. But they are very enthusiastic. And, even with so many women playing together, they swear that they don't fear an outbreak of collective PMS. "Even with PMS, we are taking it easy, because we have a lot of desire to show off the band," Sabrina, saxophonist and publicist, says enthusiastically. . . . To have just women, the members of Damas de Ferro believe, has another advantage: "when we pass

the hat, just with the girls, we hope that people will give more money," Sabrina says playfully. (Maior 2014)

The band members were understandably vexed by the article. Schavarosk explains, "We had said a lot about musical influence, but there was a moment when we were joking and said a bunch of crap, and he took this crap and made the article about it. He ignored that we had spoken about music. This was the tragic beginning of our band. It was this totally machista article talking about our makeup" (interview 2014). She stresses the need for the band to play well in order to prove itself as a musical ensemble that could be taken seriously on the same level as the predominantly male bands: "I want the band to play well because I don't want people to think, 'oh an all-women band—of course they play badly,' like 'they drive badly'" (interview 2014).

Members were subject to questions of self-presentation that their male counterparts had never had to deal with, such as, should an all-female band attempting to prove female competence perform with a particularly feminine self-presentation? Band members confronted the prejudice that dressing in a feminine way might be perceived as unserious. Schavarosk recounts, "We play out looking beautiful . . . But someone once said to us . . . 'why do even you wear makeup? If I were you, I would play dressed in garbage with messy hair'" (interview 2014). They perceive an all-women band playing in the street as more daring and activist than for other bands because of the real dangers and stereotypes attached to "street women." Creating female-friendly, safe spaces in the streets is an activist action in a city, country, and world they view as profoundly machista.

While an all-male band can easily elide political positions on gender, the demographic makeup of Damas inevitably provoked questions. Like the banned female singing voice in Iran, an all-women brass band is "overdetermined" "as 'political' regardless of . . . intentions" (Hemmasi 2017, 418). Simone Regina, writing of an all-female bloco in media outlet *UOL*, recounts that "many people say that we shouldn't have a bloco without men because that's exclusion. Without men people think it's radical feminism, but without women they think it's natural" (de Almeida 2016). Neofanfarristas have come to recognize that much of the privilege to engage in instrumental performance in popular music is another element of the "patriarchal dividend" (Connell 2009). The formation of Damas, in and of itself, calls attention to the lack of women in music, highlighting how lack of female role models, perception of instrumental music making as unfeminine, and predominance of men and machismo in the music industry undermine the growth of female musicians and deprive them of their capabilities. Damas trumpeter Ana Martins argues that "machismo diminishes the self-esteem of women ... The fact of being a woman playing—this is already feminism, a force. It is a political transformation in the sense of deconstructing the vision of machismo" (interview 2015).

Damas has often played for events specifically related to gender and sexual orientation rights, as well as other leftist causes, and has composed original songs with titles like "Ovulation" (Ovulação, CW.Ch5.Ex3).[5] Schavarosk aims for the band to play a role of "support of woman by woman. All women should support each other, and it doesn't matter what kind of life your female comrade lives. She is also a woman and should be embraced" (interview 2014). Criticizing White, middle-class feminism, she argues that Damas must place itself in support of the liberation of Black and gay women and women's sexual liberty, playing at the Carioca version of Dykes on Bikes and the Slut Walk (Marcha das vadias). Damas prioritizes creating a queer-friendly space, and there are several lesbian and bisexual women in the band as well as a trans woman on tuba.

Damas de Ferro is a stage band that shows through example that an all-female band is capable of occupying performance spaces dominated by men. With international tours and increasingly visible performances in the major venues of the city like Bola Preta and Circo Voador, the band has clearly been successful. Despite Damas' engagements with political causes, especially those related to feminism, I often heard neofanfarristas outside the band criticizing Damas de Ferro, arguing that the band should take a stronger stand on feminism or that it should abandon political causes all together. Most of the band members dismiss such criticism as itself antifeminist because outsiders sought to impose their own visions of the roles an all-female band should play. Haas, who played with band between 2014 and 2016, argues, "feminism is for women ultimately. It's for the liberation of women, and women can liberate themselves in whatever way they want. If what they want is to have a band that can play on big stages for huge crowds that love them, then that is feminism. It's not something for someone else to decide for the band" (interview 2016).

Mulheres Rodadas: A Feminist Bloco for Sexual Freedom

In late 2014, a Brazilian man received attention for uploading a picture onto a right-wing web page of himself with a sign reading "I don't deserve a woman who's been around" (*não mereço mulher rodada*). "Mulher rodada" literally means a "spun woman," and the term is intended to shame sexually promiscuous women. A virtual protest emerged with an internet Tumblr account that showed gifs of women spinning with ironic humorous phrases, including "I've been around but I haven't been with you."

Carioca journalist Renata Rodrigues conceived of a bloco of mulheres rodadas that would challenge machismo through carnival, transforming the subjects of sexual liberty and violence against women into performance art through music, dance, signs, political chants, and fantasias. In contrast to Damas de Ferro, Mulheres Rodadas would assume an explicitly feminist stance, the first brass bloco or band in Rio de Janeiro to do so. They would publicly promote the validity and freedom of women's sexual choices without shame, whether women chose monogamy, polyamory, abstinence, marriage, or anything else. The focus on women's freedom of choice was already a prominent theme in street carnival that year with Comuna que Pariu, a samba bloco allied with the Brazilian Communist Party (PCB), with its annual enredo: "the place of a woman is . . . wherever she wants" (*o lugar da mulher é . . . onde ela quiser*). Due to the effort of Mulheres Rodadas and others, such demands have exploded in street carnival and other festivities.

Not knowing of Damas de Ferro, Rodrigues first contacted another band that grew from Voadora's oficina, Ataque Brasil, and this all-male band pointed her to Damas de Ferro. The two bands joined forces to produce the music for the bloco and promote the cause of the mulheres rodadas. In the tradition of Céu na Terra and Orquestra Voadora, they taught their music freely to those interested in showing up to the bloco. They initially allowed men to participate, but only if they played in drag. Taking place for the first time on Ash Wednesday in 2015 with two thousand foliões, Mulheres Rodadas received international press in its first year from the *Washington Post, New York Times*, and the BBC (British Broadcasting Corporation), with media attention focused on redefining the roles of women in carnival.

On the occasion of the bloco's first parade, the BBC contrasted samba school *passistas* (young dancers) with Mulheres Rodadas, claiming (somewhat falsely) that "the higher profile a woman has in one of Rio's samba schools the scantier the attire. But this year, women are claiming the spotlight for very different reasons, in street carnival parades with feminist mottos" (BBC 2015). In the BBC video, a folião of the bloco can be seen reporting the familiar belief that the street carnival is a free space for criticism as opposed to the regulated spectacles of the samba schools: "Those who don't feel they live up to the beauty standards imposed by the media can come to the street carnival. It's a lot more sincere and

FIGURE 5.2 Hula-Hoopers mocking the idea of being a spun woman on February 10, 2016, at the Bloco das Mulheres Rodadas. Photo by author on February 11, 2016.

allows you to be whoever you want" (BBC 2015, CW.Ch5.Ex4).[6] By seeking to provide a space in which women can be "who they want to be," they foster an oppositional space to promote alternative femininities in carnival in contrast to those modeled by the samba schools (Brunet 2012).

Rodrigues defends the use of the carnival bloco as an instrument of critique through drawing on the satirical traditions of carnival: "Carnival is a good opportunity to subvert lots of things. There is a lot of serious stuff in this theme, but the path we choose is to make fun and show that the idea of categorizing a woman is passé and the basis for a joke" (Villela 2016). With images and fantasias of Frida Kahlo, Rosie the Riveter, and other famous feminists, they use the repertoires of carnival to make clear what is at stake. The bloco has especially featured songs playing with the idea of the circle or spinning, such as the axé song "A roda" (The circle) by Sarajane (1987), and sexual liberty, including "Eu também quero beijar" (I also want to kiss) by Cidade Negra (1999). For women who did not want to participate as musicians, Hula-Hoop (*bambolê*) dance choreography provided another opportunity to play with the theme of spinning (figure 5.2). Adopting a song from the Women's Spring based on Caetano Veloso's

"A luz de tieta" (1998), they sang against Eduardo Cunha, the speaker of Brazil's lower house of congress who was seeking to further criminalize abortion, "Eta eta eta eta, Eduardo Cunha wants to control my cunt."

In the first year, the bloco was recognized by UN Women for its denunciations of prejudice and promotion of women's' rights (ONU Mulheres 2015). Soon after, in 2016 after the coup against President Dilma Rousseff, the neofanfarrismo movement satirized hegemonic gendered identities through musicians' participation in the online campaign that satirized President Michel Temer's wife. The right-wing *Veja* magazine praised Marcela Temer as "beautiful, demure, and of the home" (*bela, recatada, e do lar*) in contrast to Rousseff, whose "managerial style" they viewed as unbecoming of a woman. Mulheres Rodadas members and other neofanfarristas posted carnival pictures of themselves with the hashtag #belarecatadaedolar with men in drag and women drinking in the streets and playing brass instruments, criticizing the normative "gender order" of the new regime (Connell 2009). They mocked the moral panic about what the right called the left's "gender ideology" (*ideologia de gênero*), which they feared would subvert traditional conceptions of gender.

Mulheres Rodadas has since strongly taken up the themes of sexual assault and consent. They used the bloco's public visibility to educate foliões and promote the sexuality of carnival only in its freely consensual forms. They have given voice to the "Não É Não" campaign (No means no), and in 2020 they paid homage to the popular feminist performance of the 2019–20 Chilean protests, "A Rapist in Your Path" (*Un violador en tu camino*), chanting the refrain in Portuguese, "It wasn't my fault, nor where I was, nor how I was dressed." They were involved in the formation of the "Atenta e Forte, Comissão de Mulheres Contra a Violência no Carnaval" (Attentive and Strong, Commission of Women Against Violence in Carnival). The commission produced a manifesto against assault during carnival that has been disseminated and publicly read by blocos in Rio, São Paulo, and Brasília. Mulheres Rodadas has also brought their ensemble to musically mobilize feminist protests, especially the #EleNão protests in 2018, organized by women nationwide against the prospect of Bolsonaro's presidency. In these ways, beyond musical education, the bloco has also focused explicitly on what Rodrigues calls the "political formation" of the participants, promoting public conversations and debates on topics of gender inequality and resistance as well as meeting with political organizations, candidates, and leaders.

Some within the brass movement initially critiqued the bloco's methods of portraying its feminist causes. They were critical that Mulheres Rodadas allowed the participation of males who have even occupied musical leadership roles. While men defend their participation through dressing in drag, others point out that doing so is a common carnival practice, one that has been increasingly critiqued as gender appropriation, as discussed in the final section of this chapter. Over the years, male leadership in Mulheres Rodadas was eliminated as the bloco sought out professional female musicians from the worlds of samba and choro for these roles. The bloco has been the only women-led neofanfarrista group to hold regular oficinas to prepare female musicians to play with them.

Though disagreements regarding the most effective methods of challenging patriarchy have emerged and fostered new debates, Carioca women have certainly been engaging in the neofanfarrismo movement in ways that have asserted the musical and leadership capacities of women. Since my fieldwork, the ranks of female musicians has continued to expand and new all-women bands have furthered the cause, such as Calcinhas Bélicas (Warrior Panties) and Bloconcé, which plays exclusively Beyoncé covers. Ju Storino, who musically supported the Lula Livre campaign (chapter 4) and organizes of the nonprofit Todas por Todas (All Women for All Women), has in recent years opened Orquestra Voadora's bloco with a demand for a free, accessible carnival for women and a warning that the bloco "does not tolerate sexual assault." Often in direct engagement with questions relating to women's rights, women have used brass to amplify their voices regarding issues that directly affect them and women everywhere.

NEOFANFARRISMO IN FAVELAS

Neofanfarristas are far from unaware of the enormous class, racial, and geographical gulfs that separate them from favelados, Cariocas who live in one of Rio de Janeiro's one thousand favelas. Seeing the city from above is to behold a patchwork of modern apartment buildings interspersed with hills (morros) rising above the richer flatlands and covered by clusters of the dilapidated red brick buildings of favelas. While favelas are traditionally situated on the dramatic hills that rise around Rio, these poorer communities exist in the flatlands of the peripheries as well, scattered around the Center, South, and West zones of the city. Janice Perlman suggests that the oppression of favelados has long been justified by what she calls the "myth of marginality"—that they are "outside the system," violently preying on the happiness and well-being of the "moral" middle classes, thus "justifying" their own exclusion. She argues that the myth of marginality contributes to self-blame, senses of moral failure, the creation of scapegoats, and divisions between poor people, making solidarity and resistance extremely difficult. Children in Rio's favelas are from a young age labeled as unworthy, dangerous, and at risk of falling into drug trafficking and violence.[7]

As expectant host of the 2014 World Cup and 2016 Olympics, Rio de Janeiro inaugurated a massive campaign in 2008 to wrest control from the drug gangs with "pacification" police unit occupations (UPP), which have been extraordinarily violent. Suspicion of the UPPs inside the favelas and by many on the left is high, while the right has largely celebrated the forceful control imposed by the state. Many of my interlocutors spoke of a perpetual civil war in Rio, referring to a "divided city" (*cidade partida*) and likening the situation to apartheid. Some favelas that have become safer for some have been gentrified by the lower middle classes, as well as by hippies, hipsters, and travelers who find the rest of the city too expensive.

Outside of Favela Brass, no neofanfarrista I have met was raised in a favela, although some chose to live in safer central favelas to cut living costs. Voadora trombonist Márcio Sobrosa speaks of the difficult relationship with favelas that he believes neofanfarristas must engage:

This city isn't just where we live here—in Santa Teresa, Lapa, the South Zone. The city is enormous. Every day poor and Black people die . . . We live in the same city and do nothing. How can we manage to create a bridge with these communities? Orquestra Voadora once went to play in the Maré [favela] . . . We blocked the street and the UPP wanted to pass. The whole community was happy to manifest in a ludic way . . . through playful, theatrical, and beautiful parades that reclaim spaces, not through violent confrontation with the police. How can we empower them to express themselves, manifest, and create visibility? Orquestra Voadora, all the South Zone, no one wants a city like this. We are a single city! (Interview 2015)

Indeed, when neofanfarrista bands play in favelas they often articulate discourses of "empowerment," sometimes in affiliation with social projects, NGOs, and government sponsorship. Seeking to deconstruct the myth of marginality, they consider performances in these spaces to be modes through which alternative ludic relationships can be expressed beyond recourse to familiar scenes of violence by importing an alternative soundscape of public participation.

These endeavors can result in genuinely joyful interclass and interracial experiences for all involved. A child in the Complexo do Alemão favela told me after a performance of the Orquestra Voadora bloco in the favela, for example, that he had heard of Orquestra Voadora but did not believe it was quite real until he saw something so beautiful with his own eyes. But I have also found that these events can be rife with class and racial antagonisms as well as tensions with drug gangs and police alike. A different model of musical engagement with favelados is Favela Brass, a social project brass band in a favela that draws on street carnival and eclectic brass repertoires. In this section, I compare these two forms of musical engagement with excluded favela populations and examine their effects in relation to the movement's larger efforts to build a soundscape of public participation in Rio de Janeiro.

Brass Invasions of Favelas

On December 15, 2015, the Tropa do Afeto (Affect Troupe) theater group, composed of clowns and a brass band organized by neofanfarristas, invaded the favela of Gramacho, a poor community that lives near and even in a gigantic abandoned landfill. The landfill had been a major employer even as the Blacker residents lived in trash, but it had been shut down the year before, ending employment for many. The intent of the musical action was to involve the favela's children that the troupe would encounter in practicing the performative experience of resistance to forces that oppress them. The action would be, according to a leaflet passed out beforehand, a "poetic act made by a collective of people, actors and non-actors, that makes possible, through the nose of the clown, the exercise of horizontal dialogue with the population . . . for the poetic act must involve the population."

After dressing in full clown regalia, we musical clowns began parading in the streets of the favela, inviting children and residents as the parade advanced. We played through the common repertoires—Orquestra Voadora's music, frevo, marchinhas, and funk carioca. We painted children into clowns and invaded bars, social centers, and other community spaces, carnivalizing the favela. We invited people into the streets beckoning through their windows, bringing to my mind DaMatta's statement that, "Ordinarily we should see the street from the house, but at Carnival we observe houses from the street" (1991 [1979], 106). Clowns hugged residents and "ridiculized" them, painting their faces and inviting them to join the impromptu carnival. One child in a wheelchair received a particularly large display of clown attention, as the clowns held hands and started dancing around him, while the band played directly to him (figure 5.3). They shouted to

FIGURE 5.3 Musical clowns playing with a boy seated in a wheelchair.
Photo by author on December 14, 2014.

the gathering crowd, "Everyone, this space is yours," inviting them to act upon the imagination of taking possession of their public spaces.

Midway through the parade, the band brought everyone down to crouch on the ground, and one of the actors in a monkey costume began to sing: "I won't turn myself into a king, because being a king is a lie. I don't want to be a lie. I want to be with the people." After some repetitions, everyone began singing this refrain and we started marching again. Once we arrived in an open space at the end of the favela, the clowns began playing with the children and letting them try instruments, while the brass band led a conga line. One of the clowns, presenting himself as the "captain," abruptly stood up and yelled "This game is over!" The people started to boo, and the monkey character who had earlier sung against being a king jumped on a car and started inciting the people to reject the captain's authority. Careful precautions had been taken to protect the captain as the children rushed toward him, genuinely angry that he had arbitrarily declared the end of this rare carnivalesque moment in the favela. The children helped the monkey character approach the captain and cut off his beard. Then they ripped off the captain's clothes to reveal a man in a diaper, reducing this character of authority to an infant. The people rejoiced at their victory, the band started playing again, and we all marched back to the entrance of the community (CW.Ch5.Ex5).[8]

Brazilian radical theater theorist Augusto Boal famously critiqued "bourgeois theater" as fundamentally oppressive because actors dramatize questions of morality to passive spectators and provide senses of moral completion rather than foundations for action. In his *Theater of the Oppressed* (1979), Boal asserts that theater should transform spectators into "spect-actors" who are actively engaged in shaping theatrical performance and their outcomes. Boal conceives of this process as a manifestation of a process Paulo Freire (1970, 67) calls "conscientization" (*conscientização*), or gaining the critical consciousness necessary to revolt against oppression through dialogic pedagogical practices. This particular action might be seen as an example of what Boal calls "invisible theater," a theatrical enactment in which people do not expect theatrical action and unwittingly become spect-actors in the drama as they take part in its unfolding.

For Boal, "the theater itself is not revolutionary; it is a rehearsal for the revolution" (1979, 122). Like other street and radical theater companies in Brazil, Tropa do Afeto owes some lineage to Boal's ideas. In using music and clowns to involve the unsuspecting children in engaging in a morality play of invisible theater, the troupe sought to engage the children as spect-actors, planting the seeds of revolt through performative experience. With the monkey's song of love for the people and rejection of kings, the children identified with the monkey's populism and ultimately rejected the captain's elitist authoritarianism. When the captain proclaimed the end of carnivalesque playing, the children connected this experience of arbitrary authority to their own lives in a profoundly unequal society. In being allowed to attack the captain and literally disrobe him of his authority, they engaged in a form of revolutionary action toward an authoritarian figure. For saxophonist Michel Moreau, one of the organizers of the action, the music was inseparable from the dramatic action, enabling the children to take part as spect-actors in the event:

> Tropa do Afeto makes a link with the people to strengthen their cultural initiatives. We had thought about music together with the action . . . We thought about certain songs to accompany the dramaturgy. This community that we are visiting has never seen a fanfarra of this style . . . Music really adds to the affective potential of the theater. We conceived the sonorization of the action. (Interview 2015)

In this way, the troupe members position themselves as theatrical and musical facilitators for enabling a conscientization of the favela children.

This event was one of many neofanfarrista engagements in favelas I experienced. While the dramatic action and roles in the Gramacho action were far more elaborate than most favela performances, the general logic was similar: favela residents are racially and economically excluded from mainstream society and are in need of outside empowerment. Neofanfarristas create a peaceful and ludic happening through which favelados can reclaim the spaces of the favela beyond the systems of control of the drug gangs or the UPP. In collaboration with other social projects, neofanfarrista bands can draw visibility and audibility to their causes and work to politicize favelados.

Despite the vocabulary of horizontalism, these forms of instrumental activism are relatively top-down hierarchical engagements in which a cultural vanguard aims to enact the liberation of the oppressed. Freire's and Boal's models rely on facilitators who provide dialogic models for engagement that allow the oppressed to creatively criticize and resist their domination. But these models presume enlightened and benevolent facilitators who act as a dialogical vanguard and propose their own view of cultural action upon the favelados. Such a vertical model of cultural activism does not necessarily originate from the practices, cultures, or leadership of the oppressed. It brings outside models from the Whiter middle classes with implicit assumptions about the validity of certain cultural forms of action over others and the supposed alienation of the working class.

I have also seen class and racial tensions explode at neofanfarrista performances in favelas. At a performance in the Complexo do Alemão favela in early 2016, two young women from the favela interrupted the brass performance, yelling on the microphone to decry the invasion of Whiter people from the South Zone. As more young favelados moved in to seize control of the microphone, it seemed for a while that the entire event would be shut down. At another action in late 2014, the Orquestra Voadora bloco led a massive parade through the Complexo do Alemão favela that accidentally entered into drug gang territory with tables set up openly selling hard drugs in labeled bags. Some Voadora musicians even began buying drugs from the favela vendors.

What happened next was mass confusion, and reports varied regarding what transpired. It was clear to some that we had to leave, and the musicians departed hastily while playing Fela Kuti's "Expensive Shit." Shots may have been heard in the distance from another gang that disapproved of the festivity occurring in this gang's territory. Another report claimed that the UPP police had been called to put a stop to the trade and that the loudness of the bloco had helped police localize where the drugs were being sold. The bloco arrived back to the center of the favela in safety, but it remains unclear what exactly unfolded. Some neofanfarristas defended our presence as having "pacified" an insecure and violent situation. But, like the "itinerant gentrification" explored in chapter 3, the arrival of privileged bodies loudly celebrating in a favela cannot be assumed to guarantee safety. Lack of knowledge of internal dynamics, power structures, and local tensions can exacerbate the cross-class and cross-racial contact that neofanfarristas celebrate (CW.Ch5.Ex6).[9]

The desire to spread art beyond the reach of the Whiter middle classes to those who live in favelas and peripheries is no doubt laudable. These actions represent a rejection of the forces that segregate Rio de Janeiro into a city that is simultaneously one of the most privileged and excluded in the world. They also, however, cross barriers of exclusion and privilege that lay bare tensions at play in Carioca society that are not simply silenced through raucous celebration, and their imported soundscapes can even exacerbate these tensions. Moreover, these engagements are generally one-off, top-down encounters, special events in which neofanfarristas enter a favela, celebrate, and retreat back into their relatively privileged homes. By contrast, what kind of empowerment might be possible in the forging of a local and permanent culture of neofanfarrismo in the favela?

Favela Brass

During the 2016 Olympics, the city administration garnered criticism for constructing walls on the sides of the freeway that connected Rio de Janeiro's international airport to the Center, which obscured the view of favelas from visitors' first impressions of the city. But with Tom Ashe's project Favela Brass playing sixteen performances in sixteen days during the Olympics—with coverage by Globo, the BBC, NBC, the *Guardian*, and *Al-Jazeera*—he hoped that the Olympics would give visibility to a positive manifestation in the favelas. When Favela Brass first performed at the 2016 HONK! RiO in a quite different moment of international visibility, the band would be a unique feature of the festival as the only ensemble to hail from a poor community with Blacker membership.

Ashe, a well-known musician in Rio's alternative brass movement and the jazz and samba scenes, points out that import taxes and lack of local production make brass instruments in Brazil two to three times the cost that they would be in his native England. Subtract the earning power of favela residents, and these prices leave the hope of participating in neofanfarrismo all but impossible. In some favelas and poorer neighborhoods, musical education may come through the samba schools, but they do not teach brass. Otherwise, the dominant musical soundscape consists of the electronic sounds of funk carioca. In positioning his project as a model of social inclusion, Ashe aims to offer solutions about how the myth of marginality might be deconstructed and how the cultural capital gained through the project might lead to economic capital and resources otherwise limited to the middle and upper classes. What social and political work might a brass band of favelado children accomplish to help close the gaps of extreme inequality that plague Rio de Janeiro?

At the beginning of my fieldwork, I lived with Ashe at the project in the Pereira da Silva favela as a volunteer trumpet teacher for three months. Pereira da Silva is a small favela located near the Center between the Santa Teresa and Laranjeiras neighborhoods. Like other hilly favelas, the view of the "marvelous city" from Pereira da Silva is spectacular. This favela had been known in the 1990s as a violent place controlled by drug trafficking, but, as one of the first posts of the UPP, it became a "success model" for pacification. Residents impressed upon me that there was little violence or strife within the favela. They insisted that I was much more likely to get robbed in the streets of the surrounding richer neighborhood of Santa Teresa (which proved, unfortunately, to be true).

Pereira da Silva is the most gentrified favela of Santa Teresa. Like other "safer" favelas in the South Zone, it had become a place where middle-class Whiter bohemians sought low rents near the center of the city—even international students and artists, such as Ashe himself—as the cost of living surged in middle-class neighborhoods. Pereira da Silva gained international visibility in the past twenty years through the Morrinho project ("little hill" or "little favela"). Morrinho is a miniature favela art project made out of the bricks used to build favela homes, representing the conditions of daily life in the favela as well as the aspirations and dreams of residents. Begun as a childhood game in 1998, Morrinho grew into a large-scale structure that attracts tourists to the favela. It has been replicated at the Art Museum of Rio (MAR) and presented at forums and exhibits in Europe as a demonstration of creative response to oppressive circumstances. A brick made for Favela Brass at Morrinho shows that the band has been imaginatively built into this artistic imagining of the community (figure 5.4).

Ashe was drawn to Rio for what he calls its "healthy" live music culture, which he saw as moribund in England. Because of the widespread pervasiveness of live music in the city, he was shocked to witness how little access to formalized

FIGURE 5.4 A brick for Favela Brass at Morrinho in Pereira da Silva.
Photo by author on December 16, 2015.

musical education there was, especially for the poorer and Blacker populations, despite the widespread romanticization of their musicality:

> Music is so central in the culture and the social life, and so it's very surprising that there are real serious holes in the music education system in Rio. And there's a divide—people who have got money to buy instruments and pay for individual lessons learn to play wind instruments. Because of the high cost of instruments and because of the lack of any kind of decent provision of instrumental music lessons in school, it makes it almost impossible for [poor] children to learn wind instruments. (Ashe 2016b)

Ashe taught a workshop in the center of the city that provided free music lessons, but, given the location alone, it was only richer people who took advantage. He concluded that the only efficient way to spread musical education to the favelas was to go directly to them.

Ashe views the lack of musical output from contemporary favelas as a direct result of lack of opportunity. Mangueirinha (Carlos São Vicente), the percussion instructor of Favela Brass, had himself first learned music through a social project in a poorer community. He expresses similar sentiments: "It's important to work with favela children that have few opportunities in real life. Opportunity doesn't arrive very easily. If you look for it, you won't find it" (interview 2014).

Diversification: Neofanfarrismo of the Excluded **189**

Ashe expresses hope that "Favela Brass will be a lesson to show that we need a musical education system in Rio that is gonna cultivate its latent talent. I don't know if people in Rio think kids in favelas are a lost cause. But if you give them lessons they'll kick the door down" (2016a). He uses the band's presence in the soundscape of Rio de Janeiro to make a statement about the "latent talent," or what Perlman calls "capability deprivation," of favela youth. The name "Favela Brass" itself aims to resignify the term favela, often negatively stigmatized and used with derision toward particular places in the city and their residents. If such a band could be organized in such oppressive social circumstances, Ashe argues, favelas cannot be wholly "marginal" (Perlman 2010).

Favela Brass has grown tremendously since its founding in 2013. When I began volunteering at the school in late 2014, the band's repertoire was limited, as was the skill of the few students who were learning to play horns. Ashe was introducing music theory, teaching students to read pitch through solfège shape systems, and using Portuguese mnemonics to teach them to read rhythms. He brought the students to perform at Boitatá rehearsals and experience the professional music world. He invited guitarists and cavaquinho players to lead rodas de samba so that the children would learn Brazilian sambas in a traditional context. A rotating cast of international volunteers from the United States, Europe, and other parts of South America offered private lessons on a variety of instruments. The band started out playing for events in the favela, such as game days during the 2014 World Cup and their own favela carnival parade in 2015. As the band's profile increased, it started playing gigs throughout the city, at private schools, the British consulate, and music festivals. By the time of the Olympics, I was amazed to see that the project had grown to have thirty or so regular students with an eclectic and well-executed repertoire, and it has since grown further and expanded to nearby public schools.

The school does not generally reflect standard gendered divisions reinforced by samba schools. At the time I volunteered there, it was about even between girl and boy musicians, and there was no particular socialized gender division in choosing an instrument. Ashe explains that in the favela, "brass is completely alien, which is good for us. We haven't inherited the idea that boys play trumpet and girls play flute. There's no baggage that way. They're all just picking up trumpets and playing them, and it works absolutely fine" (interview 2014). In this respect, Favela Brass has much in common with the street carnival and neofanfarrismo movement in which female participation on a diversity of musical instruments is far more common than in the normative gender order of the samba schools.

For Ashe, because of their community-building capacities in poor areas, Favela Brass "is a kind of samba school. Samba schools are kind of like British brass bands a hundred years ago. They have a big social function of bringing people together in low-income communities" (interview 2014). The musical aesthetics of Favela Brass, however, resonate with and are largely based on those of neofanfarrismo, a mix of the brass movement's phases of cultural nationalism and internationalist musical eclecticism. Ashe maintains that the movements to revive traditional genres since the 1990s are mostly limited to the Center of the city and the Whiter middle classes that freely circulate in these spaces. His goal is to bring the students of Favela Brass "along with" the traditional music and street carnival revival movements of the rest of the city: "we want to reconnect them just like the rest of the city with traditional samba music, ditto carnival music. They're learning the marchinhas, rather than enredo. Come carnival, they will be a part of traditional street carnival" (interview 2014). Beyond these repertoires, Ashe and the teachers aim to broaden the children's horizons to other repertoires beyond the favela as an "exercise of citizenship." Mangueirinha explains:

> In the favela, samba, funk, *charme*, and soul were born—all the genres of Black music that Black Brazilians introduced to Brazil. But it's good also for the favela to have knowledge of MPB, rock, and classical music because all good music is good to hear . . . They need to know first what is in their own country, living with and respecting others. For this reason, it wouldn't be interesting to focus on just one rhythm . . . If they respect the other rhythms of the other states certainly they are being citizens. (Interview 2014)

As well as directing the Vila Isabel samba school, Mangueirinha is the percussion leader of Cordão do Boitatá, the brass bloco that launched the alternative brass movement and its initial aesthetics of diversified cultural nationalism, and his aesthetic goals in Favela Brass resonate with the first stage of the brass movement (chapter 2).

Beyond these engagements with the diversity of Brazilian music, Ashe introduces global musical styles so that students may also be international citizens, engaging with musical eclecticism in ways similar to neofanfarrismo's embrace of cannibalism. A jazz trumpeter, Ashe integrates traditional New Orleans jazz and the second line tradition in the repertoire. Favela Brass builds affinities with New Orleans's rich musical culture also born out of poverty and legacies of slavery, encouraging a transnational dialogue with the larger Afro-diasporic experience of creative responses in oppressive environments. Ashe has transcribed and taught the children modern second line music, and Rebirth standards now resound around Pereira da Silva. He explains that, "One of the revelations was just how much the kids like the second line stuff. They just call it jazz. They prefer to play it. They like samba percussion, but there aren't too many people in Rio doing second line. It's theirs—it's something completely new . . . We wanna move toward where people in Rio can see New Orleans music going on in the streets of Rio" (interview 2017). The logo of Favela Brass even uses the traditional purple, green, and gold colors of New Orleans.

This diversity of styles mixes together in Favela Brass's repertoire, representing a more cannibalistic, eclectic approach that has developed as the project has grown in tandem with neofanfarrismo's increasing musical diversity. In their version of "Chariots of Fire," a song associated with the Olympics, the band goes between a funk carioca beat and a samba rhythm. They might then move to a contemporary second line song, an old Dixieland tune, or a maracatu song, and then fall back into a familiar set of marchinhas. Ashe explains that the mixing of traditions is the long-range goal of Favela Brass:

> It's a big aim of the project to create the conditions where they might be able to come up with new stuff through the combination of the traditions they're learning. New Orleans and Rio both face a similar danger of becoming caricatures of themselves. In Rio, you have this samba school cliché and the roda de sambas that play the same stuff in the same way. In New Orleans, you have traditional jazz which hasn't shifted forward a lot . . . [Favela Brass] is basically mixing swinging acoustic live music traditions. (Interview 2017)

As the Olympics approached, Ashe considered the possibility that Favela Brass could participate. Including Favela Brass in the Olympics would represent a success story for Pereira da Silva and an example to favelas elsewhere, and they set the goal of performing in the opening ceremonies. Ashe wrote on his blog that the opportunity represented an entrepreneurial lesson: "If we did make it, it would teach the children that if you really go for stuff, there's a good chance you will make it" (2016a). Favela Brass could represent an opening of horizons to alternative representations of favelas to the outside world when it descended upon Rio de Janeiro. In the end, Favela Brass did not make it quite to the opening ceremonies—rather they played daily performances mainly in the Olympic Boulevard. The band was, however, featured on BBC prime-time television right before the opening ceremonies (figure 5.5, CW.Ch5.Ex7).[10]

While many cultural projects that aim to uplift the poor involve a strong

FIGURE 5.5 Favela Brass children at Olympic sign. Courtesy of Tom Ashe.

denunciation of poverty and the system that creates and maintains it, Favela Brass does not embrace an explicit discourse of protest or a stringent political critique. Instead, Ashe strategically employs an entrepreneurial discourse that projects a politics of respectability through cultural achievement and valorizes taking advantage of opportunities within an unequal system, activism within a neoliberal reality not framed clearly as activism:

> I wouldn't want to use the school to make a political point ever. It's about giving kids opportunities to play music. The only political statement that I would want to make is just to show that if you give kids an opportunity in a place like this, it's worth doing because it gives good result. I suppose it's activism in the sense that it's a direct action in trying to help within a context of a broad failure to provide educational opportunities for the kids, so I think we are intervening in that sense. If someone sees a video of our kids playing traditional Brazilian carnival music well in the center of Rio, that's gonna make a few people think, "why isn't there more of this?" It's more of an implicit statement. (Interview 2014)

All of the positive contributions of Favela Brass notwithstanding, like neofanfarrismo's occupations of public space, the project could also be viewed as part of the gentrification of the Pereira da Silva favela. Ashe is part of a class of local and international bohemian outsiders who have taken up cheap residence in the favela and facilitate other outsiders, like me, to live there. In the ways that he seeks to extend a middle-class movement into the favela and bring the children "along with it," Favela Brass could be seen as an imposition of Whiter middle-class value regimes and practices. The hierarchy of the organization's structure, run by a White, middle-class gringo from Britain, means that the representation and narration of poverty and opportunity are primarily controlled by an outsider. What would such a project look like if it were primarily directed by musicians from the favela, such as Grupo Cultural Afro-Reggae, an NGO founded in the Vigário Geral favela by favelados themselves with the goal of providing musical education to build self-esteem? How might the reception of the project and its possibilities for middle-class visibility change if the means of representation were more similar to that of the Morrinho project? How would Carioca middle classes respond to a brass band project that was more intent on engaging with the dominant sounds of the favela itself rather than facilitating connection to outside repertoires and spaces?

These questions in no way discount the laudable work that Favela Brass does. Providing free musical education and aspiring to use musical opportunities to gain access to social betterment are fundamentally honorable actions. This musical intervention may well lead to the production of professional musicians, people from the favela with stronger access to the rest of the city, and a proliferation of similar projects in other favelas and poorer spaces. In contrast to the one-off musical engagements of neofanfarrismo in favelas, Favela Brass represents a long-term musical engagement with developing the musical skills of favela children that helps them become active creators and performers of music.

HOMAGE OR STEREOTYPE?

In the Boi Tolo bloco during the Official Opening of Unofficial Carnival in 2017, musicians launched into the opening major arpeggio of "Mulata bossa nova," then perhaps the most overplayed marchinha in all of Rio de Janeiro. A subgroup of neofanfarrista women had begun refusing to play certain songs that they deemed offensive. On this day the majority of the musicians refused to play the song, provoking the ire of the male musicians who had called it. "Mulata bossa nova" recounts the story of Vera Lúcia Couto, who was the first Black woman to be a contestant for Miss Brazil. Despite the progressive content of the story, female neofanfarristas criticized the marchinha on the grounds that the term *mulata* was racist and associated with the oversexualization of Black and mixed-race women. They cited the possible etymological derivation of the word from "mula/o," or mule, emphasizing that the term no longer had a place in contemporary vocabulary on race relations. In many brass blocos in the 2017 carnival, "Mulata bossa nova" was nowhere to be heard.

Controversy exploded at the beginning of 2017 regarding the representation in marchinhas of excluded Others through "politically incorrect" lyrics and stereotypical treatments of Afro-descendant, Indigenous, and LGBTQ communities. Carnival in Rio de Janeiro since the 1930s has largely celebrated the supposedly positive valuation of Afro-descendant culture despite the maintenance of extreme race-based inequality, a paradox commonly known as the "myth of racial democracy." The notion that cultural appropriation could even be a sensible critique in a "racial democracy" where marginalized cultures are viewed as part of the collective national culture was for many neofanfarristas and Cariocas a novel one.

These activist musicians rejected the notion that the right to cultural representation of all Brazilians was not actually the right of *all* Brazilians—the idea that being in a largely mixed-race country made its diverse, expressive resources "fair game." They critiqued the view that carnival is a libertarian space in which "you can do anything" (*tudo pode*), and they proposed an alternative carnivalesque ethic in which the resistance of oppressed peoples that carnival celebrates needed to be taken seriously and not transformed into a joke. While racial democracy has been widely critiqued as a myth, few have asked how the paradigm creates radically different theoretical territory for the question of cultural appropriation than in more explicitly racist environments.

At stake in the controversy has been the question, what is the difference between respectful homages and negative, essentialized stereotypes in songs about and carnival costumes of excluded Others? What emerged as a debate on social media made its way into local media, forcing other blocos to question or defend their practices, and even into the international media. The *Washington Post* would report: "Many of the most beloved Carnaval songs were written in the 1930s and '40s and use language that might now be considered controversial at best—and racist at worst . . . This year, a cluster of Carnaval parade groups chose to exclude the mulata song and other anthems from their repertoires" (Sims 2017). Importantly, it was women who pressured the musicians to stop playing certain songs and forced the debate. Trombonist Raquel Lima, in the activist media collective *Ninja*, reported, "We women are learning that we have force! Mess with one woman and you've messed with all women. It doesn't matter if three guys are playing a machista song. We will come and change the tune. We were silenced for years" (2017).

This chapter has examined how excluded populations have taken part in neo-fanfarrismo, and this section explores the effects such engagements have had on some of the movement's expressive practices. Aligning their own experiences of exclusion in solidarity with those of other marginalized groups through inter-sectional analyses, female neofanfarristas have sought to reframe the acceptable repertoires of street carnival. They forced neofanfarristas and others to confront their assumptions that they are not racist, sexist, or homophobic simply because of their good intentions, a defensive mode that serves to preserve privilege akin to what Robin DiAngelo calls "white fragility" (2018). They pushed them to engage the possibility their cultural practices might play a role in maintaining and exacerbating structural inequalities and violence. Like Sarah Ahmed's "femi-nist killjoy," they have been willing to create discomfort for the cause of justice and refuse to laugh at inequality (2017). While I too found some practices and songs offensive, I recognize that some intercultural engagements may indeed be progressive and that some defenders of these now controversial songs and practices genuinely feel that they are respecting and honoring excluded cultures by seeking to give them voice in carnival.[11]

By 2017, neofanfarrismo had become an internationalist movement with frequent visitors from throughout the West. The first time that leftist American and European visitors to Rio's brass blocos witness the traditional performative practices of the marchinha "Índio quer apito" (Indian wants whistle), their reac-tions generally range from offended to horrified. During every other B section, musicians and foliões crouch down on the ground. As the drums begin marking every eighth note to heighten the drama of the moment, musicians and foliões begin screaming with their hands waving in front of their mouths in imitation of the stereotypical "Indian call" of Wild West movies[12] present in early dramatiza-tions of the song (CW.Ch5.Ex8).[13] At the end of the section, the musicians and foliões jump up on cue to play and sing the song through again. This "Indian call" happens multiple times every time the song is played, which in a bloco like Boi Tolo might be at least once per hour, as the song is one of the most popular marchinhas in Rio (CW.Ch5.Ex9).[14] It initially seemed to me that my Brazilian activist musician friends were engaging in a mass action of stereotyped and es-sentializing behavior, a performance of collective racism. What was it that I was not understanding such that these politically engaged Brazilians perceived this practice as completely acceptable?

According to Pedro Pamplona, co-founder of Cordão do Boitatá, the song's lyrics memorialize the visit of the first lady of Brazil, wife of President Kubitschek (1956–61), to an indigenous community. She had brought various gifts to the native leaders. When she attempted to put a necklace around the chief, he stood up and rose above her. In her effort to put the necklace around his neck, she let out a fart. In the song, the chief tells her in satirical defiance, "I don't wants necklace, Indian wants whistle," a line immortalized in the marchinha:

Ê, ê, ê, ê, ê,
Indian wants whistle,
If you don't give it,
There will be a fight.
Over there in the banana trees a white woman,
Brought to Indian strange necklace.
Indian saw most beautiful present.
I don't wants necklace!
Indian wants whistle!

In another possible parallel to North American stereotypes of indigeneity, the melody of the song is based on a minor pentatonic scale and uses a melodic profile uncannily similar to the Atlanta Braves' "Tomahawk Chop." Beyond the melodic cliché, the lyrics themselves primitivize the "native" speaker as a kind of "noble savage." The lack of articles and incorrect grammar in my translation are approximations of the original Portuguese lyrics and imitate a "pidgin" Portuguese used to represent "natives" who have not mastered the colonial language. Indeed, Marchinhas are famously politically incorrect, as journalist Ruy Castro observes:

Nothing could be less politically correct than the marchinhas. Their lyrics were "offensive" to any group you could imagine: blacks, Indians, homosexuals, fat people, bald people, stammerers, adulterers, ugly women, husbands in general, bosses, civil servants—for every one of these types, several crushing marchinhas were composed. But they were so funny or absurd that, incredibly, no one seemed to take offence. (2004, 88)

Neofanfarristas too seemed not much worried about these questions during my original fieldwork from 2014 to 2016. Many interpreted "Índio quer apito" as a song of defiance to the neocolonial system in which an Indigenous leader mocked a symbol of White power and rejected her propitiating gifts. They viewed the performance of the songs as a gesture of solidarity with indigenous people, while others understood the performance and interpretation of various Others as an inherent aspect of carnival to "turn the world upside down." Most musicians perceived my pushing on the question of the ethics of representing exotic Others as generally annoying (*chato*) and an imposition of my American binary racial thinking on Brazil's complex map of racial identification. A trombonist summarized the ambivalent feelings many neofanfarristas expressed:

> Here you can make this [Indian call] gesture. There are so few Indians—there is no one to complain about this . . . Carnival marchinhas have a ton of prejudices. There's homophobia—"A cabeleira do Zezé" implies that you can't be gay. But it's to play with the homosexuality of carnival . . . There *are* heavy things in the lyrics. We *are* preoccupied with these questions. We are not alienated people. We have political consciousness of rights and minorities, with affinities for differences. Even still, we play these songs. You can only understand it like this: If you stop playing all the songs, there won't be any songs. In carnival, you can do anything. (Anonymous interview 2014)

Claire Haas's comment expressed my and other foreigners' confusion at the refusal of a supposedly "activist" movement to engage with identity politics:

> While it doesn't surprise me to see playboyzinhos with Indian feathers, it does surprise me to see in the ranks of neofanfarrismo, people with some real politics, taking on the identities of people who are more oppressed than them and not questioning it . . . If you want to honor and respect indigenous people, there are ways of doing it that don't perpetuate stereotypes about them. (Interview 2016)

In the debate that raged over social media in 2017, many Brazilian musicians did come to express opinions similar to Haas's claiming that the stereotyped gesture was offensive. One woman on social media claimed, "'Índio'. . . contributes to the alienation of the white folião who dances without trying to engage more profound questions. . . . It's making fun and nothing more . . . Given that many feel offended, why the necessity to reproduce [all this]?"[15] But others argued that without this song, there would be no consciousness of native peoples in Rio's carnival repertoires and native peoples would lose their "representivity." For them, the essence of carnival is liberty of expression on which this debate infringed. Citing Caetano Veloso's "É proibido proibir" (It's prohibited to prohibit, from 1968), they claimed that such political correctness was anathema to the spirit of carnival and used the hashtag #RIPcarnaval.

The marchinha "Cabeleira do Zezé" (1964), by João Roberto Kelly, came under fire as inciting violence against homosexuals. The song's narrator wonders if the long hair of a man implies that he is gay, climaxing in the repeated line "cut his hair off" (*corta o cabelo dele*). When Céu na Terra had performed the song with Kelly in a commemoration of the composer's marchinhas before this debate erupted in 2017, only one of the bloco's musicians had worried that its politically incorrect lyrics would cause a scandal. Another of the bloco's musicians had defended to me the song's "liberatory" function, which had allowed people to publicly sing about homosexuality in an era before its wider acceptance. Dismissing the political critiques as what might later be called cancel culture, he relates,

> This song was received fifty years ago as something completely liberatory; these days, the politically correct come knocking on the door saying "no" . . . You must play [brincar] with religiosity . . . We live in crazy times. Before you had more liberty . . . These aren't homophobic criticisms—they are ways of playing with homosexuality, with the possibility of saying "fag" [*viado*], "slut" [*vadia*], or "lesbian" [*sapatão*]. These days you can't say these things. You [must] say "homosexual." (Anonymous interview 2015)

But in the debate on social media that raged in 2017, many pointed out that hetero-cis people "playing" with the idea of violence toward homosexuals was far from innocent play, claiming that the song incited violence. One woman on social media responded to such viewpoints: "We can no longer find it normal to sing 'cut off his hair.' Traditions that kill must end!" Famed stilt walker Raquel Potí has taken to screaming "leave [*deixa*] his hair alone" instead (Guimarães 2020). Kelly's song "Maria sapatão" (Maria the Lesbian), which sings of a woman who is "Maria by day and João by night," was also criticized. Another woman on social media argued, "it's one thing for a gay man to cry 'fag' [viado], but it's another for the macho oppressor who, when he wants to offend his friend, calls him a 'little fag.'"

While there was a range of debate on these two songs considered above, most asserted that the marchinha "Ó teu cabelo" (1932) was irredeemably racist. In this song, the presumably male and White singer of the lyrics exoticizes and fetishes a sexualized mixed-race woman:

Your hair doesn't lie mulata
Because your color is mulata,
But because your color isn't contagious mulata
Mulata I want your love.

You really have a flavor of Brazil.
Your soul is the color of indigo.
Mulata, little mulata, my love
I was named your intervening tenant.[16]

Whoever invented you, my knock-out
Made a consecration.
The moon envying you made an ugly face,
Because mulata you're not from this planet.

A woman on social media described her visceral reaction against the song: "Whenever they play 'Ô teu cabelo' . . . I get extremely uncomfortable and normally my reaction is to stop dancing right away." A Black woman in the social media discussion claimed that because of such songs, "Carnival is a racist environment."

All of these now controversial songs were standard marchinhas in the alternative brass movement during my fieldwork, canonized in the repertoire of Boitatá and Céu na Terra. In response to the critiques that exploded in 2017, some musicians argued they should retire the songs and resurrect some of the many forgotten and inoffensive sambas and marchinhas that are not part of standard repertoire, while others suggested that they begin composing new marchinhas with playful but inoffensive lyrics. Voadora's saxophonist, André Ramos, recorded himself playing a newly composed marchinha and posted it on the Voadora student Facebook page. He invited students to make up their own lyrics and argued that "many people believe that nothing can be questioned in carnival, but we as musicians have to do what's possible to work with these questions. Carnival is political, and positioning and lack of positioning are political acts" (*Ninja* 2016).

Local media coverage showed that while Boitatá, Mulheres Rodadas, and others had pulled "Índio," "Ô teu cabelo," "Maria sapatão," and "Cabeleira do Zezé" from their repertoire, other blocos reacted defensively and charged them with "censoring" carnival, even raising the specter of the military dictatorship. The president of the oldest brass bloco Bola Preta (1918) responded: "We don't consider these marchinhas offensive. Those who composed them didn't have that intention. Carnival is a big play. This polemic isn't going to bring us anywhere and will devalue carnival" (Ramalho 2016). Countering this traditionalist view with reference to Hobsbawm's "invented tradition" (1983), activist and scholar Djamila Ribeiro argues in "Your discourse doesn't lie, racist" (in reference to the line, "Your hair doesn't lie, mulata" in "Ó teu cabelo"),

It's no argument to say that these songs are part of a tradition when all traditions are invented. People don't want to do work to become better people. If the target groups of these marchinhas feel offended, it's time to rethink. To have fun with the derision of Others shouldn't be understood as fun. Times change and people evolve, which is good. Voices of the past must be exactly in the historical time in which they were present. (2017)

The *Washington Post* reported that João Roberto Kelly himself, the author of many marchinhas, even composed a new marchinha lambasting the Mulheres Rodadas and defending his songs:

I want a mulher rodada.
A virgin woman has nothing.

I want a wise woman
Vibrant, awesome
To teach me many lines
To create marchinhas for carnival.

I want to see feminism,
Not as a fad and without passion,
That understands the play
Of my "gay boy" and my "lesbian."
(Xexéo 2017)

The last line refers to his marchinhas "Cabeleira do Zezé" and "Maria sapatão" that were criticized in the controversy. Kelly seems to desire a reappropriation and possession of the mulher rodada, referring to the bloco that had grabbed media attention by asserting female sexual liberty considered above. He seems to ridicule women who are concerned with these issues as "virgins," those who haven't "been around enough" and cannot get his jokes.

While some defendants of these marchinhas claimed they were being censored, reporters acknowledged that it was nearly impossible to truly ban music in carnival because of the spontaneous and chaotic nature of the blocos: "even a previous discussion—and apparent consensus—doesn't mean that a song will be taken out of the repertoire, because of the very structure of the blocos, where each person arrives with their instrument and ends up altering the program on the spot" (de Almeida 2016). During a visit in 2020, I found that "Ó teu cabelo" had mostly disappeared but that the other songs mentioned here had fallen out of favor but were still played at times.

The debate sparked in 2017 went beyond lyrics to the question of fantasias. Some neofanfarristas began to take issue with costumes that stereotyped traditionally excluded Others, especially dressing as native peoples, wearing Afros, sporting Blackface, dressing as medieval Arabic characters, cross-dressing, and dressing as a *nega maluca* ("crazy Black woman," a character associated with minstrelsy [Bishop-Sanchez 2016, 58]). For many carnival participants, the very questionability of these practices was shocking. One woman on social media, evoking "racial democracy" justifications, asked, "But isn't carnival the time for people to play? For people to be what they always wanted to be? Can a person not dream about being Indian? Being Black? Being White? Being Arab? Because here in Brazil no one is pure blooded."

Orquestra Voadora's bloco has a variety of theme days for rehearsals, and one of them is devoted to the celebration of native peoples in which the entire bloco dresses in "native" fantasias. While some may use these fantasias for only their ludic potential, others use them to launch critiques. One Whiter woman dressed as an Índia criticized Brazilian colonialism, wearing the Brazilian flag as a cape with "Return to the Indians and Ask for Forgiveness" written in place of "Order and Progress." Despite these expressions of solidarity, some native Brazilians have repeatedly argued that masking as Indian is a racist caricature, not a fantasia, with the internet campaign #Índionãoéfantasia. By contrast, in 2020, Whiter actress Alessandra Negrini was under threat of being *canceleda*, in reference to "cancel culture," for dressing as an Indigenous Brazilian in a carnival bloco accompanied by Indigenous leaders in explicit solidarity with them. Because the intent was political, her defendants, including Indigenous commentators, argued the act could not be considered cultural appropriation. No clear best practices have reached consensus in the neofanfarrismo community, but the fact of the controversy is a notable departure from the previously libertarian ambience.

The neofanfarrista band Black Clube has also been subject to critique regarding racial appropriation, as a Whiter band playing "Black music." Until 2016, the band's mascot was a *bléque pau* ("Black power") image of a stoned-looking Black man with an Afro, and band members often wore fake Afros in performance (figure 5.6). Due to a series of public critiques, the band did eventually change the mascot, but some of the band members I interviewed were indignant about the controversy. One of them reflects, referencing the homage argument,

> I do this with reverence and reference . . . When something is done with respect and the intention of lending homage, this kind of thinking doesn't make sense. We want to create a world in which things increasingly mix. The more we can surpass certain barriers I think the more people will do things together . . . We don't do this to be cool or usurp anything from anyone. We do it because we like this music, because we have idols in this music. If you are going to say that it's not legitimate for me to practice capoeira, of course it is. I chose this for myself. I chose that culture as my culture . . . Here in Brazil we have this relation with Black music. Are we going to end up just playing White music? (Anonymous interview 2015)

FIGURE 5.6 Standard showing former mascot of Black Clube.
Photo by author on February 9, 2016.

Diversification: Neofanfarrismo of the Excluded **203**

But where is line between homage and stereotype? The line of thinking cited above can also be used to justify Blackface, which I also witnessed (rarely) in the alternative brass blocos during carnival. Like in the United States, Brazil has a history of White performers ridiculing Black cultural expression through "Blackface," which is generally used in its English term in Portuguese (Herzman 2013; Bishop-Sanchez 2016). While musicians and foliões in the brass movement were debating the acceptability of these practices perhaps for the first time, such criticisms of cultural fantasias by Black and Indigenous authors in Brazil are not new. Djamila Ribeiro's post "Black Woman is not a Carnival Fantasia" rebukes Blackface and argues against the homage hypothesis: "Painting oneself black has no defense; it's offensive . . . we don't need and don't want this kind of 'homage' . . . Respect our humanity" (2015).

In general, discussants were much more likely to question the acceptability of cultural and racial fantasias than another common carnival practice—male-to-female cross-dressing. With its dominant reference being drag rather than minstrelsy, cross-dressing is generally defended as more progressive, an opportunity for a man to deconstruct gendered identities and experiment with the fluidity of gender. Recall that men are permitted to participate and even assume leadership roles in the feminist bloco Mulheres Rodadas if they are willing to cross-dress. Though many men report that dressing in drag allows for experimentation to negotiate and subvert gendered identities, it is common to see apparently machista men (so-called playboyzinhos) in drag without any subversive intention, and Judith Butler argues that "there is no necessary relation between drag and subversion" (1993, 384). Such debates go to the heart of the perennial question of whether carnival practices of inversion effectively subvert established roles and hierarchies or provide a "safety-valve" moment of playing with them that ultimately reinstates their fixity and ridicules the performed Other. Since my initial fieldwork, male-to-female cross-dressing has increasingly been critiqued as gender appropriation of female and trans identities.[17]

Activist Gabriela Monteiro admonishes readers that "if your fantasia need justifications, it probably has problems" (2016). She advises foliões to ask themselves if their fantasia "in some way reinforces stereotypes of groups oppressed by patriarchy/racism/capitalism?" She critiques the belief that cross-dressing is inherently a progressive action in a machista society, and she describes her own lack of clarity regarding the moral complexities of the question, recounting how she had gone to dialogue with transgender people on the subject: "they told me a lot of things—[from the belief] that this behavior reinforces a transphobic fetish to [on the other hand] an emotional testimony that I heard from a girl that the first time that she had an excuse to dress as she wanted was in carnival. The fact that there are diverse opinions doesn't weaken the necessity for discussion—on the contrary."

As Monteiro acknowledges, clear and unambiguous best practices for engaging the subjects of historically excluded categories, their musical genres, and their costumes are elusive and up for debate, and the line between homage and stereotype is hazy. Brazil is an extremely mixed country, and the cross-cultural, cross-racial, and cross-gender encounters that may emerge from engagements with alterity may result in progressive race relations and solidarities. But, as Monteiro argues, if these repertoires and practices are approached without questioning and dialoguing, they easily risk stereotyping, racism, or essentialism. It was, in particular, the lack of debate and reflexivity around these issues that I had found surprising in a self-defined activist movement during my initial fieldwork. It is clear that such work has begun.

CONTESTING THE DEMOGRAPHICS AND REPERTOIRES OF NEOFANFARRISMO

This chapter has explored several submovements within neofanfarrismo that have sought to diversify the movement's demographics and cultural politics beyond its Whiter, middle-class, and male origins, and increase the participation of female, poorer, and Blacker communities. While the diversification of the movement could be understood as a logical extension of the discourse of social inclusion in neofanfarrismo, the addition of these voices has also begun to transform and disrupt the movement, setting off fault lines between participants. Women's strong participation in neofanfarrismo pushed their excluded perspectives into the movement. Some of them aimed to strengthen solidarities with other excluded groups, including Afro-Brazilian, Indigenous, and queer communities. Beyond the development of projects that assert the agency and place of historically excluded communities within the alternative brass community, this participation has initiated the work of self-criticism regarding the status and rights of excluded Others within the movement's own repertoires and expressive practices.

Why did this debate come to the fore in 2017, after marchinhas and fantasias caricaturing the marginalized have long had a place in the alternative brass movement and Brazilian popular culture? I would suggest that the gradual increase of political positioning within the movement since the 2013 protests (chapter 4) has made explicit contestations more possible. The internationalism of the movement has put neofanfarristas in conversation with diverse perspectives on race and gender, such as Black Lives Matter and so-called "cancel culture." And the shift toward a cannibalistic approach to repertoires has undermined the importance of "authenticity" and respect for tradition of the earlier moment of cultural rescue in the brass movement (chapter 2).

More broadly, over the 2010s consensus politics collapsed in Brazil, making national myths more open to question. 2017 was the first carnival after the impeachment against Rousseff installed right-wing president Temer with an all-male, all-White cabinet, eventually leading to the more explicit racism of Bolsonaro. As avenues to political power became foreclosed to the left, perhaps we can see this preoccupation as a shift to exercising cultural power instead. Moreover, if racial democracy has been a hegemonic discourse used to pacify the masses, but if the hegemonic powers have come to embrace explicit White supremacy instead, perhaps these musicians are responding to a collapse of racial democracy itself as an official discourse. In critiquing cultural appropriation, they are also contending with a growing awareness of their movement's own predominant Whiteness, a category that is rather nonsensical in a supposed racial democracy. Instead, they offer an alternative Whiteness in Brazil, one that seeks to be in true solidarity with the marginalized by not presuming a right to identities that are not their own.

Since my fieldwork, this focus on inclusion of marginalized communities has continued apace. Orquestra Voadora has recently begun, for example, to orient its oficina and bloco to be more structurally accessible to people with disabilities (see Snyder 2022). Creating a group formed by participants, band members, and professionals dedicated to accessibility, Voadora launched a program sponsored by the National Arts Foundation (FUNARTE) in alliance with a larger project called "Acessibilifolia," a neologism bringing together the words for "accessibility" and "revelry." In the video episodes about the program posted by the band, "Inclusion and Revelry" (*Inclusão e folia*), Voadora saxophonist and project director André Ramos recounts how the bloco and oficina always had people with disabilities taking part. But in 2018, the band began to consider how to specifically create accessible pedagogies and spaces in rehearsals and performances to remove barriers for participation.

As Camila Alves, one of the participants interviewed in the episodes, notes, street carnival is as inaccessible as the city itself. In street carnival, packed crowds fill urban spaces with crumbling infrastructure rarely designed for people with diverse visual, aural, movement, and cognitive disabilities (CW.Ch5.Ex10).[18] For the 2019 bloco performance, Voadora created a section (*ala de acessibilidade*) specifically designed for people with disabilities with access to their support needs to take part. While this project is still in its early stages, the band has used the time of the pandemic to further develop accessibility strategies. They aim to continue the development of an always more authentically inclusive neofanfarrismo movement, one open to many more excluded communities than when it initially emerged.

SIX

Consolidation

The HONK! RiO Festival
of Activist Brass Bands

In August 2015, San Francisco's Mission Delirium, the brass band I co-founded in 2013, was set to play at midnight for an estimated two thousand people on Praia Vermelha in the South Zone's Urca neighborhood. I had managed to organize a tour for the band to participate in the first HONK! RiO Festival of Activist Brass Bands,[1] and this would be our first show. But police had been called by organizers of a nearby event to prohibit the arrival of unlicensed beer sellers. They told us we could not play without authorization, which would likely not have been granted had it been requested. After hours of negotiation to no avail and threats of arrest, an impatient audience of thousands of people who had neither beer nor music began pleading with us to play in opposition to police orders.

Many members of our American band had played in intense protest situations with the police before, and we decided to play knowing that it could mean a police assault. One of the event organizers caught the audience's attention with the "the people's mic" (*microfone humano*), the use of which had been popularized through the global Occupy movement. He alerted the crowd that we would defy the order but that we should be ready for any police reaction. The first drum hit of our version of the Bollywood classic, "Kise dhoondta hai," hit the crowd like a bottle of champagne coming uncorked as the tense police situation was diffused through exuberant partying. Cariocas began couple dancing in recognition and appreciation of our arrangement of the Brazilian forró "Feira de mangaio" mixed with hip-hop beats (CW.Ch6.Ex1, CW.Ch6.Ex2).[2] After Mission Delirium played, some audience members told us that though the first edition of what would become an annual festival would officially start a week later, this was the best opening an activist brass band festival could hope for. The police would, in the end, violently shut down the event at 6 a.m. by pointing a gun at the head of the bassist of Bagunço in the middle of the band's set that followed Mission Delirium's.

Many of the political tensions of this story presented exactly the kinds of questions around which the HONK! RiO Festival defined its activist discourse. What can the public do in public space, and who has the power and right to order public events? How is police repression of street culture related to the larger governance of this Olympic city? How activist and socially inclusive is it to throw free parties in rich, Whiter neighborhoods like Urca?

For four days later the next week, Rio de Janeiro's streets, plazas, favelas, suburbs, beaches, and nightclubs were filled with brass band music to celebrate the first annual HONK RiO! Festival of Activist Brass Bands. Inspired by Boston's HONK! Festival of Activist Street Bands, which was founded in 2006 and has expanded around the globe, twenty-one brass bands made up of three hundred musicians hailing from Rio, São Paulo, Chile, the United States, and France entertained thousands of music fans. Environmental Encroachment came from Chicago, priding itself at the time for having traveled to every HONK! festival. Rim Bam Bum hailed from Chile to represent another South American country at the festival (figure 6.1). Almost all of the brass bands and blocos discussed in this book as well as many others have played in the now annual HONK! RiO festival. Under the banner of activism, they have every year since filled the streets with the diverse repertoires of the city's neofanfarrismo movement, as well as new sounds brought by traveling bands, until interrupted by the Covid-19 pandemic. After the first edition of this festival of neofanfarrismo, Globo, in reference to HONK! RiO, asserted that 2015 would be remembered as the year that "carnival never ended" (Carolina Ribeiro 2015). Yet for neofanfarristas, part of HONK!'s purpose was to distinguish neofanfarrismo from its carnival origins. How and why would a movement that emerged from carnival seek to distance itself from the local annual festivity, embrace a transnational movement, and consolidate itself around activism?

The founding of the HONK! RiO festival in 2015 represented a culmination point in the ever-changing transformation of neofanfarrismo. A community that emerged at the turn of the millennium with the revival of brass blocos, initially

FIGURE 6.1 Rim Bam Bum from Santiago, Chile, at HONK! RiO in Praça XV.
Photo by Carolina Galeazzi on August 6, 2015.

prioritizing cultural nationalism and retaking the streets during carnival, had become an internationally oriented and year-long movement self-defined as activist. Since my initial fieldwork, neofanfarrismo has also grown beyond its Carioca origins into a genuinely national movement by taking part in the international HONK! festival movement. After this inaugural festival in Rio, annual HONK! festivals expanded in Brazil to São Paulo (2017), Brasília (2018), Belo Horizonte (2019), and Porto Alegre (2019). Bands hailing from around Brazil, France, the United States, Germany, Argentina, Uruguay, and Costa Rica have since visited Rio to play in the festival and the new festivals in other Brazilian cities.

In this final chapter, I explore the founding of the HONK! RiO festival as a consolidation of this musical social movement. I argue that rather than simply importing the festival from the United States, neofanfarristas have cannibalized it, transforming international models with their unique cultural spin and integrating their local practices of carnival and activism. In turn, they have transformed the global HONK! movement, as Carioca repertoires, organizational forms, and practices have spread around the world through this mobile musical network. Explicitly adopting the language of cannibalization in the festival's origin story, neofanfarristas destabilize center-periphery narratives that portray globalization as the simple adoption of homogenized American practices, similarly to their approaches to diversifying repertoires discussed in chapter 2.

Locally, HONK! RiO represents this musical social movement's entrance into a process of institutionalization with the building of official ideologies, messaging, and events. While HONK! RiO has published no mission statement about what constitutes activism, it has used the festival web pages and social media to promote certain ethical visions and construct a genealogy of the movement.[3] Self-selecting individuals from a variety of bands in the city volunteered to be part of the production team and craft the language and events of the festival. While a certain degree of centralization of the movement has taken place through the festival, horizontalism remains an important value and organizational model in the festival by relying on volunteer labor and open production teams rather than a hierarchical leadership. HONK! RiO has furthered the contentious debate about what constitutes musical activism, putting neofanfarristas in conversation with a broader international community of musicians concerned with the cultural politics of public festivity and musical social movements. But for the vast majority of neofanfarristas, participating in the festival has meant signing on to the established discourses generated by the production team even as they were ostensibly up for debate.[4] Many bands that did not view themselves as activist, for example, would take part anyway.

Noriko Manabe suggests that politicized festivals communicate their politics on a spectrum between "informational" and "experiential" models. In the informational approach, politics are didactic, explicit, and hierarchically communicated, while the experiential festival asserts its politics through its organization, providing "an immersive experience that enables a participant to envision an idealized future" (2015, 264), and has "greater attraction for the unconverted" (290). Compared with informational festivals such as Live Aid, HONK! RiO and the larger HONK! festival circuit are further to the experiential end of her spectrum, as I have portrayed instrumental activism as less concerned with semantic critique than with fomenting critical experiences. As trumpeter Gert Wimmer asserts, "HONK! brings the question of activism to practice. It's not a question of saying 'I am in favor of this or that,' but rather 'I will organize in this way'" (interview 2015). The festival frames itself as a horizontally produced event, open to diverse perspectives and the possibility of being shaped by them. Various "informational" and didactic points of view do, however, enter into the space, and they appear in the official messaging of the festival.

It is in the tension between unity and fragmentation that the festival is dynamically produced. Conflicts between these two models of festival activism go to the heart of the question of how this musical social movement articulates its politics, one that forms a contentious debate at the center of the movement and festival. In the broader HONK! network and in neofanfarrismo, the relative lack of explicit, "informational" positioning has produced deep controversies on just how "activist" the festival and movement are, but organizers fiercely defend the "experiential" model as a nondogmatic enactment of musical activism. In HONK RiO! and the broader HONK! circuit, all the topics considered in this book— the soundscape of public participation, repertoire diversification, instrumental protest, inclusive pedagogies, and demographic diversification—remain topics for dynamic debate and practice at the festivals.

I was fortunate during my fieldwork to be part of the production team of the first HONK! RiO Festival, during which I participated in the discussions where we crafted the discourses and event plans of the festival. Acting at once as a festival organizer, ethnographer, and touring musician, I organized Mission Delirium to tour to Rio, where we recorded our first album, *Mission Delirium: Live in Rio* (2015). The day after the festival, I hosted a bilingual colloquium (*roda de diálogo*) on the discourses and practices of activism in neofanfarrismo and the HONK! festivals, where academics, musicians, and fans debated the very topics of this book. This chapter is focused primarily on my ethnographic engagement with the production of the first edition and our initial conversations regarding what it would mean to hold an international activist street festival in Rio de Janeiro and unite neofanfarrismo around activism. It also draws on my visit to the third edition of the festival in 2017, recent interviews, participation in the transnational festival circuit in the United States since 2012, and the volume I coedited with Reebee Garofalo and Erin Allen, *HONK! A Street Band Renaissance of Music and Activism* (2020), which considers the HONK! movement globally.

THE INTERNATIONALIZATION OF HONK!

In calling the festival HONK! RiO, neofanfarristas positioned themselves within the lineage of an international movement launched in the United States. This was perhaps a surprising move for leftist Latin American movements that are often quite critical of North American influence. The Somerville Second Line Social Aid and Pleasure Society Brass Band, a community band dedicated to New Orleans music, founded the first HONK! Festival of Activist Street Bands in 2006 in the Boston area of Somerville and Cambridge, Massachusetts. HONK! Festivals have since been founded in Seattle (HONK! Fest West), Austin (HONK!TX), Providence (PRONK), New York City (HONK NYC!), and even Wollongong, Australia (HONK! Oz)—with newer related festivals sprouting up in many other cities. As of the pandemic, there were 22 HONK! festivals on four continents, with another being planned in Uganda. Alternative brass band festivals had already been in existence in Europe, especially in France and Italy, such as Montpellier's annual festival or Rome's Sbandata. No alternative brass band festival name or idea, however, has spread around the world like HONK!.

The "About HONK!" page of the website of Boston's festival does not claim itself as an origin but rather as a convergence point of diverse international and activist alternative street music movements, with language that resonates strongly with neofanfarrismo:

> Throughout the country and across the globe, a new type of street band move-ment is emerging . . . reclaiming public space with a sound that is in your face and out of this world . . . these bands draw inspiration from sources as diverse as Klezmer, Balkan and Romani music, Brazilian Samba, Afrobeat and Highlife, Punk, Funk, and Hip Hop, as well as the New Orleans second line tradition, and deliver it with all the passion and spirit of Mardi Gras and Carnival. Acoustic and mobile, these bands play at street level, usually for free, with no stages to elevate them above the crowd and no sound systems or speaker columns to separate performers from participants. These bands don't just play for the people; they play among the people and invite them to join the fun. They are active, activist, and deeply engaged in their communities, at times alongside unions and grassroots groups in outright political protest, or in some form of community-building activity . . . At full power, these bands create an irresistible spectacle of creative movement and sonic self-expression directed at making the world a better place. (HONK! Fest Website)

When I arrived in Rio de Janeiro and found brass bands playing in the streets many of the repertoires I had heard in the alternative brass movement in the United States, HONK!'s vision of a worldwide street band movement seemed prophetic.

Reebee Garofalo—snare player in Somerville Second Line, popular music scholar, and one of the original organizers of the Somerville festival—commented to me during the 2017 HONK RiO! that it felt uncanny to him that "it couldn't help but feel like I had something to do with this festival in a completely foreign country" (interview 2017). Inserting itself into the increasingly transnational HONK! network, Rio's festival is a node in what Garofalo, Allen, and I call, drawing on Deleuze and Guatarri's metaphor of fungal growth (2004 [1980]), a "rhizomatic" movement, "having no one point of origin but rather limitless horizontal points of connection" (2020). In Rio, the American HONK! movement is not viewed as the root of a family tree but as a foundation for horizontal dialogue with diverse street brass movements from around the world, forming a broader and ever more diverse transnational musical social movement. Highlighting the independent evolution of neofanfarrismo before taking up the HONK! label, American trumpeter and former Rio resident Bill Brennan refers to the intersection of the American HONK! movement and neofanfarrismo as a "convergent evolution" (interview 2014, CW.Ch6.Ex3).[5]

Os Siderais Goes to Boston

The original HONK! festival had sought to include international bands since its beginning, reaching out initially to European bands. With the inclusion of Os Siderais at the Boston HONK! in 2013, one of the primary Carioca brass bands involved in the recent momentous June 2013 protests, the original HONK! forged a link with a musical community in Brazil that practiced street culture manifestations the magnitude of which the American founders of HONK! likely had not imagined. The Boston festival organizers found Os Siderais' political activities the right fit for the festival and funded much of the band's tour costs through crowdfunding (CW.Ch6.Ex4).[6]

When I arrived in Rio in 2014, I quickly moved in with Juliano Pires, tubist and trombonist in Os Siderais and Orquestra Voadora and soon-to-be founder of HONK! RiO. He was already living with Bill Brennan, an American trumpet player he had met at HONK! in Boston from the Rude Mechanical Orchestra (RMO), New York's protest brass band founded in 2004. From my housing situation alone, the level of international networking of alternative brass band musicians that had already been achieved in Rio was palpable. I played often with Os Siderais, and the band members related to me the inspiring experience of their tour to HONK! in Boston. Many of the initial planning meetings for HONK! RiO happened at our house.

While neofanfarrismo had already been in a process for several years of searching for new sounds and musical sources, Os Siderais trumpeter Gert Wimmer relates that the trip to Boston was a spark for looking further into new styles:

"HONK! is an opportunity for you to evolve very quickly because you hear the most diverse kinds of music . . . It opened up a bridge of exchange with North American brass bands" (interview 2015). This musical exchange wasn't only from the Americans to the Brazilians. RMO's trumpet player Bill Brennan recounts, for example, the band's hosting of Os Siderais in New York City:

> We invited them and Environmental Encroachment to one of the houses and we swapped some songs. We learned [Os Siderais' original song] "Blues cigano," which the RMO called "Os Siderais Blues" because they didn't want to use the word "cigano," [meaning "gypsy," which they viewed as derogatory]. Juba [Juliano Pires] organized a political action in New York, even though he was there for less than a week, pulling together the two bands for a solidarity action with the Brazilian June 2013 protests. We marched around with a bunch of signs saying that New York stands with Brazil. Juba filmed the whole thing and made a video out of it. (Interview 2014, CW.Ch6.Ex5)[7]

Indeed, in American HONK! festivals, it is now not uncommon to hear neofan-farrista arrangements played by American bands, including "Os Siderais Blues."

Beyond the Boston festival's exceptional musical diversity and hospitable welcoming, Os Siderais was struck by the notion of an activist street music festival. Touring to HONK! in 2013 only months after the June protests that sparked politicization in the neofanfarrismo movement, the band appreciated the open celebration of activism in the context of a festival. Unlike carnival, one did not have to argue about whether HONK! was "alienated" or "engaged," since it presumed engagement in the very title of the festival. Pires explains,

> In HONK!, it's great that they assume a political discourse, because in this world people often believe they don't need to position themselves. People in HONK! assume such a beautiful idea: we can change the world. They took this idea and put it in the name of the festival itself . . . You can't do HONK! without this even if activism is not a word that will explain everything. (Interview 2014)

Though the idea of an activist festival was certainly inspiring for a band that wanted its own musical community to take more activist stances, saxophonist Gabriel Fomm relates,

> The activism [in Boston] is very "light" because of the relative social conditions and power relations. Our tradition in Rio is much more explosive because of

carnival . . . The activism that we saw was almost cute—to support the community gardens, a much lighter street occupation . . . The question of activism in Boston is difficult because it is a superprivileged city in every way. We went to play in the poorest area and it seemed almost upper-middle class compared to Rio. (Interview 2015)

Their critiques notwithstanding, Os Siderais returned to Rio de Janeiro inspired by their experiences at the original HONK! and were committed to organizing a version of the festival in Brazil. Armed with the idea that musicians could collectively produce a festival devoted to activism, they would produce the first HONK! RiO festival less than two years later.

Controversies of Activism in the HONK! Network

Journalist Amelia Mason asserts that "the giant musical block party that is HONK! is a celebration of what is probably the most vibrant incarnation of the protest music tradition in America today" (2017). As opposed to lyrically based protest music, Garofalo suggests that "we might think of HONK! bands as the ground game of progressive music" (forthcoming). Indeed, HONK!'s activist credentials in the United States go far back, representing a consolidation of a network of brass bands with histories of participation in protest beginning in the 1960s, from the Vietnam War to the alter-globalization protests, the anti-Iraq war protests, the Occupy/anti-austerity movements, and Black Lives Matter. Part of the original intention of the first festival in 2006 was to forge a space of connection and networking for bands that defined themselves as in some way political, as the Somerville band had recently musically mobilized to play in the protests against the second Iraq War.

However, the positioning of activism in HONK!, as in neofanfarrismo, has also long been an issue of controversy due to the participation of less clearly activist bands.[8] Despite the festival's explicitly activist connections, the HONK! network also emerged within less politicized, countercultural spaces, including Burning Man, Nevada's large week-long countercultural festival. Bands formed by brass musicians on the "playa" (festival grounds), such as the Burning Band and the Orphan Band, had already been connecting musicians from throughout the United States in one of the world's most famous countercultural spaces. Tracy Johnson of Environmental Encroachment (the Chicago band that attended the first HONK! RiO) explains: "There are certainly a lot of Burners in the HONK!

community. You see the [Burner practices of] leave no trace, radical inclusion, radical self-reliance, decommodification, the barter system. It's one thing to expect gifts, but at HONK! you don't have to ask for anything. Everything is offered. It's like a gift community" (interview 2015). Indeed, I have heard some participants describe HONK! as a mix of band camp, Occupy Wall Street, and Burning Man.

While bands such as the Somerville Second Line band, Vermont's Bread and Puppet Band, San Francisco's Brass Liberation Orchestra (CW.Ch6.Ex6.),[9] and New York's Rude Mechanical Orchestra all prioritize engaging in left-wing protest, such bands have never been the majority at Boston's festival, just as the focus on instrumental protest of Os Siderais and BlocAto has never been the primary focus of neofanfarrismo. As in neofanfarrismo, many bands do not identify with the term activist, and a familiar "engaged/alienated" split animates the community. Some of the bands that more narrowly define instrumental activism around engagement in protest and see their bands as political projects first and foremost view the term "activist" in the festival title as a misnomer at best and an appropriation at worst. They believe that the festival is far from politically destabilizing and has quickly grown to be "merely countercultural," a festive space divorced from political engagement. Festival organizers in Boston have responded to such critiques and have increasingly sought to reframe the activism of the festival toward protest since 2014 by organizing political actions in which the bands touring to the festival participate musically in "days of action." Anually since 2015, they have organized hundreds of musicians to play outside of an ICE (Immigration and Customs Enforcement) immigration detention center for those destined for deportation (Allen 2020, CW.Ch6.Ex7).[10]

Beyond instrumental protest, HONK! in Boston stresses social inclusion and occupation of public space as intrinsic to its activism, aiming to build what I called a "soundscape of public participation" in chapter 3. For Garofalo, a HONK! band is one that is fundamentally an open and democratic project that strategizes to create musical spaces of interaction that are accessible and fulfilling for both the amateur and the professional, a goal common to many of Rio's brass blocos and bands: "At the heart of HONK! practice is the notion that culture—and, in particular, music-making—should be part of everyday life (not a series of specialized, regulated events and not simply a commercial enterprise), and an equally powerful sense that anyone can participate" (2011, 18). While many bands, like Rio's carnival blocos, do strategize to be multilevel projects, the presence of professional bands in the HONK! and neofanfarrismo circuits shows that the high standards of some bands contrast with the participatory ethic so often prized in the movement. American HONK! organizers have created the "School of HONK" in Cambridge, Massachusetts, to bring some of these pedagogical ideas to fruition beyond the festival with a year-round weekly class for learning instruments and eclectic brass repertoires (Leppmann 2020). Not unlike Voadora's oficina, this free, multilevel, and multigenerational class with up to two hundred members is a weekly event in which participants engage in workshops, learn songs, and parade through the city.

HONK! in Boston is a nonprofit event supported by the local community through lodging, food, volunteer labor, and donations. Organizers provide housing to all musicians by working with community members to open up their houses to traveling musicians, what Mike*Antares (2020) calls HONK!'s "hospitality activism" in a time of rising housing costs and commodifying homestays. The festival portrays itself as grassroots and outside of the logic of consumerist, sponsored festivals, though organizers do ambivalently partner with the Oktoberfest sponsored by Harvard Square Business Association, "exactly the kind of commercial event" they had aimed to avoid (Bell 2020, 181). The festival is produced by a volunteer team of musicians, rather than paid agents, who take on the work of organizing it. During HONK!, major open public spaces within Davis and Harvard squares are saturated with unavoidable sounds and images of the festival's free events. The festival's annual "Reclaim the Streets for Bikes, Horns, and Feet Parade" from Somerville to Cambridge intervenes on the public with openly left-wing messages and countercultural art. All the bands parade with activist groups intermixed, including Occupy Boston, Veterans for Peace, and Food Not Bombs.

None of the bands are paid for profit, though they often receive some financial aid from crowdfunding to make the trip, especially for those from afar like Os Siderais. At the Somerville festival, a limited amount of money based on financial support from the city and crowdfunding is available to traveling bands and bands of more marginalized communities such as Black bands from New Orleans, which the Somerville festival have made a point to regularly include given the popularity of their repertoire at HONK!. Other HONK! festivals have fewer resources to pay musicians, even those traveling from afar, and many bands self-fund their trips to HONK! festivals. For a professional performance band like Mission Delirium, this has meant putting gig proceeds mostly into touring rather than paying out individual musicians, which is how the band managed to tour to HONK! RiO. Amateur and multilevel bands that make less money from gigs or do not play profitable gigs at all in favor of protest or community events may depend on their own members' finances, creating inequities and challenges that vary from band to band. Brazilian bands that made international trips earlier in the 2010s often benefitted from state cultural money available during the Workers Party boom times, but these sources have largely dried up since the financial crisis that descended in 2012. In tension therefore with the activist drive to decommodify art is the dependence on a system in which the festival does not fully cover performers' costs and is most available for participation to those with the means to participate in a labor of love, often driving away diverse professionals who expect to be compensated for their art.

Many of the critiques of neofanfarrismo discussed in this book are thus also applicable to HONK! in the United States. Like neofanfarrismo, HONK! is a relatively privileged and Whiter movement that has had limited success in diversifying despite stated goals and good faith attempts, with notable exceptions, such as the consistent presence of Black New Orleans second line bands and Haitian Rara bands from New York at the Boston HONK!. While activism has been a controversy within the original HONK!, subsequent HONK! festivals until Rio de Janeiro chose to skirt the issue all together. As new HONK! Festivals emerged in several other cities—all ongoing festivals that receive many of the same traveling bands—they maintained many of the organizing and aesthetic principles of the Boston festival. All until Rio, however, dropped the "activist" label from the festival, finding that the political framing of the Boston festival was somewhat of a lightning rod and might alienate its public and musicians. Losing this focus on activism, Austin's HONK!TX has gone so far as to consistently invite a New Orleans-themed band from the US military.

By 2019, the founders of HONK!, fearing that an exponentially expanding festival circuit around the globe organized independently in each locale might lose the original vision, published a list of requirements for using the term "HONK!": "HONK!" Festivals should be non-commercial, free of charge, in accessible public space, without amplification and staging, and lacking in corporate sponsorship, but the founders did not include the stipulation of explicitly embracing "activism" (Snyder, Allen, Garofalo 2020). Given this wide diversity of possible interpretations, the choice of neofanfarristas to reinsert the word activist (ativista) into the HONK! RiO festival title represents a marked affinity with a controversial idea within both the Brazilian and American alternative brass communities about instrumental music as an agent of social and political change.

Debating Instrumental Activism at the
First HONK! RiO Festival

As the brass band community recovered from the carnival "hangover" (ressaca) in February 2015, we began to hold preliminary conversations about organizing the first HONK! in Rio de Janeiro. Central questions included how to frame the festival, build an organizing model, raise funds, and publicize. De facto head organizer Juliano Pires had doubts about using the term "activism" because of the lack of unity around it but felt that it was an important frame to position the festival, especially in light of the legacy of the Boston HONK! and the diverse, critical practices of many neofanfarrismo bands. HONK! RiO would be a consolidation of the neofanfarrismo movement with all its diverse strains of influence, including carnival blocos, professional stage bands, and local and transnational protest movements. But the question was, as in Boston's HONK!, how to unite neofanfarrismo around activism when not all the bands viewed themselves as activist?

We established somewhat regular meetings with representatives of the participating local bands to plan the schedule and frame the vision through consensus process. We determined that we would try to obtain city permission to play in all the outdoor locations where bands would play stationary in the streets, but that we would attract more than enough people to hold events without permission. We managed to obtain permission for almost all the public spaces except for the parades, which we reasoned would be mobile and therefore would run less risk of being shut down. Producer Renata Dias obtained authorization from the city by framing HONK! RiO as a profitless event with the "intention to unite the fanfarras and bring important subjects about social problems to the public" (interview 2016).

As we planned the events and language of the festival, our concern was to model it on the format of the Boston HONK! and its discourses of activism, while integrating elements that were unique to the Brazilian history. In the Boston HONK!, the unfolding of events over the festival days had been ritualized over the years, and Rio de Janeiro followed elements of Boston's model and adapted it to its local context. We planned an opening Thursday night in Praça XV near the imperial palace with all twenty-one bands, inaugurated by Mission Delirium (figure 6.2). Friday night featured protest bands in the Gamboa neighborhood, hosted by Prata Preta, with performances by the protest bands BlocAto do Nada and São Paulo's Fanfarra do MAL (*Música, arte e liberação*). An impromptu per-

FIGURE 6.2 Bagunço at opening night of HONK! RiO.
Photo by Carolina Galeazzi on August 6, 2015.

formance of some Mission Delirium members as San Francisco's protest band Brass Liberation Orchestra (which had several overlapping members) provided an international protest band to the mix.

A day of performances on Saturday in different spaces of bohemian Santa Teresa was modeled on the simultaneous performances in the Boston HONK!. "Honkinho" ("Honk" in the Portuguese diminutive), in homage to the Boston HONK!'s "instrument petting zoo," playfully introduced children to instruments. Honkinho has since organized children's bands and provided a stage to Favela Brass. A parade of the bloco Céu na Terra was planned for late Saturday in Santa Teresa to descend to the entertainment center of Lapa. The inclusion of this bloco paid homage to the street carnival movement as the origin point of neofanfarrismo rather than HONK! itself. A massive Sunday parade on Ipanema beach modeled on Boston's parade and featuring all the bands marching along the beach with different community and activist organizations was to close the festival.

In the outdoor shows, three to fifteen brass bands were scheduled to play stationary one after another in free street performances for fans and people from the neighborhood. When these events occurred, they were unavoidable spectacles to passersby with crowds of thousands of people filling the streets. A central concern was to spread these free performances beyond the confines of the more privileged Center and South Zone neighborhoods, to "occupy" the entire city. Free events were also planned in peripheral neighborhoods and cities, as well as favelas, and these initiatives have expanded in subsequent years.

In the run-up to the festival, we invited the bands to describe their involvements in activism, which we would publish on Facebook. Most had played in protests, were involved in education or performance projects in lower-income areas and favelas, or promoted historically marginalized musicians. For many bands, the very fact of playing in the streets was celebrated as activist because it created a noncommodified and accessible soundscape of public participation in music in a privatizing city. But for some bands that were part of the neofanfarrismo community, this request presented a challenge. Bruno de Nicola recounts,

> For the production of HONK!, an encounter of engaged fanfarras, I was responsible for Cinebloco. Juba [Pires] came to ask me to send material about something social that we had done, like play in a favela, for children, in a hospital. Nothing. Cinebloco hasn't done anything of the sort. Playing in the street—maybe three of four times in the beginning to gain a bit of visibility. It's the most mercenary fanfarra. [As a band], we are not preoccupied with society or the street. (Interview 2016)

Though involvement in protest actions was an important legacy for many of the bands that participated in the festival, it was not an active component of the inaugural festival, nor was there any explicit comment on the World Cup and the Olympics. On several occasions when head organizer Pires defended the "activism" of the festival, he said that while some of the bands may not identify with the term "activism," it was the production and organization of the festival itself that was activist. Grounding the framing of activism in a rationalization akin to Manabe's "experiential model," he reflects,

> I saw in Boston also that there were many bands that weren't activist. For me, the question of activism is much more in the process of production and the concept of collective organization, the process of constructing the festival . . . We are producing collective work with many volunteers from the city. (Interview 2015)

In other words, for Pires, the festival's activist credentials rely on organizing outside of the system of capitalist sponsorship on which most festivals depend. Orquestra Voadora's American tuba player Tim Malik points out that the name in Brazilian Portuguese "HONK RiO!" sounds remarkably close to the city's megafestival "Rock in Rio" with the aspirated initial "Rs" in "Rock" and "Rio" and the "ee" following "HONK:" "The play on words of HONK! RiO is perfect. Rock in Rio is totally corporate. So there's definitely a mocking of that" (interview 2015).

At the final festival show on the Arpoador beach, Bagunço's drummer told the audience that HONK! RiO's successful realization showed that "we can do anything." Raising funds on the independent online platform of Kickstarter, we managed to pay for the costs of the festival without contracting sponsorship, which is often perceived as a necessary evil to be able to organize an official bloco in carnival. Creating similar barriers to participation for working musicians as in the American festivals, no musicians received payment except to remunerate costs, but all were housed by community members. Defending these organizational methods as forms of activism, the HONK RiO! website claims,

> Although the lineup of brass bands doesn't consist exclusively of activist or politically-engaged marching bands, the coming together of artists and city residents in order to bring about a better world is something inherent to the process of organizing HONK!. It is organized and carried out by the brass band musicians themselves. And through this process, the principles of human rights, social justice, ecology, and a more active, participatory society come to permeate the entire festival. . . . For this collective undertaking, they involve the local communities and work alongside them to develop the capacity and consciousness for improving the city in a multitude of ways. They demonstrate that every individual is capable of coming together with others to accomplish great, transformative things in the service of a better world. It is a crash course in constructing a society in a way that flies in the face of the paternalistic, "top-down" approaches of governments or businesses and runs counter to the homogenizing logic of a passive, consumption-oriented society. (HONK! RiO 2015)

Like several others critical of this relatively vague activism, Voadora trombonist Marco Serragrande failed to see anything particularly activist about HONK! RiO: "I don't see them raising a flag for any cause. What kind of activism is this? . . . It took me a while to understand the festival as activist. I thought it was a festival of fanfarras and just that" (interview 2015). In the colloquium following the festival, I invited participants to think through the festival's use of the term "activism," what it meant in Rio, and the significance of connecting to the legacy of the Boston HONK! festival. I recounted the contested history of the term "activism" in the HONK! festivals and controversies surrounding it. I asked participants if it would be helpful for HONK RiO! to develop an official definition of activism given this important history and the tendency for it to be vague and contested. Or, is it preferable to leave activism as an open concept that could be determined by participants themselves? No official answer emerged from the discussion, but participants did feel that simply using the word "activist" had a performative function because it inspired people to think about brass bands in relation to their political and social powers and act upon such imaginations. Renata Dias suggests that HONK! RiO "opened the minds of musicians in relation to the question, what is activism? A member of a fanfarra can now ask themselves, in what way is my fanfarra activist? What kind of activism? . . . You make people think . . . Neofanfarristas are starting to think more about 'what can my band do beyond its sound, beyond its musical quality'?" (interview 2016).

These conversations have since evolved. While organizers maintain that the intent of the festival remains activist, the name changed in 2018 from "Festival of Activist Fanfarras" to "Activist Festival of Fanfarras," suggesting that the festival was activist even if not all participants subscribed to the label, and again in 2019 to "Festival of Engaged [engajadas] Fanfarras." Pires explains that "ativista" described a more oppositional politics than was realistically shared in the community, while "engajado" still captured the diverse social and political initiatives of the bands in a less polarizing way. In following years, roda de diálogos have since grown in participation with up to one hundred participants debating diverse topics, from the international politics of street occupation to how to care for fellow musicians struggling with drug addiction and how to increase female participation, as well as sexual assault and structural racism in carnival. In years since, the festival has produced prefestival "ataques" with social movements that publicize the festival and highlight the efforts of leftist social movements (Moreau and Pitrez 2020).

With the deepening of political crises and increased polarization discussed in chatper 4, musicians began to use the platforms of the festival for more explicit, "informational" political positioning, including denunciations of Temer, Crivella, and Bolsonaro. Likewise, American bands have paraded in Rio de Janeiro in homage to Black Lives Matter. In 2017, female neofanfarristas organized participating women to form a "bLoka," a feminization of the word bloco with a leftist "k," which was an exclusively female jam session before the annual parade. The presumption of activism has continued to shape a dynamic debate led by festival participants rather than one defined by an absolute mission statement. For many in the international HONK! movement, the movement's democratic and nondogmatic approach to activism is itself a theoretical contribution to what can be considered musical activism. Pushing back against the critiques that these festivals are not explicitly political enough and essentially arguing for Manabe's experiential model, Boston HONK! organizer Trudi Cohen argues that "to define an activist band in broad terms rather than limited terms benefits us" (Andrews 2017), an approach that resonates with HONK! RiO's.

Cannibalizing HONK!

As Somerville festival organizer Reebee Garofalo mused upon visiting HONK! RiO, "At first I was shocked that they wanted to throw a HONK! festival since Brazil needs another music festival like it needs a hole in the head, but then I understood that it was the activism of our festival that drew them the most" (interview 2017). But "activist" was not the first term proposed for the title of the HONK! RiO festival. Pires had suggested calling it the "HONK! RiO Festival of Cannibalist Brass Bands [Antropofágicas]" in reference to his idea that neofanfarrismo represents an aesthetic and ethical cannibalization of the brass band (see introduction). If this name had prevailed, it would have presented an obscure reference for international bands, but Brazilians would have understood it as celebrating a uniquely Brazilian interpretation of musical eclecticism and countercultural style that neofanfarrismo had come to embrace. While the name did not prevail, in publicity materials for the festival, HONK! RiO explicitly defines itself as a "cannibalization" of the global HONK! network and positions neofanfarrismo as distinct from the local carnival. Through HONK! RiO they aimed to mark neofanfarrismo as an independent movement within the local live music landscape of Rio de Janeiro.

Indeed, with the first edition of HONK! RiO held in August 2015, the polar opposite season of carnival, the festival offered a major public manifestation of a consolidated brass band mobilization outside of the festivities. Before the festival occurred, Carol Schavarosk had hoped that HONK! RiO would "separate fanfarras from carnival. It's still very linked. People playing brass in the street, for those who see it from the outside, it seems like carnival. There must be more distinction between what is a bloco and what is a 'brass band,'" using the English term (interview 2014). For festival volunteer Renata Dias, this goal was certainly met by the festival: "HONK! RiO brought the idea to the foliões that love carnival that fanfarras play more than just marchinhas . . . They already think differently" (interview 2016). When Prata Preta, a brass bloco that primarily plays marchinhas and sambas (chapter 2), was invited to play in the first festival, the bloco rejected the invitation, perceiving the distinction as important: "They invited us to play in HONK! RiO . . . We thought that it wasn't appropriate to play because it had nothing to do with us. We are not a fanfarra. A carnival bloco is different" (Fábio Sarol interview 2015). The concern with separating HONK! from carnival is not only aesthetic but ethical. Though I have shown that many of neofanfarristas' theories of activism have an origin in what Pires calls the "principles of carnival," HONK! RiO is anxious not to be overly "carnivalized" with purely ludic activities and seeks to distinguish itself from carnival through its activist commitments.

Despite all this, HONK! RiO also positions itself within the history of the city's brass bloco revival by inviting "homaged" blocos to play during the festival, pointing to multiple points of origin in a typically rhizomatic fashion. Céu na Terra was invited the first year, Boi Tolo and Prata Preta in the second, and Songoro Cosongo in the third. Since these are open blocos in which anyone can play, these experiences were especially inspiring to international participants who had never experienced the explosive, participatory mobilization of thousands in the streets that occurs in Rio's brass blocos. In the second edition of the festival, HONK! RiO organizers explained the importance of carnival to the movement's origins on social media:

> HONK! RiO is inspired by the movements of fanfarras and street bands from outside Brazil in recent decades, but we also give total reverence and honor to our traditional street carnival, [which is] free, democratic, and spontaneous. Here the HONK! festival happens with our imprint [cara], and it is no accident that many people confuse fanfarras with carnival. A fanfarra is a fanfarra . . . but carnival is ours! Because of this, the 2016 HONK! RiO Festival pays homage to two great Carioca carnivalesque cordões: the Cordão do Boi Tolo and the Cordão do Prata Preta, blocos that mark the history of the city with irreverence, tradition, and clear political positioning: the streets are ours. Let's occupy them! (HONK! RiO Facebook 2016)

This reclaiming of carnival by HONK! RiO indicates a relationship similar to that of the broader neofanfarrismo movement to Brazilian music traditions described in chapter 2, in which the musically eclectic urge does not reject cultural rescue and tradition but rather cannibalizes them and mixes them with other sources. While HONK! RiO represents a culmination in the transformation of the brass bloco revival into an internationally oriented movement, it also turns back to its origins and constructs a genealogy that positions carnival as the origin of it all.

In the years since its founding, HONK! RiO has forged new international partnerships that have influenced Rio's community but have also influenced the larger international HONK! movement. The tour of Austin's Minor Mishap to HONK! RiO for the second edition of the festival in 2016 led to the invitation of Os Siderais to Austin's HONK!TX the following year and other Brazilian bands in years following. Os Siderais toured through New Orleans, diving into second line and traditional jazz scenes, before opening HONK!TX with a workshop on the bloco concept. In the description of the event, an organizer from Minor Mishap describes the rationale:

> One of my favorite things from our trip to Rio de Janeiro was seeing various bands merge into blocos and then parade through the city—all joining in on each other's songs. We're hoping to foster more of this sense of community here in Austin and what better time than during HONK!TX? You are all invited to participate! The Super Band Merge, or bloco, will . . . be chaotic, but we hope it will be glorious chaos rather than frustrating chaos. (Honk!TX Facebook 2017)

Brazilian bands have become common at HONK! festivals in the United States. As more international bands visit the Brazilian festivals, these international influences, repertoire exchanges, intercultural experiments, and practices of activism will only continue to cross-fertilize in the years ahead (CW.Ch6.Ex8).[11] As Environmental Encroachment's trombonist Mike Smith observes, "Brazil already had a HONK! culture that we could bring a few things to. Now they're bringing things to our HONK! culture" (interview 2015).

In 2017, HONK! RiO organizers would launch the free Oficina do HONK in preparation for the "Bloco do HONK" in homage to Boston's School of HONK!. The open ensemble has continued beyond the initial festival as "BLONK." BLONK plays songs from a variety of the local and international bands who have participated in the festival to provide an open bloco for anyone present at the festival to participate whether or not they play in a performing band, paralleling the rise of formalized "pickup" bands at other HONK! festivals (CW.Ch6.Ex9).[12] They pay homage to circulating repertoires of the global HONK! movement and cannibalize them with unique fusions. In the neofanfarrismo community, BLONK is now a not-to-be-missed element of street carnival, as the city's carnival mixes further with the transnational HONK! universe. HONK RiO!, in other words, represents not a movement with a distant, linear origin in the city's carnival. Rather the two events represent a dynamic feedback loop of mutual influence, two heightened manifestations of neofanfarrismo every year.

BLONK, like many other Carioca bands, has also begun travelling to the burgeoning national network of Brazilian HONK! festivals in São Paulo, Brasília, Belo Horizonte, and Porto Alegre. During my initial fieldwork, Carioca bands already traveled to perform in other cities, especially nearby São Paulo and Belo Horizonte, and a few brass bands from other Brazilian cities visited Rio de Janeiro. But while HONK! RiO clearly represented a culmination of transnational affinities, I did not expect that the festival would rapidly provoke the spread of Rio de Janeiro's neofanfarrismo movement to the status of a genuinely national movement, albeit one somewhat regionally limited to the country's Whiter Southeast and South. HONK! has not (yet) taken off in Northeastern or Northern cities, even Brazil's capital of brass, Recife. In contrast to the "modern" Southeast, Northeastern cities have long been positioned as traditional sources of Brazilian culture and are defined by local heritage regimes that are likely to make the process of transnationalization slower. Similarly, although the American brass capital of New Orleans has experienced a similar diversification within an alternative Whiter brass scene comparable to neofanfarrismo (Snyder 2021a), New Orleans has not yet felt the need to throw its own HONK! festival with its already full cultural calendar.

As HONK! in Brazil follows a Southeastern/Southern geographical trajectory, the part of the country most marked by the dominant Whiteness that supported Temer and Bolsonaro, its profile as a movement of middle-class alternative Whiteness becomes even clearer. In a country where festive Blackness has been commodified as authentic heritage, the Whiter cities of the Brazilian Southeast and South that have thrown their own HONK! festivals are those known for their "lack" of public festivity. São Paulo has been known as the "tomb of samba," and Paulistas have also described a narrative of an absent local carnival in their youth, with the festivity being a time to travel to more "authentic" carnivals. São Paulo, Brasília, and Belo Horizonte were the capitals of B-Rock in the 1980s and '90s, more concerned with following international trends than "cannibalizing" rock in the model of Recife's mangue beat. Brasília, the federal capital built in the 1950s, was built in a "modernist" mold that has made it Brazil's most car-based city, known for its lack of public spaces. All of these places have experienced a street carnival "revival" that has integrated revivalist and eclecticist brass movements in ways comparable to and often inspired by Rio de Janeiro. They are places where people without the weight of heritage have embraced the alternative carnivalesque instead, and they are deserving of further research.

The programs of recent HONK! RiO festivals reveal a proliferation of Brazilian touring bands from these other cities. As these bands learned of Rio's festival and began traveling to it, the pattern established in the United States of inspired traveling bands forming their own local festivals has decidedly taken off in Brazil. These developments have created a HONK! festival circuit comparable to the American version with a shared consciousness of being part of a translocal movement. In the nationalization of neofanfarrismo, the Carioca word neofanfarrismo itself has been disseminated around the country, as well as other neofanfarrista vocabularies, such as "cracudagem," "cannibalization," and "ocupar." The bLoka has become a leaderless traveling collective with a standardized repertoire that is present at each Brazilian HONK!, offering an exclusive space for women to participate in music without men. While forging common national repertoires and vocabularies, each of these cities has adapted, or "cannibalized," the festival to its local needs, practices, and urban architectures. Like nearby *gaúcho* Uruguay and Argentina, Brazil's furthest south major city, Porto Alegre, is also one of its Whitest, with 80 percent White, 10 percent Black, and 10 percent mixed. Porto Alegre based the route of its final parade on the city's Museu do Percurso do Negro, a guided walk through the city that spotlights local Afro-Brazilian history. The parade integrated the bands with artists who at particular places along the way recounted stories of Afro-Brazilian history and resistance. HONK!'s anti-dogmatic approach to activism has provided a performative invitation to action, an open format with which new festivals can interpret the label and manifest it on their own terms.

During the pandemic in 2020, Brazilians participated in large numbers in the virtual international event launched by the Somerville festival called HONK!United, a "virtual world rally" that expanded the possibilities for translocal dialogue that had previously occurred only through travel (Snyder, Garofalo, and Allen 2022). Segments from Rio and São Paulo were featured first in the broadcasts organized by Somerville, positioning the Brazilian manifestations as central rather than peripheral to a network that originated in North America (CW.Ch6.Ex10).[13] A bilingual workshop was organized with Brazilians from several cities' HONK! festivals to discuss music and activism in comparison with the scene in the United States. All those around the world who participated in HONK!United are now aware of the participation of the raucous neofanfarrismo movement in the HONK! network without ever traveling to Brazil.

TRANSLATING HONK!
RIO INTO UNIFIED POLITICAL ACTION

While instrumental protest may not have been a primary focus of the first HONK! RiO festival in 2015, the networking and consolidating of the movement around activism had immediate impacts on the movement's ability to organize a protest outside of the festival setting. Many neofanfarrista bands and musicians had increasingly acted as tactical musical support groups for various social movements and protests as political crises grew in the 2010s, but, as I have shown, few issues broadly unite the movement. The possibility of a clampdown on the raucous street culture of Rio de Janeiro, however, is a mobilizing issue by which all neofanfarrista bands feel affected and around which neofanfarristas can be quickly politicized. In preparation for the Olympics, the city mounted a crackdown on unofficial street music and carnival events in 2016. As repression against unpermitted street activity increased that year, neofanfarristas would unite to protest for the right to play in the street, mobilizing the activist discourses promoted in HONK! RiO. This final episode shows the fluidity between various musical, carnivalesque, and activist repertoires of neofanfarrismo enacted in new scenarios, as the musical social movement positioned itself in opposition to Olympic Rio de Janeiro.

The 2016 Official Opening of Unofficial Carnival began on January 3 in Praça XV with the "anarchist" brass bloco Boi Tolo leading a massive unruly parade through the center of Rio de Janeiro to celebrate its tenth anniversary. The parade was open and cordless without clear direction, and I joined the mass of people with my trumpet. As more people arrived, the bloco grew increasingly crowded and began dividing into different sections, with some minibands stopped in the street while others marched off spontaneously in other directions. As our minibloco found its way back to the main crowd, we noticed that a line of riot cops had formed behind the main section of the bloco.

The riot cops arrested an unlicensed beer seller, and a trombonist began playing the Darth Vader "Imperial March" while a tubist faced off with the police (figure 6.3). As we arrived in the Cinelândia square, I watched as more disputes arose between beer sellers and the Municipal Guard police. Then gas bombs, flash bombs, and rubber bullets started to go off, contributing to a near stampede as musicians and foliões dispersed. The celebratory soundscape dissipated into the sounds of explosions and cries, and the massive crowd was withered within minutes. A small group began to regather defiantly, playing Sérgio Sampaio's famous countercultural song, "Eu quero é botar meu bloco na rua" (1972) with foliões singing the titular refrain, "I want to put my bloco in the street," a line that proclaims a will for cultural production unencumbered by the authorities. A diminished Boi Tolo emerged from the smoke of gas bombs meandering toward the Museum of Modern Art, the traditional grounds of Voadora rehearsals (CW.Ch6.Ex11).[14]

Boi Tolo is a famously illegal bloco due to its resistance to the regulations of official blocos (chapter 3), but police attacks on unofficial carnival blocos had been until that point, musicians told me, without precedent. In the preceding year, however, I had seen an uptick in repressive practices, from the prohibition on beer sellers at cracudagem to the police-enforced cancellation of outdoor rehearsals for no apparent legal reason and the episode before the first HONK! RiO discussed at the beginning of this chapter. A consensus in the neofanfarrismo movement emerged that the city administration had chosen this particular occasion to send a message: in this year of the Olympics, unofficial street culture would not be tolerated in the Olympic City.

Neofanfarristas interpreted the attack as one on the precarious beer sellers

FIGURE 6.3 Boi Tolo tubist defiantly plays in front of the municipal guard before police attack on January 3, 2016. Photo courtesy of Alexandre d'Albergaria.

FIGURE 6.4 Police beating folião who plays outside of the enclosed official carnival.
Artwork by Matheus Ribs.

who sold beers other than Ambev-owned Antarctica, the official beer and sponsor of street carnival—a message from the company that threats to its monopoly would not be tolerated. For neofanfarristas, the notion that a private company would use the state to manage a carnival event for its own profit and violently enforce its monopoly was akin to the privatization of street carnival. Heineken, not owned by Ambev and with its red star, would jokingly emerge as the "beer of the resistance." Images and memes were shared on social media that pointed the finger at Antarctica and its attempts to control carnival and repress unofficial events (figure 6.4).

One brass bloco and neofanfarrista band after another published repudiations of the repression on social media. The brass community organized a nonviolent action that would bring together many musicians on January 14. When I arrived in Cinelândia for the action, musicians-turned-protesters were creating banners proclaiming "Carnival is Not a Marketplace" and "In Repudiation of the Daily Violence of the Municipal Guard." The brass band community had organized a New Orleans-influenced "jazz funeral" for Zé Pereira, a traditional personification of carnival (chapter 2), adapting a subversive New Orleans tradition of "mock

FIGURE 6.5 Image of jazz funeral for Zé Pereira.
Photo by author on January 14, 2016.

jazz funerals" that ironically performs the death of an institution or practice (Sakakeeny 2010). "Mourners" brought a coffin with a dead Zé Pereira on a stick and placed it at the base of the stairs of City Hall (figure 6.5). The band began to slowly play the New Orleans jazz funeral standard, "Just a Closer Walk with Thee," while carrying Zé Pereira's coffin around the square. Arriving back at the steps, we then launched into the traditional carnival march of "Zé Pereira," as protesters removed the doll from his grave and made him dance excitedly above the crowd in a ceremony of death and resurrection. We then marched through the Center of the city with the bands' standards, including that of HONK! RiO, and a huge banner against police violence (CW.Ch6.Ex12).[15]

IMPACTS OF MOVEMENT CONSOLIDATION

This final story illustrates many of the workings of the neofanfarrismo movement, its modes of social cohesion, its use of collectively known musical resources in protest, and the ways it has interacted with hegemonic power since the consolidation of the movement around activism through HONK! RiO. First, though the police attacked Boi Tolo, the action triggered a cohesive and collective response of solidarity from representatives of almost the entire brass community, indicating the collective consciousness of a shared movement. Musicians viewed what happened to Boi Tolo, an open bloco in which most had played, to be relevant to all neofanfarristas. Second, a potential response of political protest was already latent within the musical repertoires of contention of the brass musicians when they were attacked. Though this protest was novel in that it articulated a response to the very viability and rights of existence of the brass movement, the experiences of playing in protests provided musicians with ready-made musical tools of response, from playing the "Imperial March" to melodic soccer chants that called the mayor a dictator.

Third, Rio's brass community has such a large, collective, eclectic pool of repertoire on which to draw that an interband musical protest required little training or preparation. The choice to hold a mock jazz funeral with classic jazz funeral songs for Zé Pereira brought together a Black practice from New Orleans, little known beyond the Crescent City, with classic, local music for the iconic figure of Rio's carnival. During the protest action, neofanfarristas collectively played particular songs, from MPB protest classics to satirical marchinhas, to underline the contentious tone of the action, drawing on both national and international repertoires for strategic ends and combining them creatively. Lastly, Boi Tolo's

FIGURE 6.6 March uniting various brass bands and blocos with their standards against police repression of playing in the streets. Photo by author on January 14, 2016.

discourse of occupation of public space and opposition to regulations and city control turned in this moment from a relatively tolerated subcultural movement into an oppositional movement against the city administration. Neofanfarristas believed their soundscapes of public participation were being repressed by the state in favor of private interests. They generated a frame for action that laid the blame on Antarctica and a larger ploy to privatize carnival. Blocos like Boi Tolo that sought mostly to exist outside of the official carnival became more politicized when their actions no longer came to be tolerated in the Olympic City.

The HONK! festival's consolidation of neofanfarrismo as a musical social movement framed around activism had aided in producing a collective response of much of the brass community to militate for the right to play in the streets. The mobilization constituted an unintended consequence of the festival's consolidation of the community around the ambiguous discourse of activism. While HONK! RiO promulgated its politics more through an experiential model of activism rather than an informational one, we might see the festivals' experiential activism as captured best in the dual meanings of Portuguese verb *experimentar*, which means both "to experiment" and "to experience." That is, rather than a didactic, informational, or monologic form of activism, instrumental activism's horizontality and lack of firm discourses promote a dialogic form of activism that is dynamically constructed by its participants. Around the world, HONK! festivals present experimental spaces in which musicians can try new models of musical activism and push the festivals toward new forms of engagement—be they musical protests of ICE in Boston, feminist performances like the bLoka, or the episode in which musicians quite literally raised the HONK! banner to defend Rio de Janeiro's street carnival. Rejecting distinctions between the ludic and this revolutionary in this musical social movement, they proclaimed, as can be seen in figure 6.6, that carnival is at once revelry and struggle.

CONCLUSION

Carnival Strike

A year before the attack on Boi Tolo and the campaign organized against the repression of street culture recounted in the previous chapter, Orchestra Voadora saxophonist André Ramos had told me, "In the beginning of neofanfarrismo it was just 'woo-hoo, let's party.' But when you encounter a violent police unit, it will force political questioning whether you want to participate [in politics] or not. It all stops being mere play very quickly" (interview 2015). His comment is a microcosm of the transformation this book traces: the brass revival that emerged in the boom times of Workers Party control of the 2000s grew increasingly politicized with the rise of neofanfarrismo and the many crises the country confronted beginning in the 2010s. The movement began to use its repertoires to act as an oppositional musical force.

I have argued that neofanfarrismo extended the "principles of carnival" to a theory and practice of activism by promoting revival, experimentation, inclusion, resistance, diversification, and consolidation. In doing so, these musicians have sought to produce a musical social movement that challenges the neoliberal rationale of the Olympic city of Rio de Janeiro at a time of political crisis in Brazil and throughout the world. I have documented transformations of the movement in the quarter century from carnivalesque to activist, nationalist to internationalist, and led by predominantly male musicians of the Whiter alternative middle class to a much broader range of communities. And I have illustrated some of the creative and critical engagements of Rio's brass band community as musicians have militated for a more democratic, public, egalitarian, diverse, and safe city. So just how politically impactful has all this been?

Considering the HONK! Festival in Boston, Rosza Daniel Lang-Levitsky and

Michelle Hardesty argue that the festival's activism is largely "antipolitical": not necessarily hostile to the contestation involved in political work, but not clearly taking a side.[1] Antipolitical movements are vague in political positioning, using strategies that "support whomever benefits from a lack of open conflict (generally those whom the status quo rewards) and defuse movements organizing for change" (2020, 187). Arguing that the Somerville HONK! Festival is largely antipolitical, they portray how the festival has been pushed by the minority of political bands that attend it toward more contentious stances and actions, such as the sound action at the ICE detention center, rather than leading oppositional politics.

The critique of the original HONK! festival as antipolitical resonates with critiques of neofanfarrismo examined throughout this book. HONK! RiO's activism might read as the essence of antipolitics: "The festival's activism is based on the initiative of each person involved . . . in which all people encounter each other, dialogue, dance, play, act, and transform urban space" (HONK! RiO Facebook). In Raymond Williams's terms, it is worth asking how we can distinguish between emergent, alternative movements that are easily woven into dominant culture and those that are tangibly oppositional. While evaluating the success of social movements with clearly defined targets, goals, and campaigns is quite difficult, it is not even customary to judge the success of cultural movements on such goal-oriented terms. How can we assess the tangible impacts of a musical social movement such as neofanfarrismo, which does portray itself as oppositional but is characterized by diffuse, horizontal, and open definitions of activism?

It is worth recounting the accomplishments of the movement in an effort to answer this murky question. Neofanfarrismo has played a vital role in transforming the aesthetics of Rio de Janeiro's enormous carnival beyond cultural nationalism toward an embrace, theoretically, of any genre by disinheriting the official heritage regimes and espousing an alternative carnivalesque. The movement has provided a space for the reentrance of the Whiter middle classes into carnival and various new spaces of the city. Participants have worked to democratize access to music education through oficinas and free bloco rehearsals, leading hundreds if not thousands of Cariocas to consider themselves musicians for the first time. Neofanfarrismo has reframed carnival as a year-long movement in which volatile, experimental street parties are available for participation beyond the carnival season. Through the HONK! festival circuit, brass musicians have forged a national community with transnational reach. Neofanfarrismo has helped make the fanfarra official cultural patrimony of the State of Rio de Janeiro.

On a cultural level alone, it has clearly positioned itself as an audible element on the aesthetic soundscape of one of the world's most musical cities, one that has been overdefined by heritage industries. It is not clear, however, that these accomplishments are inherently oppositional.

But beyond these initiatives, musicians have repurposed repertoires to contribute to social movement campaigns that militate for a city and country that would be dramatically different from Bolsonaro's and Crivella's right-wing visions, or even more moderate neoliberal ones. They have put questions of management of public space at the forefront of public debate as Rio de Janeiro transformed into a city ruled by the local and international profit-driven rationales of an Olympic city. They have sought to politicize carnival through incorporating social movement platforms and the unofficial carnival movement's rejection of neoliberal management. Musicians have worked to foment a soundscape of public participation that integrates marginalized populations and creates a city that sounds democracy. Neofanfarristas have sought to use music to empower marginalized populations and challenge diverse, intersectional oppressions, and these communities have increasingly occupied important leadership roles and participated in larger numbers. This story shows that the movement's Whiteness, middle-class profile, and predominant maleness likely cannot displace themselves simply by being alternative, but they can be decentered by diverse new participants. In this process of diversification, musicians have challenged all carnival participants to think critically about the ways they express relationships to marginalized Others through the repertoires and expressive practices of carnival, debates that have reached international forums. If neofanfarrismo is successful at further diversifying, it is plausible that my analysis of neofanfarrismo as a Whiter movement may in coming years be obsolete, or at least less applicable.

These are tangible contributions of an oppositional movement. I celebrate their accomplishments, but I have pointed to their limits and challenges as well. We should take nuanced accounts of activist movements to understand the real possibilities of and obstacles to creating change, especially in movements that are led by a privileged vanguard. The free soundscape of public participation, as examined in chapter 3, has been criticized by many Caricoas for devaluing the monetary value of performance. The movement's unaccountable language of horizontalism might uphold invisible hierarchies. The very real but concealed presence of monetary exchange maintains its privileged demographics and challenges simple, altruistic visions of the movement. Neofanfarristas are complicit in gentrifying urban spaces that can further marginalize vulnerable populations.

They invite depoliticized fanfarrões into their midst, and they carnivalize class and racial solidarities in ways that may produce no effective changes in socio-economic relations. Neofanfarrismo's cultural practices could be interpreted as exclusionary expressions of distinction of alternative Whiteness in contrast to the commodified hegemonic Blackness of the culture industries and the hegemonic Whiteness of conservative Brazilians. Staking out cultural space may be alternative but is not necessarily the same as creating a genuinely populist or oppositional movement.

This middle-class, Whiter community is ensconced within and limited by the systems it critiques. This is perhaps an obvious point, but I have taken it as a foundation of analysis. Understanding the subject positions at play and their relationships to power in activist movements can give us a realistic appreciation of their potential. In my analysis of the movement's prevailing alternative Whiteness, I pointed to the weight of Brazil's long legacies of cloaked racism and social divisions, illustrated ways that instrumental activism can challenge them and forge a more genuine racial democracy, and showed how these engagements are strongly limited. Like Williams, I have argued that emergent culture is neither necessarily an expression of pure resistance nor simply a commodified expression of hipness that expresses no real possibilities of resistance. Rather, the emergent is a dialectical part of the dominant, a mode of positioning that encourages new critiques and projects to materialize within the boundaries set by hegemonic relationships. Insurgent and differential citizenships (Holston 2008) in neofanfarrismo are in a dynamic, tense, and productive relationship with one another, and alternative movements navigate the realities of the world in which they find themselves, while pushing for realities not yet born. In 2021, Ramos summed up this dynamic in the case of Voadora during the years of its existence as the reality of the country and world changed profoundly around neofanfarristas in a statement that is applicable to much of the larger neofanfarrismo movement:

> Voadora got started in 2008, when the world was completely different, for the good and the bad. In 2008, Brazil was another country, full of hopes for a brilliant future, but the decade that followed showed that this [aspiration] was just in our heads. But on the other hand, it was a country filled with prejudices that were hardly discussed, as was the case all over the world. Voadora started as an all-male band not for any deliberate reason but for a structural reason. Voadora's bloco has the virtue of being a very numerous group and therefore has the potential to be very diverse. And as Voadora is a group that has been

very open to the participation of diverse people, we managed to attract people who brought [generative] conflicts to the group. They conquered space inside the group, and this is a great victory for us . . . But it is difficult to have a diverse group because there are always invisible barriers, so you have to do constant work, questioning yourself and creating the conditions for inclusion. (Interview 2021)

This transformation, or cannibalization, of an explicitly carnivalesque movement into an explicitly activist musical social movement that Ramos describes forces us to question conventional boundaries of analysis. Employing musical, festive, and political repertoires in a variety of scenarios, neofanfarristas challenge any simplistic division between the cultural and political, alienated and engaged, counterculture and activism, diversion and discipline. In neofanfarrismo, musical festivity has been a generative force for the production and mobilization of social movements and for the politicization of the musical community and their revelers. Holston (2014), Castells (2012), and others have noted the lack of durability of contemporary internationally based social movements, but the neofanfarrismo movement shows that more explicitly cultural expressions of activism are perhaps more durable in binding and sustaining resistant communities, or at least differently so. They help set the affective conditions for festive political engagement when new opportunities arise.

During my last visit to Rio in early, pre-Covid 2020, when anxieties around a stronger degree of oppression were running high and protests had waned for fear of repression under Bolsonaro, it seemed to neofanfarristas unlikely that culturally defined movements would be attacked to the same degree as more explicitly oppositional social movements with concrete programs for political change, such as the Landless Workers Movement (MST). Musical social movements generally lack the organized discipline and concrete targets of social movements, but they have a huge advantage in attracting the politically uninitiated. They provide cultural contexts for political survival during periods of demobilization and repression when politics as usual are no longer possible. As Eduardo Londoño portrays, highlighting Céu na Terra and Cordão do Boitatá in a *New York Times* article, "'Like a Scream of Resistance': Rio's Carnival in Bolsonaro's Brazil," Rio's street carnival in 2020 was marked by extremely politicized expressions against Bolsonaro. The festivities provided a heightened space for political critique when other spaces were foreclosed.

In this book, I have emphasized the inspirational capacity of discourse to produce change, arguing that critical theories and carnival theories, interpreted by movement actors, are not merely interpretative frameworks but performative models that provide rationalizations of practice. Neofanfarristas largely understand the radical "principles of carnival" as foundational ethics of practice that forge an alternative, maybe even revolutionary, new reality. Likewise, I have argued that the discourse of the "alternative" has been an engine of change within neofanfarrismo that has prevented the movement's ossification. As emergent alternatives eventually come to be cast as dominant or hegemonic, the alternative negates itself and establishes the foundations for new alternatives to emerge. Through this dialectical model of cultural change, the brass blocos emerged from the dominant worlds of carnival; neofanfarrismo broadened its repertoires, seasonal limitations, and political engagement; and excluded communities have diversified what had been viewed as an overly privileged "populist" movement.

As a point of culmination, HONK! RiO cemented neofanfarrismo's status as an activist movement distinct from but in dialogue with carnival. But in founding the HONK! RiO festival, neofanfarrismo is no more unified or static than it ever was before, as consolidation does not necessarily lead to unification. With HONK! RiO, the festival has forged new institutions and moments of mobilization through which the movement may continue to grow, evolve, diversify, and debate, creating new emergent alternatives some of which may be tangibly oppositional. While I cannot neatly conclude with a firm estimation of the movement's transformational capacities, I suggest that we can learn from neofanfarrismo's successes and challenges in building a musical social movement that challenges the neoliberal governance of contemporary cities and militates against the encroaching neofascist authoritarianism that the world now confronts.

On the other hand, is there any more proof of neofanfarrismo's oppositional status, that it is not merely antipolitical and instead poses a perceived threat, than the fact that musicians and foliões have many times been violently confronted by the police and the Olympic City's efforts to discipline them? The hegemonic cultural economy of the city relies on and commodifies the production of neofanfarrismo while affording musicians the bare minimum resources to survive, function, and organize. But, like the proletariat, neofanfarrismo is not completely confined to the boundaries set by hegemonic power but is, rather, in a tense, dynamic, and productive relationship with them. In response to the attack against Boi Tolo examined in the last chapter and the protest it inspired, producer Renata Dias positions neofanfarrismo as a part of the cultural and political economy of the city with a real capacity to challenge it. She even fantasized about a "carnival strike," a strategy that collapses boundaries between the ludic and the political:

> "See here, mayor: there will be no street blocos this year. Your tourists will come to Rio. The sponsors will come. There will be no musicians. This carnival, we will just meditate" . . . The city needs us. It depends on us. It sells itself through street carnival with plaques all over the city promoting it. It swells its chest to speak about us and doesn't support us with anything. (Interview 2016)

Shifting from indignance, she stops to reflect: "I don't know how long this will take. I don't know how many years. But I believe there will be a change. Either it will be the privatization of carnival, or it will be us saying, 'listen, the street is ours. We have rights. We will do our thing. You will have to swallow it. Or we call a carnival strike.'"

———

In fact, as the 2021 carnival arrived amid the Covid-19 pandemic, the neofanfarrismo community did call a kind of carnival strike. They launched a campaign initiated by former students of Orquestra Voadora's oficina that was quickly taken up by much of the larger street carnival community in a collective demand not to celebrate street carnival amid the previously unimagined circumstances of the pandemic (see Snyder 2021b). This agreement between carnival institutions successfully pressured the city administration to take the unprecedented decision to cancel the 2021 carnival in response to Bolsonaro's necropolitical abandonment of the country to virus denialism. The bands and blocos of street carnival urged foliões not to transgress the city's cancelation of the event and to celebrate the event at home instead under the banner of the "Carnival at Home" movement (#carnavalemcasa). In this precarious moment, they acted collectively through official and social media, using their cultural power to carnivalesquely invert the meaning of carnivalesque resistance, not as the usual freedom to party in the street, but as the responsibility to act with caution for themselves and others by staying out of the streets (CW.Con.Ex1).[2]

This book has told a story of how the street carnival community, and specifically the neofanfarrismo movement that emerged from it, consolidated a capacity for this kind of collective political action. Despite the efforts of the "Carnival at Home" campaign, in the months following the 2021 carnival, infections rates rose precipitously in Rio de Janeiro and the country's death counts tragically reached 4,000 per day. Clandestine carnival parties surely contributed to the devastation, but the immeasurable impact that neofanfarristas and other street carnival institutions had in lessening the contagion by uncharacteristically convincing each other and their foliões to stay home on this occasion literally saved lives.

APPENDIX

Carioca Bands and Blocos Discussed in the Book

MOVEMENT	BAND/BLOCO	YEAR FOUNDED	REPERTOIRE
Precursors	Bola Preta	1918	Carioca classicism
	Banda de Ipanema	1965	Carioca classicism
Brass bloco Revival	Cordão do Boitatá	1996	Carioca classicism/ NE regionalism
	Bloco da Ansiedade	1997	Frevo
	Escola Portátil	2000	Carioca classicism/Choro
	Bloco do Céu na Terra	2001	Carioca classicism/ NE regionalism
	Cordão do Prata Preta	2004	Carioca classicism
Neofanfarrismo	Songoro Cosongo	2005	Latin/Cannibalist
	Cordão do Boi Tolo	2006	Spontaneous/Cannibalist
	Orquestra Voadora	2008	Cannibalist
	Amigos da Onça	2008	Axé/Cannibalist
	Fanfarrada	2009	Latin/Cannibalist
	Monte Alegre Hot Jazz Band	2009	Trad Jazz
	Go East Orkestra	2010	Balkan
	Os Siderais	2011	Cannibalist
	Super Mário Bloco	2012	Mario video game music
	Cinebloco	2012	Cinema music
	BlocAto do Nada	2012	MPB/Funk carioca
	Black Clube	2013	"Black Music"
	Damas de Ferro	2013	Cannibalist
	Bagunço	2013	Cannibalist
	Favela Brass	2014	New Orleans second line
	Ocupa Carnaval	2014	Politicized Marchinhas

NOTES

INTRODUCTION *An Alternative Movement in an Olympic City*

1. CW.Int.Ex1. "Orquestra Voadora Carnaval 2019." Footage of 2019 Orquestra Voadora, carnival. www.andrewsnydermusic.com/introduction.html/.

2. Lei Ordinária 8488.

3. CW.Int.Ex2. Orquestra Voadora. "Hino da Orquestra Voadora" (The Anthem of Orquestra Voadora). www.andrewsnydermusic.com/introduction.html/.

4. Most of this book's cited interviews were conducted in Portuguese, with a few conducted in French and Spanish, and were translated into English by the author. A few were conducted in English. Aside from Portuguese, this international movement includes native speakers of primarily these three other languages. All other texts originally in Portuguese were translated by the author if not otherwise noted.

5. In recent years, debate has emerged regarding the capitalization of racial categories, and it is increasingly common to capitalize "Black" to discuss Black cultures and identities that have often experienced erasure. There is less agreement about the capitalization of "White," with some arguing that capitalizing "White" in response to "Black" favors an "all lives matter" approach to the issue. Others have argued for capitalization of "White" from a different perspective, suggesting that capitalizing works against the racial invisibility that is a privilege of Whiteness. As this book focuses on the salience of race in constructing community, I have chosen to capitalize both terms, while recognizing criticisms and viable alternatives.

6. In response to Gustave Le Bon (2007 [1895]) and others who viewed crowds and social movements as irrational mobs, social movement scholars in the 1960s and 70s tended to downplay the role of culture in order to argue for the "rationality" of social movement actors. Indeed, the "disciplined" left in the twentieth century often disavowed counterculture as an impediment to revolution. Since the "cultural turn" of the 1980s, music, emotion, and culture have been valorized for their roles in social movements, but often in ways that are functionalist and treat music as a "resource" for social movement mobilization (Eyerman and Jamison 1998).

7. In contrast to an "arborescent" model, in which a hierarchical tree form represents origin of descendant "branches" to a common root, Deleuze and Guatarri's notion of the rhizome (1980 [2004]) is a model of influence that stresses multiple "horizontal," or planar, interactions between various nodes with endless entry and exit points, any of which may be connected to any other.

8. "Wilson Witzel." *Greg News*. www.youtube.com/watch?v=NoYsmi4zcRU13.

9. While Brazil is less racially polarized between Black and White communities than, for example, the United States, the country's race relations exist on a hierarchical continuum, or spectrum, of racial identification in which Whiter communities are afforded more privileges than Blacker ones. For this reason, "Blacker" and "Whiter" emphasize the relativity of racial formation in a country as racially mixed as Brazil.

10. Though *negrx/a/o* (Black) and *brancx/a/o* (White) are commonly used terms in Brazil, "Blacker" and "Whiter" are not translated "emic" terms used by neofanfarristas or prominent in Brazilian critical race studies, but I find them useful to discuss communities that are not homogenous but are racially distinct from others. *Negritude* (Blackness) and *branquitude* (Whiteness), however, are increasingly used in Brazilian scholarly, activist, and music circles. There is a multitude of racial terms and categories in Brazil, but I maintain that understanding Blackness and Whiteness relationally is key to understanding the aesthetics and ethics of the neofanfarrismo movement in relation to the country's broader cultural and poltical histories of relations between Afro- and Euro-Brazilian heritage. I generally refer, however, to cultural traditions and individuals, when I know how they racially identify, and as "Black" or "White," or other terms, to reference their racialization as such.

11. Such reactionary racial politics against racial democracy have existed since the very origins of its national embrace, as Barbara Weinstein (2015) has shown in her study of São Paulo's revolts against Vargas, which were motivated by the urge to protect São Paulo state's Whiteness as the "color of modernity."

12. One could argue there might be many forms of alternative Whiteness and Blackness in a country as politically and racially diverse as Brazil. In my use of alternative Whiteness in this book, I am racially situating neofanfarristas' emic use of the world "alternative" as middle-class, countercultural, and leftist. Readers should note that "alternative whiteness" is not a prominent term in the neofanfarrismo community and could be used with different meanings in other studies.

13. Bourdieu (1984 [1979]) famously argued that middle classes craft exclusionary conceptions of taste to maintain social distinction from lower classes. Likewise, neofanfarristas' aesthetic preferences are formed in their social positions in relation to other communities, if not determined by them.

14. In other words, I am asking, in the framework of anthropologist James Holston

(2008), to what extent neofanfarrismo succeeds at participating in "insurgent citizenship," the diverse struggles that emerged during the dictatorship to overthrow Brazil's unequal sociopolitical landscape, rather than merely being a cultural expression of one sector of Brazil's "differentiated citizenship," the perpetuated systems of inequality based on legacies of class, race, and gender privilege.

15. Indeed, Starr and Waterman argue that two distinct and "conflicting agendas," to challenge the status quo and to create a market category, are inherent to alternative music scenes more broadly (2017, 524).

16. More broadly, an emerging body of scholarship has shown the brass band to be a tremendously adaptable ensemble with a great diversity of local, populist, and alternative manifestations around the world (Flaes 2000; Reily and Brucher 2013; Sakakeeny 2013; Abe 2018; Snyder, Allen, and Garofalo 2020).

17. While the word "fanfarrão" appears to have an etymological relation to the word "fanfarra," many disavowed any relation of the words. Trombonist Marco Serragrande told me, "'Fanfarrão' has nothing to do with brass instruments. At least, the slang means someone who just wants to have fun and who is not preoccupied with responsibility. It has nothing to do with music" (interview 2015).

18. See Queiroz 1992; Vianna 1995; McCann 2004.

19. Local scholars, journalists, and graduate students in Rio with whom I have been in conversation are increasingly devoting attention to street carnival and neofanfarrismo (see, for example, Fernandes and Herschmann 2014; Fernandes 2019; Belart 2021). The Carioca podcast *Batuques e Confetes* has featured many of these scholars.

20. Other scholars have shown that the music of carnivals in the Americas has become increasingly diversified around new and varied affinities in the past several decades (for example, Guilbault 2007). In Brazil, scholars have indicated how the proliferation of regional genres, decentralized access to recording technology, and the rise of postnational subjectivities and diasporic music making have fragmented senses of national identity rooted in Vargas-era brasilidade (Vianna 1995; Dunn and Perrone 2001). Other recent analyses of contemporary Brazilian popular music have highlighted the role of adapting and reformulating traditional musical resources with global forms of popular music (Moehn 2012).

21. For example, Eyerman and Jamison 1998; Rosenthal and Flacks 2011.

22. I build on William Roy's observation that "the effect of music on social movement activities and outcomes depends less on the meaning of the lyrics or the sonic qualities of the performance than on the social relationships within which it is embedded" (2010, 2).

23. In examining musicians' efforts to create this soundscape, this book builds on recent work in sound studies by asking what role acoustic sound plays in shaping senses of the public (see Sakakeeny 2010; Abe 2018; Cardoso 2019).

ONE Revival: The Death and Life of Street Carnival

1. CW.Ch1.Ex1. *Porta dos Fundos.* "Blocos." A satiric sketch about the world of alternative brass blocos. www.andrewsnydermusic.com/ch-1-revival.html/.

2. The terms *retomada* (retaking), *renascimento* (rebirth), *revitalização* (revitalization), and others are also common, with the prominent "re-" prefix implying the sense of creating an older tradition anew.

3. The participatory brass blocos that were founded at this stage do not use one unifying ensemble term in Portuguese beyond the generic "bloco." I have also heard *bloco de sopros* (wind instrument bloco) and *bloco de fanfarra*, but fanfarra usually refers to a smaller formation, as discussed in the following chapter.

4. See also Teresa Caldeira's study of São Paulo (2000), which paints a picture of Brazilian cities as mired in deepening urban segregation, stark inequality, and a retreat of the upper-middle class to suburban spaces.

5. Using music to brand public spaces has been, of course, part of much broader effort to revitalize historical urban centers around the world in the new millennium after many had been abandoned in the latter half of the twentieth century. See, for example, Peterson's discussion of downtown Los Angeles (2012).

6. Drives to "clean up" the city have a long history in Rio, especially in periods of international attention (Meade 1997; Sheriff 1999).

7. See also Kennelly 2013 for an account of how the neoliberal management of the 2010 Olympics in Vancouver, Canada, branded the city and left marginalized populations further vulnerable.

8. The anxiety surrounding the supposed loss of the authentic Carioca carnival is not new. Beatriz Jaguaribe claims, "Ever since the nineteenth century, the lament of the loss of an 'authentic' carnival has been repeated in press accounts just as the critique of its commercialization has also been voiced by intellectuals and artists" (2014, 113).

9. Eyerman and Jamison (1998) argue that activists often "mobilize tradition" for new critical ends, and Stuart Tannock suggests that nostalgia is not beholden to the right, but rather that it is "a valuable way of approaching the past important to all social groups" (1995: 453).

10. "Saudade" is a foundational, and famously untranslatable, element of aesthetics and affect in the Lusophone (Portuguese-speaking) world. Lila Gray refers to it as a "a philosophical-historical-poetic topos of longing" that "exists as a way of being in the present and *feeling* the past . . . while dreaming for a future" (2013, 83).

11. Angélica Madeira argues that in the context of ascendant neoliberalism and embrace of international capitalism, the middle-class urban youth of the 1980s "sought to go beyond nationalism, cultural or biological heritage [through] the international language of rock . . . Cultural nationalism was regarded as outdated" (2011, 97–98).

12. Much of this critical scholarship has been in reaction to the "salvage ethnography" of earlier ethnomusicology and anthropology, which sought to "rescue" cultural manifestations based on assumptions of modernity as unidirectionally destroying traditional, authentic culture. The oft-cited "invention of tradition" (Hobsbawm and Ranger 1983) emphasizes that traditional practices that appear as authentic manifestations have specific origin stories that once established their aura of authenticity. Developing these ideas, Barbara Kirshenblatt-Gimblett defines heritage as "a new form of cultural production of the present that takes recourse to the past" (1995, 269) that is produced anew rather than "rescued" from the past, creating a "selective tradition" (Williams 2001 [1961]).

13. Robert Flaes portrays the brass band historically as a "tried and trusty mainstay of power, both as emblem and weapon" (2000, 9).

14. Indeed, Larry Crook argues that "the bands represented the first musical institution in Brazil with a truly nationwide scope and popular appeal" (2009, 115).

15. In recent decades, bandas de música have experienced a revival due to competitive band meetings (encontros) and government support. Some of them play arrangements of popular Brazilian and international songs as well as more traditional repertoires (Reily 2013), perhaps providing a reference for neofanfarristas even if they tend to downplay the influence of traditional band culture in Brazil on their own movement.

16. Discussing the song known as the first carnival samba, "Pelo telefone," Marc Hertzman writes that "Military bands played instrumental versions, revelers sang parodied versions, and Carnival societies feted guests and members to seemingly endless repetitions of the catchy tune" (2013, 101).

17. See Andrade 2012; Jaguaribe 2014; Herschmann 2013.

18. Micael Herschmann (2013) also credits the decline of street carnival to the fall of Rio de Janeiro as the primary cultural engine of Brazil, the growth of carnival in Salvador and Recife, extreme violence in the city in the 1980s and 1990s, and its status as one of the centers of resistance to the dictatorship and repression of the resistance. Benjamin Cowan notes that "the dictatorship fretted that carnival celebrations in Rio emphasized scenes of libertinism, where eroticism and sex are exploited, giving the impression of an atmosphere of open orgy" (2016, 240).

19. This national embrace of a form of hegemonic Blackness, one that received cultural representation in the form of samba's exultation but lost the capacity to critique Brazilian race relations in the process, paradoxically maintained a racial hierarchy that concealed but still privileged hegemonic Whiteness. This transition was a major shift from the earlier Brazilian ideology of "Whitening" (branqueamento) that explicitly celebrated Whiteness after Brazil abolished slavery in 1888 and sought to Whiten itself through European immigration and miscegenation.

20. Such low esteem for the samba schools also appears in academic literature on the subject. Alison Raphael has provocatively claimed that samba schools "have been used

as a convenient vehicle through which the larger society has coopted and undermined a genuine manifestation of popular culture" (1990, 73). Robin Sheriff (1999) views the construction of the sambódromo as the most recent "theft of carnival" in a long history of commodification and appropriation, and her interlocutors speak of its construction as the final death of the "real" carnival. Ruy Castro celebrates the blocos and quips that the sambódromo "may be the greatest spectacle on earth, but that's what it is, a spectacle. The real carnival is the one in which people enjoy themselves, and don't just watch others having a good time . . . and when it appears suddenly in your street, it takes the whole neighborhood along with it" (2003, 106).

21. Writing before the construction of the sambódromo, DaMatta contrasts the street carnival, which for him includes the samba schools, to domestic indoor carnivals. The opposition between carnivals in Rio today, however, generally opposes the street carnival of the blocos to the sambódromo and the samba schools.

22. Samba-enredo, or a samba that tells a story, is the primary musical genre of the samba schools. Each school composes an enredo each year in an attempt to win the competition.

23. Turino's oft-cited model distinguishes between participatory and presentational fields based on numerous qualifications, such as open versus closed forms, division between audience and musicians, tolerance versus intolerance for mistakes, and levels of openness to multilevel participants among other vectors, though he admits that there is a great deal of variation and hybridity between these fields in musical traditions around the world. See Snyder 2019b for a critique of Turino's model.

24. These Blacker "suburban" blocos, also known as *blocos de embalo*, are also connected to the birth of the Blacker *pagode* samba scene that emerged in the 1970s, which critiqued the commercialization of the samba schools from a perspective of what could be called alternative Blackness.

25. Rita Fernandes, president of the Sebastiana League of blocos, refers to Banda de Ipanema and a few other middle-class carnival groups born during the dictatorship as isolated "acts of resistance," distinct from the veritable "movement" of street carnival revival that would emerge at the end of the dictatorship and redemocratization process (2019, 186).

26. CW.Ch1.Ex2. Cordão do Boitatá. "Teaser Carnaval Cordão do Boitatá." Performance by Cordão do Boitatá. CW.Ch1.Ex3. Céu na Terra. "Cristo Nasceu na Bahia 2020." Animations of Céu na Terra based on performance footage. www.andrewsnydermusic .com/ch-1-revival.html/.

27. A sustained analysis of Boitatá's presentational and participatory performances can be found in Lacombe 2014. Also see Snyder (2019b) on presentational and participatory performance in neofanfarrismo.

28. A manifestation of Bahian carnival in which trucks blast music in the streets.

29. This quasi-Freudian definition that implies that the fantasized self is more real than the social self resonates with DaMatta's own: the fantasia "reveals much more than it conceals. Representing a hidden desire, the [fantasia] creates a synthesis between the closeted person, the social roles he or she plays, and those he or she would like to fill . . . Carnival costumes create a social field of encounter, mediation, and social polysemy" (1991 [1979], 40–42).

30. A central shopping district famed as a place to buy carnival fantasias.

31. Jaguaribe contextualizes the revival of the street carnival as part of a larger rationale of reviving the city as a center of tourism, portraying it as part of "the re-democratization of civil society and the ever increasing prestige given to manifestations of popular culture; the force of the tourist industry that envisioned, in street carnival, a lucrative form of seducing potential visitors; the media coverage of the street carnival that extolled the comeback as an 'authentic' demonstration of the city's joyful spirit; and the sponsorship of businesses combined with the patronage of the municipal authorities that not only close the street for the merry making but also offer guides, map, and itineraries of the partying" (2014, 125).

32. CW.Ch1.Ex4. *Porta dos Fundos*. "Carlos." Satire of samba school. www.andrew snydermusic.com/ch-1-revival.html/.

33. CW.Ch1.Ex5. *Porta dos Fundos*. "Carnaval do Crivella." Satire of samba school. www.andrewsnydermusic.com/ch-1-revival.html/.

34. CW.Ch1.Ex6. *Porta dos Fundos*. "Carnaval 2019." Satire of samba school. www .andrewsnydermusic.com/ch-1-revival.html/.

35. CW.Ch1.Ex7. *Porta dos Fundos*. "Carnavírus." Satire of samba school. www.andrews-nydermusic.com/ch-1-revival.html/.

TWO *Experimentation: To Play Anything*

1. CW.Ch2.Ex1. Orquestra Voadora. "Ferro Velho." Original composition by Tim Malik. www.andrewsnydermusic.com/ch-2-experimentation.html/.

2. The use of the term "old guard" (*velha guarda*) is a playful reference to how early sambistas and choro players of the 1920s and '30s had come to be identified by later generations (McCann 2004).

3. Neofanfarristas' reactions against globalization resonate with a critique of the domination of the global North in scholarly accounts that attribute the heightened diversification and circulation of repertoires around the world to "globalization" in a way that portrays "peripheral" countries as passive receptacles of global hegemonic influences. In this view, globalization is the "recent regime under which nonwestern peoples are dominated and represented by the West" (Taylor 2007, 113–14). In contrast, Martin Stokes has argued that the term "cosmopolitanism" helps foreground the limitations of "globalization," emphasizing "music as an active and engaged means of world making, not simply

a response to forces beyond our control" (2007, 10). Theories of "glocalism" have also shown how global entanglements have produced a diversity of new hybrid forms around the world, but here I suggest that understanding communities' own vocabularies about musical circulation is more enlightening.

4. In these respects I draw on Matt Sakakeeny, who argues that circulation generates new cultural forms by reaching both into the past and diverse locations of the present (2013), and Thomas Turino, who argues that there are many continuities between colonialism, nationalism, and cosmopolitanism, though they are often understood in opposition to one another (2000).

5. Like the musicians about whom Martin Stokes writes in the context of Turkey, Rio's brass movement is made up of "burgeoning (but unstable and vulnerable) middle-classes who perceive themselves at a distance from the old nation-state modernizing projects, and in search for new means of cultural distinction" (Stokes 2007, 8).

6. See the Appendix for a timeline of relevant blocos and bands discussed in this book and especially in this chapter.

7. Though Andrade was White, "race" here is being used to refer to a national Brazilian race that elides racial distinction.

8. Bryan McCann, underlining the long-lasting importance of the decades in which these positions became dominant cultural frameworks, suggests that, in Brazil, "Innovation occurs within the patterns established between the late 1920s and mid-1950s. After fifty years of reiteration and revision, these patterns have acquired a range of meanings and the density of tradition" (2004, 245). As Michael Denning (2015) argues, the pattern of vernacular music rising to prominence occurred globally in the 1920s and '30s.

9. Christopher Dunn argues that in MPB political alienation from leftist causes took on a cultural component: "a symptom of alienation would be cultural inauthenticity—the production and consumption of cultural products divorced from 'national reality'" (2016, 170).

10. Christopher Dunn (2016) has argued that Tropicália put to rest the divisions between cultural nationalism and musical imperialism, while Frederick Moehn (2012) shows that cannibalist discourse is the predominant metaphor for Rio's popular musicians in their musical experiments with Brazilian and international music, as they aimed to resist being labeled either as folklorists or as global imitators.

11. See Albuquerque Jr. (2014) on the "Invention of the Northeast" as a space of nostalgia with foundational status within Brazilian national narratives.

12. Companion website. Repertoire of Cordão do Boitatá and Céu na Terra. www .andrewsnydermusic.com/repertoires.html/.

13. CW.Ch2.Ex2 Cordão do Boitatá. "O trenzinho do caipira." Boitatá's interpretation of Heitor Villa-Lobos's composition. www.andrewsnydermusic.com/ch-2-experimentation .html/.

14. CW.Ch3.Ex3. Céu na Terra. "Carnaval 2014." Performance of Céu na Terra bloco playing maxixe. www.andrewsnydermusic.com/ch-2-experimentation.html/.

15. CW.Ch2.Ex4. Bandão da Escola Portátil. "Gaúcho." Performance of big band at Escola Portátil choro school at Uni-Rio. www.andrewsnydermusic.com/ch-2-experimentation.html/.

16. For McCann, regionalism militates "not for opposition to a larger Brazilian national character, but for a special place . . . *within* that character . . . [Regionalism] communicated a part—a crucial part—to the whole. The implication was that only the chosen could live these cultures, but that all Brazilians could and inevitably did benefit from them, because they kept essential elements of the national soul" (2004, 120).

17. CW.Ch2.Ex5. Bloco da Ansiedade 2020. "Madeira que Cupim não Rói." Carioca bloco specializing in frevo music from Recife. www.andrewsnydermusic.com/ch-2-experimentation.html/.

18. CW.Ch2.Ex6. Cordão do Prata Preta. "Turma do funil"/"Cachaça não é água." Performance of marchinhas by Cordão do Prata Preta. www.andrewsnydermusic.com/ch-2-experimentation.html/.

19. Companion website. Selection of repertoire of Orquestra Voadora's band and bloco. www.andrewsnydermusic.com/repertoires.html/.

20. For a documentation of alternative brass bands in Portugal, see Moniz (2020).

21. More broadly, K. E. Goldschmitt (2020) shows how in the mediated popular music realm, traditional tropes of Brazilian branding began to fade in the 2000s and 2010s in favor of a broader diversity of genres from Brazil circulating on the world stage.

22. CW.Ch2.Ex7. Songoro Cosongo. "Perez Prado, Mambo No. 5." Performance by Songoro Cosongo bloco that specializes in diverse Latin genres. www.andrewsnydermusic.com/ch-2-experimentation.html/.

23. In Hispanic America, *bolivarianismo* refers to a political ideology of anti-imperialism and cultural solidarity with the rest of Latin America. See also Herschmann and Cabanzo on Songoro Cosongo's "alternative cosmopolitanism" based on Latin American solidarities rather than identification with the hegemony of the Anglo-American popular culture world (2016).

24. CW.Ch2.Ex8. Rim Bam Bum. "Danza del Guerrero." Performance by Chilean brass band that notably visited Rio de Janeiro in carnival 2014 and HONK! RiO 2015. www.andrewsnydermusic.com/ch-2-experimentation.html/.

25. Roberto DaMatta (1979 [1991]), in his study of Rio de Janeiro's carnival, compares at length the Carioca manifestation with New Orleans Mardi Gras. Annie Gibson suggests that Brazilian immigrants in New Orleans are "perhaps unique among immigrant groups there, [as] they have found moments in which they do not need a cultural translation dictionary" (2015, 146). Also see Snyder (2021a) for a comparison of the neofanfarrismo movement with New Orleans' Whiter carnival brass movement.

26. CW.Ch2.Ex9. Monte Alegre Hot Jazz Band. "Washington and Lee Swing." Carioca New Orleans-style trad jazz band. www.andrewsnydermusic.com/ch-2-experimentation .html/.

27. CW.Ch2.Ex10. Orquestra Voadora. "Elefante." Original composition by André Ramos. www.andrewsnydermusic.com/ch-2-experimentation.html/.

28. CW.Ch2.Ex11. "Dumb and Brass e Maracatuzeiros." Performance by French band in collaboration with maracatu percussionists in Recife, Brazil. www.andrewsnydermusic .com/ch-2-experimentation.html/.

29. CW.Ch2.Ex12. Go East Orkestar. "Guča 2012." Carioca Balkan band performing Brazilian and Balkan songs at famed festival in Serbia. www.andrewsnydermusic.com /ch-2-experimentation.html/.

30. CW.Ch2.Ex13. TechnoBrass. "Dark Brejo." Carioca band's brass interpretation of techno music. www.andrewsnydermusic.com/ch-2-experimentation.html/.

31. CW.Ch2.Ex14. "Super Mario Bloco." Bloco devoted to playing the music of Mario Bros. video games. www.andrewsnydermusic.com/ch-2-experimentation.html/.

32. That the alternativeness of playing these popular genres is inherently relational and contextual is well illustrated by comparison between this use of global popular music in Rio's carnival with American high school bands, which often play pop covers but are viewed as highly mainstream.

33. CW.Ch2.Ex15. Gangbé Brass Band vs Orquestra Voadora. "Batalha de Fanfarras." Famed Béninois brass jams with Orquestra Voadora in Rio de Janeiro. www.andrewsnyder music.com/ch-2-experimentation.html/.

34. CW.Ch2.Ex16. Céu na Terra. "2016 Marrabenta Brasil Moçambique." Collabora- tions with Mozambican musicians playing popular marrabenta genre. www.andrewsnyder music.com/ch-2-experimentation.html/.

35. Hermano Vianna (2011) refers to these marginalized genres as the "parallel music of Brazil," suggesting that the music industry of Brazilian popular music, which owes much to the aesthetic boundaries created by the MPB aesthetic, has been destabilized in the past three decades due to the decentralization of recording and distribution. He argues that the introduction of these new genres to the Brazilian popular music landscape "is the product of social inclusion conquered by force . . . Brazil will have to get used to this forced, messy, and bottom-up 'inclusion'" (2011, 248).

36. Though the Black American genres that influenced "Black music" were in some cases, like funk and soul, explicitly political, Christopher Dunn argues that the dismissal of "Black music" by leftists "is remarkably similar to ways in which [Brazilian nationalist] leftist critics regarded the hippie counterculture [and Tropicália] of the early 1970s, which they regarded as alienated, inconsequential, and beholden to cultural products and styles from the United States" (2016, 151).

37. CW.Ch2.Ex17. Amigos da Onça. "Carnaval 2015." Footage of Amigos da Onça bloco

in the middle of the night in Center of Rio de Janeiro. www.andrewsnydermusic.com /ch-2-experimentation.html/.

38. CW.Ch2.Ex18. Fanfarrada. "Coração Black." Original composition by Pedro Paulo Júnior based on Carioca funk rhythms. www.andrewsnydermusic.com/ch-2-experiment ation.html/.

39. CW.Ch2.Ex19. Bagunço. "Retirante." Original composition by João Ribeiro featuring images of 2016 French tour in which author participated as trumpet player. www .andrewsnydermusic.com/ch-2-experimentation.html/.

40. See Ribeiro (2020) for a discussion of the cultural tensions regarding the timing of carnival and carnivalesque events.

THREE Inclusion: Whose Rio?

1. Feld defines acoustemology as the "local conditions of acoustic sensation, knowledge, and imagination embodied in the culturally particular sense of place" (1996, 91).

2. For example, Marié Abe's notion of "resonance": "the capacity of sound to implicate all vibrating bodies and objects within its proximity" (2018, xxiii), which, although "necessarily fleeting and provisional, nonetheless allow us to imagine ourselves in relation to others and the environment differently, and to embody, through our sensory experiences, yet-to-be-imagined possibilities" (35).

3. Charles Keil claims, for example, that "participation is the opposite of alienation from nature, from society, from the body, from labor" (1987, 276), and Thomas Turino asserts that "the participatory field is radical within the capitalist cosmopolitan formation in that it is *not for listening apart from doing*" (2008, 77).

4. Drawing on Michel DeCerteau (1984), Reily and Brucher argue that brass bands transform "place," identified by what is located in it, through practices of "space," or what is done in it. They write, "Bands can transform both places into spaces and spaces into places, continuously actualizing spaces during their performances and identifying places through their presence" (2013, 18).

5. Cardoso writes that "sound opens up politics of shared existence; as a matter of defining and performing the collective, politics opens up the acoustics of human and nonhuman associations" (2019, 2). As Cardoso shows, beyond objective measurement of sound used to regulate cities, "local actors have constantly drawn attention to the more subjective ear. For them, the 'signal' embedded in noise is made of 'good,' 'necessary,' 'bad,' and 'useless' decibels" (9). He documents how elites have often sought to sonically isolate themselves from urban commotion, and in Latin America they have aimed to create more "civilized" urban soundscapes akin to that of European capitals, which are contested by marginalized Others.

6. Similarly, arguing that the various Carioca street music movements indeed consti-

tute a form of musical activism, Herschmann and Fernandes suggest, "We affirm that the errant music executed in the streets is *politics*, and puts—through the gaps—the *Other* in the urban scene: these creative initiatives, therefore, articulate and generate a tension with the mediatized Rio de Janeiro, globalized capitalism, and the logic of the massive urban interventions" (2014, 42).

7. Harvey argues that the right to the city can be fomented through alternative practices, creating moments of "spontaneous coming together in a moment of 'irruption;' when disparate heterotopic groups suddenly see, if only for a fleeting moment, the possibilities of collective action to create something radically different" (2012, xvii). Harvey (2012; 2013) claims that the global social movements that have surged since the global financial crisis of 2008, of which the 2013 Brazilian protests are considered a part, have resulted in the emergence of "rebel cities" that contest the neoliberal structuring of the city through popular occupations of city space.

8. "Choque de ordem" (shock of order) is a term used to refer to police actions that violently impose order, control, and pacification.

9. The law (Lei 5429) guarantees the freedom to perform in public without permit as long as the performers adhere to a number of requirements including keeping the performance free, permitting the circulation of traffic and pedestrians, not using a structure or stage, having no private sponsorship, and not playing after 10 p.m. in locations where they will bother residents.

10. CW.Ch3.Ex1. "Curta! Blocos Cariocas—Boi Tolo (2015)." Short documentary about Boi Tolo bloco and its anarchic parading style. www.andrewsnydermusic.com/ch-3-inclusion.html/.

11. The name also references the many dramatic ox traditions from the northeast of Brazil, such as *bumba-meu-boi*.

12. *Globo* comments that, "As they do not follow a pre-planned route and improvise their trajectories, the unofficial blocos are testimonies of collective performances that would happen with difficulty otherwise" (Filgueiras 2016).

13. Freire (1970) argues that oppression in education is manifested through the hierarchical position of the teacher, who controls knowledge, relative to that of the student, who is dependent on the teacher's knowledge and fails to instill their own independence in the process of learning. The teacher "banks" knowledge into the student in order to prove capability according to hierarchically set standards. Freire proposes instead a dialogic approach of experimentation led collectively by the student and the teacher.

14. Circo Voador was inaugurated on the Arpoador beach in Ipanema in 1982 with an emphasis on Brazilian rock. The government viewed it as subversive and closed it in 1996. It was reopened in Lapa during the revitalization of the central entertainment district in 2004 in front of the iconic Lapa Arches. Today it is a cultural home of the Carioca left, alternative scenes, and social movements. It provides the most diverse musical offerings in

Lapa, including rock, jazz, Afrobeat, and international bands, as well as samba and more traditional Brazilian musical genres. The name of Orquestra Voadora has no intentional relation to Circo Voador.

15. Voadora's oficina is not unlike the School of HONK community music school that has emerged in Boston in tandem with the annual HONK! festival (Leppman 2020).

16. The Facebook page for the event similarly presents it as a resignification and transformation of the material reality, marginalization, and challenges of the urban world: "The word cracudagem has been resignified in Rio de Janeiro, with music, good energy, and people disposed to occupy public space with art and cultural transformation. Cracudagem is a spontaneous event without control" (*Oficina de cracudagem* Facebook page, 2016).

17. CW.Ch3.Ex2. "Cracudagem na Lapa." Student-led jam session after every oficina running late into the night. www.andrewsnydermusic.com/ch-3-inclusion.html/.

18. In addition to his distinction between presentational and participatory, Turino (2008) distinguishes between high-fidelity recording, which seeks to be true to live performance, and studio art recording, which manipulates sound for artistic ends.

19. CW.Ch3.Ex3. Fela Kuti. "Expensive Shit." www.andrewsnydermusic.com/ch-3-inclusion.html/.

20. CW.Ch3.Ex4. Orquestra Voadora. "Expensive Shit" studio recording. www.andrewsnydermusic.com/ch-3-inclusion.html/.

21. Musical examples of "Expensive Shit" are adapted from Orquestra Voadora's sheet music used by permission of the band.

22. CW.Ch3.Ex5. "Orquestra Voadora no Circo—Expensive Shit." Live performance at Circo Voador. www.andrewsnydermusic.com/ch-3-inclusion.html/.

23. CW.Ch3.Ex6. "Orquestra Voadora oficina improvisation education." Extract from student-created documentary about Voaodra oficina, *Aprendendo a Voar*, showing education strategies for improvising over Fela Kuti's "Expensive Shit." www.andrewsnydermusic.com/ch-3-inclusion.html/.

24. CW.Ch3.Ex7. Orquestra Voadora Bloco. "Expensive Shit." Performance of bloco at carnival. www.andrewsnydermusic.com/ch-3-inclusion.html/.

25. In the case of an American HONK! band, Kallman writes that "the general challenge is how to extend the benefits and participation in the band as fully as possible to everyone within it. A persistent tension emerges between the responsibility of a group (what structures it offers for participation, and how it supports inclusion of less-heard voices) and the responsibility of individual members (the ways that individual accountability is understood and practiced)" (2020, 126).

26. Jeff Packman has written of carnival's "false sense of belonging that does nothing more than placate the masses" (2010, 259), and Roberto DaMatta (1991 [1979]) has shown how the illusory mask of carnivalesque equality is easily unveiled with the elitist phrase "do you know with whom you are speaking?"

27. Indeed, Cardoso (2019) has documented the intense oppression of Blacker sound-scapes in São Paulo and the targeting of *funk* in particular.

28. Likewise, DaMatta writes that in street carnival events, the streets "suddenly become a safe and humane place" (1991 [1979], 86).

FOUR Resistance: Nothing Should Seem Impossible to Change

1. CW.Ch4.Ex1. Technobloco. "Sambódromo." Technobloco invades the sambó-dromo and denounces anti-carnival Mayor Crivella. www.andrewsnydermusic.com/ch-4 -resistance.html/.

2. CW.Ch4.Ex2. "Carinhoso." Trumpeter deescalates situation during June 2013 protests by playing Pixinguinha's love song "Carinhoso." www.andrewsnydermusic.com /ch-4-resistance.html/.

3. CW.Ch4.Ex3. "Agressão Policial." Police aggression follows Technobloco's rendition of "Carinhoso." www.andrewsnydermusic.com/ch-4-resistance.html/.

4. Many scholars of protest music generally imply that social movements "act upon" music, examining how they "mobilize" musical traditions or resources (Eyerman and Jamison 1998) or how they "do music" (Roy 2010).

5. Academic considerations of protest music have predominantly focused on lyrics to understand politicization and oppositional stances (Eyerman and Jamison 1998; Roy 2010; Rosenthal and Flacks 2011). Lyrics provide a window for understanding what Eyerman and Jamison (1998) call the "cognitive praxis" of a social movement, or how music diffuses and frames ideas to incite participation in social movements. Such studies have focused primarily on protest song traditions and the political content of the songs of popular musicians. In theorizing instrumental protest, I build on a broader shift in social movement theory that has turned away from a focus on "rationality" of social movement actors, represented in music studies of lyrics, toward emphasis on the roles of creativity, play, and emotion (Jasper 2018). This consideration of instrumental protest also follows a growing interest in sound as an element of protest (Sterne 2012; Abe 2018). In the case of Brazilian protest music, scholars have focused especially on the lyrical subtlety of the 1960s MPB festivals (Perrone 1989; Dunn 2001; Stroud 2008). Recent work by Brazilian scholars (Herschmann and Fernandes 2014; Martins 2015 and 2016) has focused on the role of music in recent protests in Rio. Trombonist Carol Schavarosk stresses, however, that the existence of explosive street protests in contemporary Brazil makes the context for interpreting protest music distinct from the models of the 1960s. "The context in the '60s and '70s was different. There were the great music festivals during the dictatorship. You couldn't have a protest. Musicians had to create lyrics with double meanings. Even then, they were arrested . . . There was no protest. You would die" (interview 2014).

6. Mic check, or the people's mic (*microfone humano* in Portuguese), is a decentral-

ized call-and-response technique to project the voice of a single protester (Castells 2012). Popularized by the Occupy Wall Street movement, it is often used in Rio de Janeiro by both protest and festive crowds.

7. CW.Ch4.Ex4. BlocAto. "Nada Deve Parecer Impossível." BlocAto plays "Carinhoso" in June 2013 protests. www.andrewsnydermusic.com/ch-4-resistance.html/.

8. The Black Bloc is an internationally known leftist tactic of dressing all in black to cover one's identity while engaging in direct action.

9. CW.Ch4.Ex5. Jornal a Nova Democracia. "Ao som de Siderais, ato lembra a Batalha da Educação no Rio em outubro de 2013." Os Siderais plays in 2014 in remembrance of violent repression of the teachers' strike one year earlier. www.andrewsnydermusic.com /ch-4-resistance.html/.

10. Guy Fawkes, who planned the failed Gunpowder Plot of 1605 against the British Parliament, is a historic figure of revolutionary action memorialized in the film *V for Vendetta* (2006).

11. Drawing a historical line to earlier urban movements of "insurgent citizenship," James Holston argues that "the crisis of urban mobility (20 cents), police violence, and evictions (especially in Rio due to demolitions for World Cup and Olympic facilities) revived the conceptual foundations of insurgent citizenship as protesters demanded radical equality (zero fare) and right to the city" (2014, 894).

12. CW.Ch4.Ex6. Ocupa Carnval. "Eu quero o fim da Polícia Militar." Footage of Ocupa Carnaval carnival parade beginning with a standard call for the end of the military police. www.andrewsnydermusic.com/ch-4-resistance.html/.

13. CW.Ch4.Ex7. Ocupa Carnaval. "Cidade maravilhosa." Satiric remake of famous song "Marvelous City" recalling the marvels of Rio de Janeiro. www.andrewsnydermusic .com/ch-4-resistance.html/.

14. CW.Ch4.Ex8. "Fora Temer—versão Carmina Burana." Orchestral musicians protest Temer presidency leading to the refrain's popularity among neofanfarristas in protest. www.andrewsnydermusic.com/ch-4-resistance.html/.

15. CW.Ch4.Ex9. Chico Buarque-Djavan-Gilberto Gil. "Clip Jingle Lula-Lá." Famed MPB musicians sing in support of early Lula presidential campaign. Lula-lá at :40. www .andrewsnydermusic.com/ch-4-resistance.html/.

16. CW.Ch4.Ex10. "Em tempos de janelas." Documentary about Ju Storino's daily protest quoting Lula-lá campaign jingle. www.andrewsnydermusic.com/ch-4-resistance .html/.

FIVE *Diversification: Neofanfarrismo of the Excluded*

1. CW.Ch5.Ex1. "Favela Brass nas Olimpíadas do Rio 2016." Favela Brass plays in the Olympic Avenue. www.andrewsnydermusic.com/ch-5-diversification.html/.

2. CW.Ch5.Ex2. "Damas de Ferro en Cuba." Footage of Damas de Ferro's tour to Cuba. www.andrewsnydermusic.com/ch-5-diversification.html/.

3. Carla Brunet (2012) argues that samba schools are important institutions that teach, regulate, and discipline idealized notions of femininity and masculinity in Brazil.

4. All-female brass bands and female musicians in New Orleans brass bands (DeCoste 2017) and the international HONK! movement (Leibman 2020) have subverted the gendering of brass and percussion as male.

5. CW.Ch5.Ex3. "Damas de Ferro: Ovulação @ HONK! 2017." Damas de Ferro playing original song "Ovulation" at HONK! in Somerville, Massachusetts, in 2017. www .andrewsnydermusic.com/ch-5-diversification.html/.

6. CW.Ch5.Ex4. BBC. "Women make their mark in Brazil's carnival." BBC reporting on first carnival parade of Mulheres Rodadas. www.andrewsnydermusic.com/ch-5 -diversification.html/.

7. Perlman argues that "Favela residents are not marginal at all but inextricably bound into society, albeit in a manner detrimental to their own interests. They contribute their hard work, their high hopes, and their loyalties, but do not benefit from the goods and services of the system. Although they are neither economically nor politically marginal, they are exploited, manipulated, and repressed; although they are neither socially nor culturally marginal, they are stigmatized and excluded from a closed class system" (2010, 150).

8. CW.Ch5.Ex5. "Tropa do Afeto—14/12/2014—Jardim Gramacho." The Affect Troupe invades Gramacho mixing brass band performance and Theater of the Oppressed tactics to engage favela children. www.andrewsnydermusic.com/ch-5-diversification.html/.

9. CW.Ch5.Ex6. "Orquestra Voadora no Complexo do Alemão—Circulando—Raízes em Movimento." Voadora plays on a different occasion in alliance with social movement in Complexo do Alemão favela. www.andrewsnydermusic.com/ch-5-diversification.html/.

10. CW.Ch5.Ex7. "Favela Brass ending BBC's show for the Opening of the Rio 2016 Olympics." www.andrewsnydermusic.com/ch-5-diversification.html/.

11. These debates resonate with contemporary academic and activist discussions regarding the ethics of cultural appropriation around the world. Many authors liken cultural appropriation to a kind of minstrelsy, what Kathryn Bishop-Sanchez refers to in Brazil as "performative race": a "'cannibalism' that draws its value from the very richness it usurps . . . It draws from the appearance of racial hegemony [democracy] but ultimately reaffirms white supremacy" (2016, 47). Eric Lott has argued that presenting the homage vs. stereotyping question as an either/or misses that cultural appropriation is often understood by musicians themselves as both: "Minstrel performers often attempted to repress through ridicule their real interest in black cultural practices they nonetheless betrayed—minstrelsy's mixed erotic economy of celebration and exploitation . . . what [I call] 'love and theft'" (Lott 1995, 6). Others have recognized the vast diversity of possible cross-cultural interactions and their potential for progressive effects, encapsulated in T.

Roberts's term "radical interracialism" (2016), in which the performance with or of the Other may yield solidarity with the Other.

12. In a parallel to the Mardi Gras Indians tradition of New Orleans, Afro-Brazilians have often found aesthetic inspiration in indigenous imagery propagated by American Wild West films, including Rio de Janeiro's Cacique de Ramos, *Blocos de índio* in Bahia, and *Caboclinha* traditions in the Northeast.

13. CW.Ch5.Ex8. "Indio quer apito se não der pau vai comer." Historic recording of marchinha played by brass bands in Rio. www.andrewsnydermusic.com/ch-5-diversifi cation.html/.

14. CW.Ch5.Ex9. Prata Preta. "Marchinha do Índio quer apito." Performance of "Indian Wants Whistle" by brass blocos in Rio. www.andrewsnydermusic.com/ch-5-diversification .html/.

15. Statements taken from this Facebook conversation are quoted anonymously.

16. This line refers to military lieutenants allied with Getúlio Vargas who were appointed by him to be "interventionist" governors over Brazilian states, underlining the domination the singer is proclaiming over the mulata.

17. Supporting the view that carnivalesque inversion in which the privileged perform the oppressed may do harm and is more tolerated than the opposite inversion, Aurélie Godet argues that, "In assessing the concrete social impact of carnival, one must . . . compare the effects of two types of symbolic disruption: the imitation of the powerless by the powerful, and the reverse. Downward travesty or 'ethnic drag' is usually tolerated, unless a certain political consciousness has already taken hold among the oppressed themselves and they are in a position to protest. The latter form of impersonation, however, is more likely to be condemned or suppressed, thus contradicting the Bakhtinian description of carnival as essentially good-humored and democratic" (2020, 13).

18. CW.Ch5.Ex10. "Um Novo Olhar. Inclusão e Folia. Episódio 03." Episode of "Inclusion and Revelry," documentary about Orquestra Voadora's efforts to make its musical and carnival activities accessible to people with disabilities. www.andrewsnydermusic .com/ch-5-diversification.html/.

SIX *Consolidation: The HONK! RiO Festival of Activist Brass Bands*

1. In Portuguese, "HONK! RiO Festival de Fanfarras Ativistas."

2. CW.Ch6.Ex1. "Mission Delirium Live in Rio de Janeiro at Praia Vermelha August 2015 playing 'Feira de Mangaio.'" Performance at HONK! RiO of Brazilian forró arranged for brass by author. CW.Ch6.Ex2. "Mission Delirium—Tandy—Live in Rio de Janeiro—August 2015." Performance at HONK! RiO of author's original song mixing Afro-diasporic 12/8 rhythm timeline with Balkanesque melodies. www.andrewsnyder music.com/ch-6-consolidation.html/.

3. On the companion website, I have included the history of neofanfarrismo as published on the HONK! RiO website. www.andrewsnydermusic.com/history-of-neofanfarrismo.html/.

4. HONK RiO! official website with footage: https://neofanfarrismo.wordpress.com/videos-e-noticias-honk-rio/.

5. CW.Ch6.Ex3. "HONK RIO—o Neofanfarrismo encontra o HONK." Video released for first HONK! RiO in 2015 entitled "Neofanfarrismo meets HONK!." www.andrewsnydermusic.com/ch-6-consolidation.html/.

6. CW.Ch6.Ex4. Os Siderais. "Episódio 5—HONK 1 EUA." Documentary about the tours of Os Siderais to American HONK! festivals. www.andrewsnydermusic.com/ch-6-consolidation.html/.

7. CW.Ch6.Ex5. "Brazilian June: New York's protest (Part 1)." Documentary of collaborations between Os Siderais and New York brass band Rude Mechanical Orchestra to protest in solidarity with Brazilian protests. www.andrewsnydermusic.com/ch-6-consolidation.html/.

8. Festival organizer Reebee Garofalo writes, "Although the term 'activist' can be controversial in describing HONK! bands, most are civically engaged in some way, if not in outright political protest then at least in some form of community-building activity. Because of their commitment to playing in the street, HONK! bands exemplify a forceful political statement about reclaiming public space in a time of profound privatization" (2012, 281).

9. CW.Ch6.Ex6. "House Keys not Handcuffs!—Ya Move Ya Lose by Brass Liberation Orchestra—HONK! 2017." Author performs with San Francisco Bay Area brass band Brass Liberation Orchestra (BLO) at HONK! in Somerville, Massachusetts. www.andrewsnydermusic.com/ch-6-consolidation.html/.

10. CW.Ch6.Ex7. "Honk! Down the Walls! /// ¡Bulla Contra los Muros! 'Matador' outside South Bay Jail." Footage of HONK! bands playing together in protest outside of an ICE detention center in Boston. www.andrewsnydermusic.com/ch-6-consolidation.html/.

11. CW.Ch6.Ex8. Mission Delirium. "Marablé." Original brass band composition by Andrew Snyder integrating maracatu and candomblé rhythms. www.andrewsnydermusic.com/ch-6-consolidation.html/.

12. CW.Ch6.Ex9. "Bloco do Honk—Homenagem ao Songoro Cosongo—HONK! RiO 2017." Bloco of HONK! pays homage to Carioca bloco Songoro Cosongo that first drew on non-Brazilian genres in 2000s at HONK! RiO in 2017. www.andrewsnydermusic.com/ch-6-consolidation.html/.

13. CW.Ch6.Ex10. HONK!United. "HONK! São Paulo Festival." Documentary about HONK! São Paulo for HONK!United global virtual festival in 2020. www.andrewsnydermusic.com/ch-6-consolidation.html/.

14. CW.Ch6.Ex11. "Confusão Centro RJ—Abertura Carnaval 2016." Unprovoked police

assault on Boi Tolo bloco during Official Opening of Unofficial Carnival in 2016. www
.andrewsnydermusic.com/ch-6-consolidation.html/.

15. CW.Ch6.Ex12. "Just a Closer Walk with Thee." Protest of police repression of street
music in Rio de Janeiro, January 2016. www.andrewsnydermusic.com/ch-6-consolidation
.html/.

CONCLUSION *Carnival Strike*

1. The term "antipolitics" references the 1984 book of the same name by Hungarian
dissident George Konrad, who argued against open confrontation with the Soviet Union.

2. CW.Con.Ex1. Marcelo Cebukin. "Este ano não teve carnaval." Original song "This
Year There Was No Carnival" released in 2021 by Marcelo Cebukin, maestro of Céu na
Terra bloco. The song features some of the leaders of street carnival, supports the campaign
not to celebrate carnival during the height of the pandemic in early 2021, and promises
a bright future. www.andrewsnydermusic.com/conclusion.html/.

BIBLIOGRAPHY

Abe, Marié. 2018. *Resonances of Chindon-Ya: Sounding Space and Sociality in Contemporary Japan.* Middletown, CT: Wesleyan University Press.

Agier, Michel. 2000. *Anthropologie du carnaval. La ville, la fête et l'Afrique à Bahia.* Marseille: Parenthèses/IRD.

Ahmed, Sarah. 2017. *Living a Feminist Life.* Durham, NC: Duke University Press.

Albuquerque Jr., Durval Muniz de. 2014. *The Invention of the Brazilian Northeast.* Durham, NC: Duke University Press.

Allen, Erin. 2020. "Sounding Solidarity at the Suffolk County ICE Immigration Detention Center." In *HONK! A Street Band Renaissance of Music and Activism*, edited by Andrew Snyder, Erin Allen, and Reebee Garofalo, 262–75. New York: Routledge.

——. Forthcoming 2023. "Brass Bands, Critical Musicking, and the Ethics of Engagement in the US HONK! Street Band Movement." PhD diss., The Ohio State University.

Almeida, Giselle de. 2017. "Mulheres ritmistas discutem machismo e racismo no carnaval." *CarnaUOL.* February 14. https://carnaval.uol.com.br/2017/noticias/redacao/2017/02/14/mulheres-ritmistas-discutem-machismo-e-racismo-no-carnaval.htm/.

Anderson, Benedict. 1983. *Imagined Communities: Reflections on the Origins and Spread of Nationalism.* London: Verso.

Andrade, Marcelo Rubião de. 2012. "Música, espaço público e ordem social no carnaval de rua do Rio de Janeiro: Um estudo ethnomusicológico (2009–2011)." Masters thesis, Universidade Federal do Rio de Janeiro.

Andrade, Oswald de. 1991 [1928]. "Oswald de Andrade's 'Cannibalist Manifesto.'" Translated by Leslie Bary. *Latin American Literary Review.* 19 (38): 35–37.

——, and Stella M. de Sá Rego. 1986. "Manifesto of Pau-Brasil Poetry." *Latin American Literary Review* 14 (27): 184–87.

Andrews, Phil. 2017. "Episode 11: Trudi Cohen and John Bell." *Street Brass Podcast.* www.podomatic.com/podcasts/streetbrass/episodes/2017-05-10T18_50_43-07_00.

Antares, Mike. 2020. "The Key of Rest: HONK!'s Hospitality Activism." In *HONK! A*

Street Band Renaissance of Music and Activism, edited by Andrew Snyder, Erin Allen, and Reebee Garofalo, 185–99. New York: Routledge.

Araújo, Samuel. 2005. "Entre palcos, ruas e salões: Processos de circularidade cultural na música dos ranchos carnavalescos do Rio de Janeiro (1890–1930)." *Em Pauta* 16 (26): 73–94.

Ashe, Tom. 2016a. "An Olympic Dream Come True?" *Favela Brass Blog*. December. www.favelabrass.org/2016/08/favela-brass-olympic-dream-come-true.html/.

———. 2016b. "Favela Brass." BBC. https://soundcloud.com/favelabrass.

Avelar, Idelber. 2017. "The June 2013 Uprisings and the Waning of Lulismo in Brazil: Of Antagonism, Contradiction, and Oxymoron." *Luso-Brazilian Review* 54 (1): 9–27.

———, and Christopher Dunn, eds. 2011. *Brazilian Popular Music and Citizenship*. Durham, NC: Duke University Press.

Bagini, Licia. 2014. "Bella ciao: De chant national à chant international." *Annals of University of Oradea, Series: International Relations & European Studies* 6: 101–14.

Bairros, Sabrina de Oliveira. 2012. "Um estudo sobre a importância das mídias sociais para os blocos de rua do Carnaval carioca." Masters thesis, Centro Universitário da Cidade.

Bakhtin, Mikhail. 1984 [1941]. *Rabelais and His World*, translated by Helene Iswolsky. Bloomington: Indiana University Press.

Barbassa, Juliana. 2015. *Dancing with the Devil in the City of God: Rio de Janeiro on the Brink*. New York: Touchstone.

Barreira, Gabriela. 2016. "Guarda Municipal Reprime Blocos Na Escadaria Da Câmara Do Rio." *O Globo*. January 3. http://g1.globo.com/rio-de-janeiro/carnaval/2016/noticia/2016/01/guarda-municipal-reprime-blocos-na-escadaria-da-camara-do-rio.html/.

Barroso, Flávia, and Juliana Gonçalves. "Subversão e purpurina: Um estudo sobre o carnaval de rua não-oficial do Rio de Janeiro." XXXIX Congresso Brasileiro de Ciências da Comunicação. Paper. September 9. São Paulo.

BBC. 2015. "Women make their mark at carnival." February 15. www.bbc.com/news/world-latin-america-31476241.

Belart, Victor. 2021. *Cidade Pirata: Carnaval de rua, coletivos culturais e o Centro do Rio de Janeiro (2010–2021)*. Belo Horizonte, MG: Letramento; Temporada.

Bell, John. 2020. "HONK! and the Politics of Performance in Public Space." In *HONK! A Street Band Renaissance of Music and Activism*, edited by Andrew Snyder, Erin Allen, and Reebee Garofalo, 171–84. New York: Routledge.

Bendix, Regina. 1997. *In Search of Authenticity: The Formation of Folklore Studies*. Madison: University of Wisconsin Press.

Bishop-Sanchez, Katherine. 2016. *Creating Carmen Miranda: Race, Camp, and Transnational Stardom*. Nashville, TN: Vanderbilt University Press.

Bithell, Caroline, and Juniper Hill. 2016. *The Oxford Handbook of Music Revival*. Oxford: Oxford University Press.

Boal, Augusto. 1979. *Theater of the Oppressed*. New York: Urizen Books.

Bogad, Larry. 2016. *Tactical Performance*. London: Routledge.

Boudjadja, Brahim. 2017. "La France en fanfare, histoire d'une réappropriation culturelle." *The Conversation*. May 4. http://theconversation.com/la-france-en-fanfare-histoire -dune-reappropriation-culturelle-76820/.

Bourdieu, Pierre. 1984 [1979]. *Distinction: A Social Critique of the Judgment of Taste*. New York: Routledge.

Brown, Hayes. 2019. "Brazil's President Tweeted Amateur Golden Shower Porn Then Asked What a Golden Shower Is." *Buzzfeed*. March 6. www.buzzfeednews.com/article /hayesbrown/jair-bolsonaro-golden-shower-tweet-carnaval.

Brunet, Carla Sacon. 2012. "Carnaval, Samba Schools and the Negotiation of Gendered Identities in São Paulo, Brazil." PhD dissertation, University of California, Berkeley.

Butler, Judith. 1993. *Bodies that Matter: On the Discursive Limits of Sex*. New York: Routledge.

———. 2015. *Notes Toward a Performative Freedom of Assembly*. Cambridge, MA: Harvard University Press.

Caldeira, Teresa. 2000. *City of Walls: Crime, Segregation, and Citizenship in São Paulo*. Berkeley: University of California Press.

Cardoso, Leonardo. 2019. *Sound-Politics in São Paulo*. Oxford: Oxford University Press.

Carvalho, Bruno, Mariana Cavalcanti, and Vjayanthi Rao Venuturupalli, eds. 2016. *Occupy All Streets: Olympic Urbanism and Contested Futures in Rio de Janeiro*. New York: Terreform.

Castells, Manuel. 2012. *Networks of Outrage and Hope: Social Movements in the Internet Age*. Cambridge: Polity Press.

Castro, Ruy. 2004. *Rio de Janeiro: Carnival under Fire*, translated by John Gledson. New York: Bloomsbury Publishing.

Certeau, Michel de. 1984. *The Practice of Everyday Life*, translated by Steven Rendall. Berkeley: University of California Press.

Connell, Raewyn. 2009. *Gender: In World Perspective*. Cambridge: Polity Press.

Cowan, Benjamin. 2016. *Securing Sex: Morality and Repression in the Making of Cold War Brazil*. Chapel Hill: University of North Carolina Press.

Crook, Larry. 2009. *Focus: Music of Northeast Brazil*. New York: Routledge.

DaMatta, Roberto. 1991 [1979]. *Carnivals, Rogues, and Heroes: An Interpretation of the Brazilian Dilemma*, translated by John Drury. Notre Dame, IN: University of Notre Dame Press.

Daughtry, J. Martin. 2015. *Listening to War: Sound, Music, and Survival in Wartime Iraq*. Oxford: Oxford University Press.

Debord, Guy. 1995 [1970]. *Society of the Spectacle*. New York: Zone Books.

DeCoste, Kyle. 2017. "Street Queens: New Orleans Brass Bands and the Problem of Intersectionality." *Ethnomusicology* 61 (2): 181–206.

Deleuze, Gilles, and Félix Guattari. 2004 [1980]. *A Thousand Plateaus*, translated by Brian Massumi. London and New York: Continuum.

Denning, Michael. 2015. *Noise Uprising: The Audiopolitics of a World Musical Revolution*. London: Verso.

Desliga. 2010. Desliga website. Accessed December 28, 2015. http://desligadosblocos .blogspot.com/2010/09/manifesto-momesco.html/.

DiAngelo, Robin. 2018. *White Fragility: Why It's so Hard for White People to Talk about Racism*. Boston: Beacon Press.

Dias, Flávia. 2017. "Feminismos nas fanfarras de rua carioca: Os estudos de caso do bloco Mulheres Rodadas e da brass band Damas de Ferro." Masters thesis, Universidade Federal do Rio de Janeiro.

Draper, Jack. 2010. *Forró and Redemptive Regionalism from the Brazilian Northeast*. New York: Peter Lang Publishing.

Drott, Eric. 2017. "Musical Contention and Contentious Music; or, the Drums of Occupy Wall Street." *Contemporary Music Review* 37 (5–6): 626–45.

Dunn, Christopher. 2001. *Brutality Garden: Tropicália and the Emergence of a Brazilian Counterculture*. Chapel Hill: University of North Carolina Press.

———. 2016. *Contracultura: Alternative Arts and Social Transformation in Authoritarian Brazil*. Chapel Hill: University of North Carolina Press.

———, and Charles Perrone, eds. 2001. *Brazilian Popular Music and Globalization*. New York: Routledge.

Ehrenreich, Barbara. 2006. *Dancing in the Streets: A History of Collective Joy*. New York: Holt Paperback.

Eyerman, Ron, and Andrew Jamison. 1998. *Music and Social Movements: Mobilizing Traditions in the Twentieth Century*. Cambridge: Cambridge University Press.

Faiola, Anthony, and Anna Kaiser. 2017. "Rio's Pentecostal mayor takes on the capital of Carnival." *Washington Post*. December 13. www.washingtonpost.com/world/the _americas/rios-pentecostal-mayor-takes-on-the-capital-of-carnival/2017/12/12/2f6c 2a70-da1a-11e7-a241-0848315642d0_story.html/.

Fanfarrada. 2016. "Fanfarrada's Facebook page." Accessed October 27, 2016. www.facebook .com/FANFARRADA/?fref=ts.

Federação Anarquista do Rio de Janeiro. ND. "Luta Libertária—Militância e Ativismo." Accessed May 4, 2017. https://anarquismorj.wordpress.com/textos-e-documentos /teoria-e-debate/luta-libertaria-militancia-e-ativismo/.

Feld, Steven. 2000. "A Sweet Lullaby for World Music." *Public Culture* 12 (1): 145–71.

———. 1996. "Waterfalls of Song: An Acoustemology of Place Resounding in Bosavi, Papua New Guinea." In *Senses of Place*, edited by Steven Feld and Keith Basso, 91–136. Santa Fe, NM: School of American Research Press.

Fernandes, Cíntia, and Micael Herschmann. 2014. *Música nas ruas do Rio de Janeiro.* São Paulo: Intercom.

Fernandes, Rita. 2019. *Meu bloco na rua: A retomada do carnaval de rua do Rio de Janeiro.* Rio de Janeiro: Civilização Brasileira.

Ferreira, Felipe. 2004. *O livro de ouro do carnaval brasileiro.* Rio de Janeiro: Ediouro.

Figueiredo, Rubens. 2014. *Junho de 2013: A sociedade enfrenta o estado.* São Paulo: Summus Editorial.

Filgueiras, Mariana. 2016. "Quando os blocos fogem da burocracia e saem vestidos de pirata." February 10. http://oglobo.globo.com/rio/carnaval/2016/quando-os-blocos -fogem-da-burocracia-saem-vestidos-de-pirata-18642160.

Flaes, Robert M. Boonzajer. 2000. *Brass Unbound: Secret Children of the Colonial Brass Band.* The Netherlands: Royal Tropical Institute.

Flanet, Véronique. 2015. *La belle histoire des fanfares des Beaux-Arts: 1948–1968.* Paris: L'Harmattan.

Freeman, Jo. 1972. "The Tyranny of Structurelessness." *Berkeley Journal of Sociology* 17: 151–64.

Freire, Paulo. 2000 [1970]. *Pedagogy of the Oppressed.* New York: Bloomsbury.

Garofalo, Reebee. Forthcoming. "HONK! Activism: Alternative Brass Bands as Political Projects." In *The Oxford Handbook of Protest Music*, edited by Noriko Manabe and Eric Drott. New York: Oxford University Press.

———. 2012. "HONK! Pedagogy and Music." *Journal of Popular Music Studies* 24 (3): 280–86.

———. 2020. "The Many Roads to HONK! and the Power of Brass and Percussion." In *HONK! A Street Band Renaissance of Music and Activism*, edited by Andrew Snyder, Erin Allen, and Reebee Garofalo, 15–27. New York: Routledge.

Gibson, Annie. 2015. "Performing Cultural Visibility: Brazilian Immigrants, Mardi Gras, and New Orleans." In *Performing Brazil: Essays on Culture, Identity, and the Performing Arts*, edited by Severino Albuquerque and Kathryn Bishop-Sanchez, 144–69. Madison: University of Wisconsin Press.

Gilroy, Paul. 1993. *The Black Atlantic: Modernity and Double Consciousness.* London: Verso.

Gluckman, Max. 1965. *Custom and Conflict in Africa.* Oxford: Blackwell.

Godet, Aurélie. 2020. "Behind the Masks, the Politics of Carnival." *Journal of Festive Studies* 2 (1): 1–30.

Goldschmitt, K. E. 2020. *Bossa Mundo: Brazilian Music in Transnational Media Industries.* Oxford: Oxford University Press.

Graeber, David. 2013. *The Democracy Project: A History, a Crisis, a Movement.* New York: Spiegel & Grau.

Gray, Lila. 2013. *Fado Resounding: Affective Politics and Urban Life.* Durham, NC: Duke University Press.

Guilbault, Jocelyne. 2007. *Governing Sound: The Cultural Politics of Trinidad's Carnival Musics*. Chicago: University of Chicago Press.

Guillermoprieto, Alma. 1990. *Samba*. New York: Knopf.

Guimarães, Cleo. 2020. "Carnaval de rua: conheça Raquel Potí, a pernalta mais querida dos blocos." *Veja Rio*. February 17. https://vejario.abril.com.br/beira-mar/saiba-quem-e -pernalta-dos-blocos/?fbclid=IwAR3NFKd-4yJ_jVv127LK7LUh3hoK74fhL4l7WHiVH MGXNwoUB3466z9iGQc.

Hall, Stuart. 1980. "Race, articulation and societies structured in dominance." In *Sociological Theories: Race and Colonialism*, 305–45. Paris: UNESCO.

Harrison, Rodney. 2013. *Heritage: Critical Approaches*. Abington, UK: Routledge.

Harvey, David. 2013. "A liberdade da cidade." In *Cidades rebeldes: Passe livre e as manifestações que tomaram as ruas do Brasil*, edited by David Harvey, et al., 27–34. São Paulo: Boitempo Editorial.

———. 2012. *Rebel Cities: From the Right to the City to the Urban Revolution*. London: Verso.

Hemmasi, Farzaneh. 2017. "'One Can Veil and Be a Singer!': Performing Piety on an Iranian Talent Competition." *Journal of Middle East Women's Studies* 13 (3): 416–37.

Herschmann, Micael. 2013. "Alguns apontamentos sobre o crescimento do carnaval de rua no Rio de Janeiro no início do século 21." *Intercom-Revista Brasileira de Ciências Da Comunicação* 36 (2): 267–89.

———. 2007. *Lapa: Cidade da musica: Desafios e perspectives para o crescimento do Rio de Janeiro e da industra da musica independente nacional*. Rio de Janeiro: Manaud X.

———, and Maria Cabanzo. 2016. "Contribuições do grupo musical Songoro Cosongo para o crescimento do carnaval de rua e das fanfarras cariocas no início do século XXI." *Revista Lumina* 10 (3): 1–16.

Hertzman, Marc. 2013. *Making Samba: A New History of Race and Music in Brazil*. Durham, NC: Duke University Press.

Hobsbawm, Eric, and Terence Ranger. 1983. *The Invention of Tradition*. Cambridge: Cambridge University Press.

Holston, James. 2014. "'Come to the street!': Urban protest, Brazil 2013." *Hot Spots, Cultural Anthropology* website. December 20. https://culanth.org/fieldsights/458-come-to-the -street-urban-protest-brazil-2013.

———. 2008. *Insurgent Citizenship: Disjunctions of Democracy and Modernity in Brazil*. Princeton, NJ: Princeton University Press.

HONK! Festival of Activist Street Bands. "About—HONK!" Accessed October 27, 2016. http://honkfest.org/about/.

HONK! RiO. "HONK! RiO Facebook page." Accessed February 27, 2020. www.facebook .com/honkrio/.

———. 2015. "HONK! RiO Wordpress page." Accessed August 12, 2017. https://neofanfar rismo.wordpress.com/historico/.

HONK!TX. 2017. "'Super Band Merge Workshop and Parade' Facebook event page." Accessed May 16, 2017. www.facebook.com/events/398786737149048/?ref=br_rs.

Jackson, David. 1996. "Three Glad Races: Primitivism and Ethnicity in Brazilian Modernist Literature." *Modernism/Modernity* 1 (2): 89–112.

Jaguaribe, Beatriz. 2016. "Branding the Marvelous City." In *Occupy All Streets: Olympic Urbanism and Contested Futures in Rio de Janeiro*, edited by Bruno Carvalho, Mariana Cavalcanti, and Vyjayanthi Rao Venuturupalli, 30–59. New York: Terreform.

———. 2014. *Rio de Janeiro: Urban Life through the Eyes of the City.* New York: Routledge.

Jasper, James. 2018. *The Emotions of Protest.* Chicago: University of Chicago Press.

Kallman, Meghan. 2020. "Leadership, Inclusion, and Group Decision-Making in HONK! Bands." In *HONK! A Street Band Renaissance of Music and Activism*, edited by Andrew Snyder, Erin Allen, and Reebee Garofalo, 117–30. New York: Routledge.

Keil, Charles. 1987. "Participatory Discrepancies and the Power of Music." *American Anthropology Association* 2 (3): 275–83.

Kennelly, Jaqueline. 2015. "'You're making our city look bad': Olympic security, neoliberal urbanization, and homeless youth." *Ethnography* 16 (1): 3–24.

Kirshenblatt-Gimblett, Barbara. 1995. "Theorizing Heritage," *Ethnomusicology* 39 (3): 367–80.

Klubock, Thomas. 1998. *Contested Communities: Class, Gender, and Politics in Chile's El Teniente Copper Mine, 1904–1951.* Durham, NC: Duke University Press.

Lacombe, Fabiano. 2014. "O Cordão do Boitatá: relação com as noções de indústria cultural, professionalismo, tradição e mudança." Masters thesis, Universidade Federal do Rio de Janeiro.

Lang-Levitsky, Rosza Daniel, and Michele Hardesty. 2020. "Why Do We Honk? How Do We Honk?: Politics, Antipolitics, and Activist Street Bands." In *HONK! A Street Band Renaissance of Music and Activism*, edited by Andrew Snyder, Erin Allen, and Reebee Garofalo, 185–98. New York: Routledge.

Laušević, Mirjana. 2006. *Balkan Fascination: Creating an Alternative Music Culture in America.* Oxford: Oxford University Press.

Le Bon, Gustave. 2007 [1895]. *La psychologie des foules.* Paris: FV Editions.

Lefebvre, Henri. 1968. *Le droit à la ville.* Paris: Anthropos.

Leppmann, Kevin. 2020. "Learning on Parade with the School of HONK." In *HONK! A Street Band Renaissance of Music and Activism*, edited by Andrew Snyder, Erin Allen, and Reebee Garofalo, 89–100. New York: Routledge.

Liebman, Becky. 2020. "Horns and Hers: The Subversion of Gendered Instrumentation in the HONK! Movement." In *HONK! A Street Band Renaissance of Music and Activ-*

ism, edited by Andrew Snyder, Erin Allen, and Reebee Garofalo, 145–56. New York: Routledge.

Livingston, Tamara. 1996. "Music Revivals: Towards a General Theory." *Ethnomusicology* 43 (1): 66–85.

Londoño, Ernesto. 2020. "'Like a Scream of Resistance': Rio's Carnival in Bolsonaro's Brazil." *New York Times*. February 26.

Lott, Eric. 1995. *Love and Theft: Blackface Minstrelsy and the American Working Class*. New York: Oxford University Press.

Madeira, Angélica. 2011. "Rude Poetics of the 1980s: The Politics and Aesthetics of Os Titãs." In *Brazilian Popular Music and Citizenship*, edited by Christopher Dunn and Idelber Avelar, 1–27. Durham, NC: Duke University Press.

Maior, Leandro. 2014. "Banda Damas de Ferro se prepara para estrear no Carnaval 2014." *O Dia*. January 4. http://odia.ig.com.br/diversao/2014-01-04/banda-damas-de-ferro -se-prepara-para-estrear-no-carnaval-2014.html/.

Manabe, Noriko. 2015. *The Revolution Will Not Be Televised: Protest Music after Fukushima*. Oxford: Oxford University Press.

Marino, Angela. 2014. "Fiesta Politics: A Rehearsal—and an Act—of Governance." *Revista* 13 (3): 69–71.

Marković, Alexander. 2017. "Gypsy Fingers are Unique! Identity Politics and Romani Musical Performance in Vranje, Serbia." PhD dissertation, University of Illinois at Chicago.

Martins, Daniel Marcos. 2015. "Música, identidade e ativismo: A música nos protestos de rua no Rio de Janeiro (2013–2015)." *Revista Vórtex* 3 (2): 188–207.

———. 2016. "Música pela Democracia: comportamentos e protesto dos músicos de orquestra no Rio de Janeiro." *Debates UniRio* 19: 38–61.

Mason, Amelia. 2017. "In an Era of Protest, HONK! Fest's Activist Roots Come into Focus." *The Artery*. October 5. www.wbur.org/artery/2017/10/05/honk-fests-activist -roots.

McCann, Bryan. 2004. *Hello, Hello Brazil: Popular Music in the Making of Modern Brazil*. Durham, NC: Duke University Press.

McKay, George. 2007. "'A Soundtrack to the Insurrection': Street Music, Marching Bands and Popular Protests." *Parallax* 13 (1): 20–31.

Meade, Teresa. 1997. *Civilizing Rio: Reform and Resistance in a Brazilian City: 1889–1930*. University Park: Pennsylvania State University Press.

Mendonça, Valéria, Pedro Figueiredo, and Pedro Neville. 2018. "Riotur estima 6 milhões de foliões no carnaval, com 1,5 milhão de turistas." *Globo*. January 11. https://g1.globo .com/rj/rio-de-janeiro/carnaval/2018/noticia/prefeitura-do-rio-espera-15-milhao-de -folioes-estrangeiros-para-o-carnaval.ghtml/.

Moehn, Frederick. 2012. *Contemporary Carioca: Technologies of Mixing in a Brazilian Music Scene*. Durham, NC: Duke University Press.

Moniz, Miguel. 2020. "The Emergence of Fanfarra Brass Bands in Portugal (1990s to present): associativism, local activism, and trans-local cultural production." In *Our Music/ Our World: Wind Bands and Local Social Life*, edited by Maria do Rosário Pestana, André Granjo, Damien François Sagrillo, and Gloria Rodriguez Lorenzo, 349–400. Lisbon: Edições Colibri.

Monnerat, Alessandra. 2017. "Mulheres colocam a mão na massa nos blocos de rua." *O Dia*. February 18. http://odia.ig.com.br/diversao/carnaval/2017-02-18/mulheres -colocam-a-mao-na-massa-nos-blocos-de-rua.html/.

Monteiro, Gabriela. 2016. "Pequeno guia para não fazer feio nas fantasias de carnaval." *Blogueiras negras*. February 2. http://blogueirasnegras.org/pequeno-guia-negro-e -feminista-para-nao-fazer-feio-nas-fantasias-de-carnaval/.

Moreau, Michel, and Maria Pitrez. 2020. "Expanding Borders: Activism, Effervescence, and Rhythms in Brazil's HONK! RiO," translated by Andrew Snyder. www.honkrenais sance.net/moreauxpitrez.html/.

Ninja. 2017. "O carnaval é político!" January 22. Accessed May 4, 2017. https://ninja.oxi mity.com/article/O-carnaval-%C3%A9-pol%C3%ADtico-1.

Ocupa carnaval. 2015. "Ocupa carnaval's Facebook page." Accessed December 10, 2015. www.facebook.com/ocupacarnaval/.

ONU Mulheres Brasil. 2015. "Pequim+20 no carnaval." Accessed March 11, 2020. www .onumulheres.org.br/planeta5050-2030/carnaval-2015/.

Orquestra Voadora. 2013. "Orquestra Voadora website." Accessed March 19, 2014. www .orquestravoadora.com.br/.

Packman, Jeff. 2010. "Singing Together/Meaning Apart: Popular Music, Participation, and Cultural Politics in Salvador, Brazil." *Latin American Music Review* 31 (2): 241–67.

Perlman, Janice. 2010. *Favela: Four Decades of Living on the Edge in Rio de Janeiro*. Oxford: Oxford University Press.

Perrone, Charles. 1989. *Masters of Contemporary Brazilian Song: MPB 1965–1985*. Austin: University of Texas Press.

Pestana, Maria do Rosário, André Granjo, Damien François Sagrillo and Gloria Rodriguez Lorenzo, eds. 2020. *Our Music/Our World: Wind Bands and Local Social Life*. Lisboa: Edições Colibri.

Peterson, Mariana. 2012. *Sound, Space, and the City: Civic Performance in Downtown Los Angeles*. Philadelphia: University of Pennsylvania Press.

Peterson, Richard A., and Roger M. Kern. 1996. "Highbrow Taste: From Snob to Omnivore." *American Sociological Review* 61 (5): 900–907.

Podber, Naomi. 2020. "Building Connections While Maintaining the Band: The Challenging Politics of Inclusion in Activist Work." In *HONK! A Street Band Renaissance of Music and Activism*, edited by Andrew Snyder, Erin Allen, and Reebee Garofalo, 131–44. New York: Routledge.

de Queiroz, Maria Isaura Pereira. 1992. *Carnaval Brasileiro: O vivido e o mito*. São Paulo: Brasiliense.

Ramalho, Guilherme. 2017. "Maria Zapatão e Zézé são banidos da folia carioca." *O Globo*. January 31. http://oglobo.globo.com/rio/maria-sapatao-zeze-sao-banidos-da-folia-carioca-20846897?utm_source=Facebook&utm_medium=Social&utm_campaign=O%20Globo/.

Raphael, Alison. 1990. "From Popular Culture to Microenterprise: The History of Brazilian Samba Schools." *Latin American Music Review* 11 (1): 73–83.

Reily, Suzel. 2013. "From Processions to Encontros: The Performance Niches of the Community Bands of Minas Gerais, Brazil." In *Brass Bands of the World: Militarism, Colonial Legacies, and Local Music Making*, edited by Suzel Reily and Katherine Brucher, 99–102. New York: Routledge.

———, and Katherine Brucher, eds. 2013. *Brass Bands of the World: Militarism, Colonial Legacies, and Local Music Making*. New York: Routledge.

Ribeiro, Carolina. 2015. "Com eventos todo fim de semana, carnaval carioca mostra que não tem fim." Globo. September 13. http://oglobo.globo.com/rio/com-eventos-todo-fim-de-semana-carnaval-carioca-mostra-que-nao-tem-fim-17457368.

Ribeiro, Djamila. 2015. "Mulher negra não é fantasia de carnaval." *Carta Capital*. February 2. www.cartacapital.com.br/blogs/escritorio-feminista/mulher-negra-nao-e-fantasia-de-carnaval-5190.html/.

———. 2017. "O teu discurso não nega, racista." *Carta Capital*. February 9. www.cartacapital.com.br/sociedade/o-teu-discurso-nao-nega-racista.

Roberts, T. 2016. *Resounding Afro-Asia: Interracial Music and the Politics of Collaboration*. Oxford: Oxford University Press.

Robinson, Dylan. 2020. *Hungry Listening: Resonant Theory for Indigenous Sound Studies*. Minneapolis: University of Minnesota Press.

Rosenthal, Rob, and Richard Flacks. 2011. *Playing for Change: Music and Musicians in the Service of Social Movements*. Boulder, CO: Paradigm Publishers.

Roy, William. 2010. *Reds, Whites and Blues: Social Movements, Folk Music, and Race in America*. Princeton, NJ: Princeton University Press.

Sakakeeny, Matt. 2011. "New Orleans Music as a Circulatory System." *Black Music Research Journal* 31 (2): 291–325.

_____. 2013. *Roll with It: Brass Bands in the Streets of New Orleans*. Durham, NC: Duke University Press.

_____. 2010. "'Under the Bridge': An Orientation to Soundscapes in New Orleans." *Ethnomusicology* 54 (1): 1–27.

Sézérat, Laurine. 2020. "Autonomous Street Carnival Blocos and Reinventing Citizenship in Rio de Janeiro." In *HONK! A Street Band Renaissance of Music and Activism*, edited by Andrew Snyder, Erin Allen, and Reebee Garofalo, 28–40. New York: Routledge.

————, and Victor Andrade. 2016. "Influência das redes sociotécnicas na formação de espaços autônomos." *Primeiro Congresso Internacional Espaços Públicos*: 1–9.

Sheriff, Robin E. 1999. "The Theft of Carnaval: National Spectacle and Racial Politics in Rio de Janeiro." *Cultural Anthropology* 14 (1): 3–28.

Sims, Shannon. 2017. "Less skin, more God and no racism: How Brazil's left and right want to change Carnaval." *Washington Post*. February 11. www.washingtonpost.com /news/worldviews/wp/2017/02/11/less-skin-more-god-and-no-racism-how-brazils-left -and-right-want-to-change-carnaval/?utm_term=.caf564618725.

Snyder, Andrew. 2021b. "Carnaval em casa: Activist Inversions in Rio de Janeiro's Street Carnival during the COVID-19 Pandemic." *Journal of Festive Studies* 3: 17–46.

————. 2021a. "Carnival Brass Bands in New Orleans and Rio de Janeiro: Disinheritance, Alternative Whiteness, and Musical Eclecticism." *Ethnomusicology* 65 (3): 519–48.

————. 2015. "Cuivres critiques: la musique comme tactique d'action directe dans la baie de San Francisco." In *Politiques des musiques populaires au XXIe siècle*, edited by Jedediah Sklower, 211–32. Guichen, France: Éd. Mélanie Seteun.

————. 2019a. "From Nationalist Rescue to Internationalist Cannibalism: The Alternative Carnivaslesque, Brass, and the Revival of Street Carnival in Rio de Janeiro." *Luso-Brazilian Review* 56 (1): 106–29.

————. Forthcoming. "'Music is Liberation:' The Brass Liberation Orchestra and Musical Direct Action." In *At the Crossroads: Music and Social Justice*, edited by Susan Asai, Brenda Romero, Andrew Snyder, David McDonald, and Katelyn Best. Bloomington: Indiana University Press.

————. 2020a. "Musical Eclecticism, Cultural Appropriation, and Whiteness in Mission Delirium and HONK!" In *HONK! A Street Band Renaissance of Music and Activism*, edited by Andrew Snyder, Erin Allen, and Reebee Garofalo, 77–89. New York: Routledge.

————. 2019b. "Playing the System: The Capitalist Industry of Participatory Music Education in Rio de Janeiro's Oficinas." *Journal of Popular Music Studies* 31 (3): 119–44.

————. 2020b. "Politicizing Carnival Brass Bands in Olympic Rio de Janeiro: Instrumental Protest and Musical Repertoires of Contention." *Latin American Music Review* 41 (1): 27–58.

————. 2022. "Revelry, Inclusion, and Disability in the Street Carnival of Rio de Janeiro." *Journal of Festival Culture Inquiry and Analysis* 1.

————, Erin Allen, and Reebee Garofalo, eds. 2020. *HONK! A Street Band Renaissance of Music and Activism*. New York: Routledge.

————. 2022. "HONK!United: A Virtual Global Festival of Activist Brass Bands during the COVID-19 Pandemic." *Music and Politics*: 16 (1): 1–28.

Sonevytsky, Maria. 2019. *Wild Music: Sound and Sovereignty in Ukraine*. Middletown, CT: Wesleyan University Press.

Songoro Cosongo. "Songoro Cosongo—Músicas." Accessed October 27, 2016. www .rodrigopaluma.com.br/songoro/musicas.html/.

Stanyek, Jason. 2011. "Choro do Norte: Improvising the Transregional Roda in the United States." *Luso-Brazilian Review* 48 (1): 100–129.

Starr, Larry, and Christopher Waterman. 2017. *American Popular Music: From Minstrelsy to MP3*. Oxford: Oxford University Press.

Sterne, Jonathan. 2012. "Quebec's Casseroles: On Participation, Percussion and Protest." *Sounding Out!* June 4. http://soundstudiesblog.com/2012/06/04/casseroles/.

St. John, Graham. 2008. "Protestival: Global Days of Action and Carnivalized Politics in the Present." *Social Movement Studies* 7 (2): 167–90.

Stokes, Martin. 2007. "On Musical Cosmopolitanism." *The Macalester International Roundtable 2007*. Paper 3. http://digitalcommons.macalester.edu/intlrdtable/3.

Street, John. 2012. *Music and Politics*. Cambridge: Polity Press.

Stroud, Sean. 2008. *The Defense of Tradition in Brazilian Popular Music*. Aldershot, UK: Ashgate.

Tannock, Stuart. 1995. "Nostalgia Critique." *Cultural Studies* 9 (3): 453–64.

Taylor, Diana. 2003. *The Archive and the Repertoire: Performing Cultural Memory in the Americas*. Durham, NC: Duke University Press.

Taylor, Timothy. 2007. *Beyond Exoticism: Western Music and the World*. Durham, NC: Duke University Press.

Tilly, Charles. 2010. *Regimes and Repertoires*. Chicago: University of Chicago Press.

Tinhorão, José Ramos. 2013 [1974]. *Pequena história da música popular: da modinha à lambada*. São Paulo: Editora 34.

Turino, Thomas. 2008. *Music as Social Life: The Politics of Participation*. Chicago: University Press of Chicago.

———. 2000. *Nationalists, Cosmopolitans, and Popular Music in Zimbabwe*. Chicago: University of Chicago Press.

Turner, Victor. 1969. *The Ritual Process*. Chicago: Aldine Publishing.

Veloso, Caetano, and Christopher Dunn. 1996. "The Tropicalista Rebellion." *Transition* 70: 116–38.

Vianna, Hermano. 1995. *O mistério do samba*. Rio de Janeiro: Editora Universidade Federal do Rio de Janeiro.

———. 2011. "Technobrega, Forró, Lambada: The Parallel Music of Brazil." In *Brazilian Popular Music and Citizenship*, edited by Christopher Dunn and Idelber Avelar, 240–49. Durham, NC: Duke University Press.

Villela, Flávia. 2016. "Mulheres Rodadas ridicularizam o machismo em bloco no Rio." *Agência Brasil—Últimas Notícias Do Brasil E Do Mundo*. February 2. http://agenciabrasil .ebc.com.br/geral/noticia/2016-02/mulheres-rodadas-ridicularizam-o-machismo-em -bloco-no-rio/.

Weinstein, Barbara. 2015. *The Color of Modernity: São Paulo and the Making of Race and Nation in Brazil*. Durham, NC: Duke University Press.

Whitney, Jennifer. 2003. "Infernal Noise: The Soundtrack to Insurrection." In *We Are Everywhere: The Irresistible Rise of Global Anti-Capitalism*, edited by Notes from Nowhere, 216–27. London: Verso.

Williams, Raymond. 2001 [1961]. *The Long Revolution*. Orchard Park, NY: Broadview Press.

———. 1977. *Marxism and Literature*. Oxford: Oxford University Press.

Williamson, Theresa. 2016. "Monopoly City vs. Singular City: Competing Urban Visions." In *Occupy All Streets: Olympic Urbanism and Contested Futures in Rio de Janeiro*, edited by Bruno Carvalho, Mariana Cavalcanti, and Vyjayanthi Rao Venuturupalli, 142–73. New York: Terreform.

Xexéo, Artur. 2017. "Uma marchinha para as mulheres rodadas." *O Globo*. February 19. http://oglobo.globo.com/cultura/uma-marchinha-para-as-mulheres-rodadas-20948179.

Yúdice, George. 2003. *The Expediency of Culture: Uses of Culture in the Global Era*. Durham, NC: Duke University Press.

Zirin, Dave. 2014. *Brazil's Dance with the Devil: The World Cup, The Olympics, and the Fight for Democracy*. Chicago: Haymarket.

INDEX

funding for, 223; instrumental activism at, 220–25; internationalization of, 212–25; international partnerships of, 226–27; overview of, 28, 210–11; parade route of, 229; unified political action of, 230–34

HONK!United, 229

horizontal education, 116–19

horizontalism, 14, 130–32, 139

hospitality activism, 218

Hula-Hoop (*bambolê*) dance, 179

Immigration and Customs Enforcement (ICE), 217

impeachment, 165–69

improvisation, 126

inclusion: within cracudagem, 132; of HONK! in Boston, 217; limitations of, 129–30; within neofanfarrismo, 129; of Orquestra Voadora, 206–7; within the street (rua), 138

"Índio quer apito," 196–99

Infernal Noise Brigade, 145

innovation, 254n8

instrumental activism: defined, 25, 217; forms of, 186; at HONK! RiO! festival, 220–25; musical quality within, 128–30; paradoxes of, 128–38; professionalism within, 128–30

instrumental protest: carnival and, 146–48; defined, 142; overview of, 144–45, 260n5; participatory musical protest within, 150–54; photo of, 145; as protestival, 147; repertoire for, 145; tactical capacities of the brass band within, 148–50; tactical performance within, 147

instruments, cost of, 133, 187–88, 189

insurgent citizenship, 249n14, 261n11

inter-class collaborations, 120–22

internal orientalism, 82

internationalist cannibalism (*antropofagia*), 24, 68–69, 71, 74, 86

International Olympic Committee (IOC), 9

international subculture, neofanfarrismo as, 87

invention of tradition, 201, 251n12

invisible theater, 185

itinerant gentrification, 136

Jackson, Michael, 100

Jaguaribe, Beatriz, 37–38, 250n8

Jamaican Rastafarianism, 100

jazz bands, 47

jazz funeral, 232–34

Joaquim, Leandro, 37, 128

Jobim, Tom, 98

Johnson, Tracy, 216–17

José da Silva, Horácio, 85

"Just a Closer Walk With Thee," 234

Kallman, Meghan, 106, 131, 132, 259n25

Keil, Charles, 115, 120, 257n3

Kelly, João Roberto, 199, 201–2

"Kise dhoondta hai," 208

Kočani Orkestar, 95

Kusturica, Emir, 96

Kuti, Fela, 98, 122–28

Lacombe, Fabiano, 103

laisser-faire group, 130–31

Landless Workers Movement (MST), 241

Lang-Levitsky, Rosza Daniel, 237–38

Lapa, 38, 39, 127, 221

Lapa Arches, 104

Laučević, Mirjana, 96

Lavoe, Héctor, 92

leadership: within Boi Tolo, 116, 131–32; within Favela Brass, 173; horizontal, 131–32; role of, 139

Lefebvre, Henri, 109

leftist revival, 41–43

Lima, Raquel, 195–96

Livingston, Tamara, 42

Londoño, Eduardo, 241

Lopes, Luis, 44

Lott, Eric, 262–63n11

Lula da Silva, Luiz Inácio, 40, 167, 168

Lula Livre (Free Lula) campaign, 167

lyrics, significance of, 195, 197, 260n5

Machado, Gustavo, 37, 58–59, 87, 146, 156

machismo, 176–77

Madeira, Angélica, 250n11

Mafort, Mathias, 24, 115, 150

MUSIC / CULTURE

A series from Wesleyan University Press
Edited by Deborah Wong, Sherrie Tucker, and Jeremy Wallach
Originating editors: George Lipsitz, Susan McClary, and Robert Walser

The Music/Culture series has consistently reshaped and redirected music scholarship. Founded in 1993 by George Lipsitz, Susan McClary, and Robert Walser, the series features outstanding critical work on music. Unconstrained by disciplinary divides, the series addresses music and power through a range of times, places, and approaches. Music/Culture strives to integrate a variety of approaches to the study of music, linking analysis of musical significance to larger issues of power—what is permitted and forbidden, who is included and excluded, who speaks and who gets silenced. From ethnographic classics to cutting-edge studies, Music/Culture zeroes in on how musicians articulate social needs, conflicts, coalitions, and hope. Books in the series investigate the cultural work of music in urgent and sometimes experimental ways, from the radical fringe to the quotidian. Music/Culture asks deep and broad questions about music through the framework of the most restless and rigorous critical theory.

Marié Abe
Resonances of Chindon-ya:
Sounding Space and Sociality
in Contemporary Japan

Frances Aparicio
Listening to Salsa: Gender, Latin Popular
Music, and Puerto Rican Cultures

Paul Austerlitz
Jazz Consciousness: Music, Race,
and Humanity

Shalini R. Ayyagari
Musical Resilience: Performing Patronage
in the Indian Thar Desert

Christina Baade and Kristin McGee
Beyoncé in the World: Making Meaning
with Queen Bey in Troubled Times

Emma Baulch
Genre Publics: Popular Music,
Technologies, and Class
in Indonesia

Harris M. Berger
Metal, Rock, and Jazz: Perception
and the Phenomenology
of Musical Experience

Harris M. Berger
Stance: Ideas about Emotion, Style,
and Meaning for the Study
of Expressive Culture

Harris M. Berger and
Giovanna P. Del Negro
Identity and Everyday Life: Essays
in the Study of Folklore, Music,
and Popular Culture

Franya J. Berkman
Monument Eternal: The Music
of Alice Coltrane

Dick Blau, Angeliki Vellou Keil,
and Charles Keil
Bright Balkan Morning:
Romani Lives and the Power
of Music in Greek Macedonia

Susan Boynton and
Roe-Min Kok, editors
Musical Childhoods and the
Cultures of Youth

James Buhler, Caryl Flinn,
and David Neumeyer, editors
Music and Cinema

Thomas Burkhalter, Kay Dickinson,
and Benjamin J. Harbert, editors
The Arab Avant-Garde: Music,
Politics, Modernity

Patrick Burkart
Music and Cyberliberties

Julia Byl
Antiphonal Histories: Resonant Pasts
in the Toba Batak Musical Present

Corinna Campbell
Parameters and Peripheries of Culture:
Interpreting Maroon Music and Dance
in Paramaribo, Suriname

Alexander M. Cannon
Seeding the Tradition: Musical Creativity
in Southern Vietnam

Daniel Cavicchi
Listening and Longing: Music Lovers
in the Age of Barnum

Susan D. Crafts, Daniel Cavicchi,
Charles Keil, and the
Music in Daily Life Project
My Music: Explorations
of Music in Daily Life

Jim Cullen
Born in the USA: Bruce Springsteen
and the American Tradition

Anne Danielsen
Presence and Pleasure: The Funk Grooves
of James Brown and Parliament

Peter Doyle
Echo and Reverb: Fabricating
Space in Popular Music Recording,
1900–1960

Ron Emoff
Recollecting from the Past: Musical
Practice and Spirit Possession on the East
Coast of Madagascar

Yayoi Uno Everett and
Frederick Lau, editors
Locating East Asia in Western Art Music

Susan Fast and Kip Pegley, editors
Music, Politics, and Violence

Heidi Feldman
Black Rhythms of Peru: Reviving African
Musical Heritage in the Black Pacific

ABOUT THE AUTHOR

Andrew Snyder is currently a postdoctoral researcher in the Instituto de Etno-musicologia at the Universidade Nova de Lisboa, having completed his PhD in ethnomusicology at the University of California, Berkeley. With an interest in the intersections of public festivity and social movements, he coedited *HONK! A Street Band Renaissance of Music and Activism* and *At the Crossroads: Music and Social Justice*, and he has published articles in *Latin American Music Review*, *Journal of Popular Music Studies*, *Ethnomusicology*, and *Yearbook for Traditional Music*, among others. A trumpeter, singer, guitarist, and pianist, he has played in a wide range of styles and ensembles, and he is cofounder of San Francisco's Mission Delirium Brass Band.